The Interpretation of Old English Poems

The Interpretation of
Old English Poems

Stanley B. Greenfield

Professor of English
College of Liberal Arts, University of Oregon

Routledge & Kegan Paul
London and Boston

First published 1972
by Routledge & Kegan Paul Ltd
Broadway House, 68–74 Carter Lane,
London EC4V 5EL and
9 Park Street,
Boston, Mass. 2108, U.S.A.
Printed in Great Britain by
Western Printing Services Ltd
Bristol
© *Stanley B. Greenfield* 1972
No part of this book may be reproduced in
any form without permission from the
publisher, except for the quotation of brief
passages in criticism

ISBN 0 7100 7340 2

For my mother and father

In a dark time, the eye begins to see . . .
That place among the rocks—is it a cave,
Or winding path? The edge is what I have.

A steady storm of correspondences!
A night flowing with birds, a ragged moon,
And in broad day the midnight come again!

Theodore Roethke
'In a Dark Time'

Contents

Abbreviations

ASPR	*The Anglo-Saxon Poetic Records*, 6 vols, ed. G. P. Krapp and E. V. K. Dobbie (New York, 1931–53)
BTD	*An Anglo-Saxon Dictionary*, ed. J. Bosworth and T. N. Toller (Oxford, 1882–98)
BTS	*An Anglo-Saxon Dictionary, Supplement*, ed. T. N. Toller (Oxford, 1908–21)
ELH	*Journal of English Literary History*
JEGP	*Journal of English and Germanic Philology*
MLN	*Modern Language Notes*
MLQ	*Modern Language Quarterly*
MP	*Modern Philology*
NM	*Neuphilologische Mitteilungen*
PMLA	*Publications of the Modern Language Association of America*
RES	*Review of English Studies*

All quotations from *Beowulf* are from Frederick Klaeber's 3rd edition (Boston, 1950). Quotations from other Old English poems are from *ASPR*, except as otherwise noted. Indications of vowel length have, except in quotations from other critics, been omitted.

Preface

This book is an effort to produce a 'handbook' for Old English critics and students, to indicate procedures that offer, in my judgment, the best hope for valid insights into the meaning of Old English poems. To this end it is both prescriptive and proscriptive, suggestive rather than definitive. Its strengths will have to be judged by its readers; its weaknesses are all too apparent to its author, and the epigraph is not without a certain ironic application to his own critical attempts.

The interpretation of Old English *poems*—not *poetry*. One of my basic tenets is that some of the main streams of modern Old English criticism tend to detract from the special nature, the unique identity, of particular poems. This is not to deny a poem's participation in the community and commonality of its Anglo-Saxon poetical and cultural heritage, but rather to draw attention, in crucial matters of interpretation, small and large, to the convergence of various kinds of poetic and extra-poetic elements in the immediate text, and to make that text speak to us across the years with the dignity and self-assurance of its individuality.

Parts of chapters 2–5 utilize sections of various articles I have published previously: 'The Canons of Old English Criticism', *ELH* 34 (1967), 141–55 (© The Johns Hopkins Press); '*Beowulf* 207b–28: Narrative and Descriptive Art', *Notes & Queries* 13 (1966); 'Grendel's Approach to Heorot: Syntax and Poetry', *Old English Poetry: Fifteen Essays*, ed. R. P. Creed (Providence, R.I.: Brown Univ. Press, 1967); 'Syntactic Analysis and Old English Poetry', *NM* 64 (1963); 'Attitudes and Values in *The Seafarer*', *Studies in Philology* 51 (1954). A small part of the discussion of *The Phoenix* in chapter 6 is taken from my *Critical History of Old English Literature* (New York Univ. Press, 1965;

Univ. of London Press, 1966). All of these have been thoroughly re-worked and adapted to the design of this book. For permission to reprint and re-use these materials, I wish to thank the various journals and publishers concerned. The section on the *Finnsburh Fragment* in chapter 2 is a different version of an article appearing in a Festschrift issue of *NM*, 73 (1972).

During the course of the academic year 1970–1, I have had occasion to try out parts of chapters 1–3 in talks at Cambridge University, Leeds University and University College, Dublin, and before the London Medieval Society and the Annual Conference of Professors and Lecturers of English held at Cambridge in April 1971. I am most grateful for these opportunities, and for the service they offered in giving shape to this book. I should in particular like to thank Professors Eric G. Stanley and Peter Clemoes, the former for reading the first four chapters and making innumerable suggestions for their improvement (he is, of course, in no way responsible for errors or difficulties that remain), the latter for his steady encouragement in the project throughout the year, especially in those 'dark times' before the 'eye' began to see. Roger Fowler read the whole book for the press, and his general criticism and comments on specific points have been invaluable to me in making the final draft.

I wish to thank also the generosity of the John Simon Guggenheim Memorial Foundation for granting me a Fellowship in 1965–6, when several sections of this book first took shape; and that of the National Endowment for the Humanities of the United States for granting me a Senior Fellowship in 1970–1 for further research and the creation of the present interpretative study. I wish too to thank Susan Fagan and Sharon Brunsman for their splendid work on the typescript. Finally, to my wife and children, who have with patience endured the many demands I have put upon them during these labours, my love and gratitude.

1

Towards a Critical Framework

Thematically and aesthetically, Old English poems seem attractive to the modern reader even though they are mainly known in translation. *Beowulf* has long been a favourite, but the shorter poems also have in recent years found their poeticized way between popular book covers.[1] Additionally, several generations of students have come to appreciate in the original the elegies, *Maldon*, religious pieces like the *Dream of the Rood* and of course *Beowulf*, and have had some contact with the scholarly *aperçus* which have expanded these poems' horizons of understanding. Such contact with and experience of Old English poetry and its literary history and criticism remain, however, largely outside the mainstream of English literary studies. This isolation is perhaps not surprising in view of the conventions governing the composition and form of Anglo-Saxon poems, so radically different for the most part from those affecting more recent poetic compositions. Nevertheless there have been some attempts to find a continuous thread between our earliest English poems and those of later origin.[2] One critical commonplace calls attention to the re-surfacing of the Old English alliterative tradition in fourteenth-century poems like *Sir Gawain and the Green Knight* and *Piers Plowman*, and to its modified revival in the verse of modern poets like Gerard Manley Hopkins and W. H. Auden. Another, in a somewhat old-fashioned way, rhapsodically links the spirit of Old English poetry with that of subsequent periods: so, for example, H. C. Wyld[3] when he says that

three qualities, a feeling for the mysterious in the loveliness of nature, a sense of the solemn and sublime, sympathy with the impulses of the human heart, pervade the whole of Anglo-Saxon poetry, and through them it establishes its kinship with that of later times. In all periods, too, our

poets have found in the sights and sounds of the external
world the mirror and symbol of spiritual experience . . . .

Latterly some Old English scholars have followed one or another
of the critical methodologies which emphasize the interpretation
and aesthetic components of individual texts and which assume or
formulate theoretical critical positions *vis-à-vis* matters of 'form'
and 'content'. Thus we can find some critical essays explicitly
placed in the modern camps of the New Criticism, or formalism,
or modern linguistics. Other Old English scholars have rejected
such approaches, preferring to follow D. W. Robertson into
critical *Kampf* under a standard of 'historical criticism'.[4] And
increasingly we find essays theorizing about special topics like
the 'oral formula', 'theme', *variation* and metre.

Under these circumstances, it seems to me an appropriate
time to attempt a view of Old English poetry in terms of general
critical theory and practice, and to establish a more broadly
based rationale for our understanding and appreciation of Old
English poems. In the following pages, therefore, I propose to ask
whether it is possible, in the light of modern critical theorizing
and analyses of English literature, to develop a critical framework
by which we may arrive at more authoritative interpretations and
assessments of the Anglo-Saxon poetic achievement. To do this
we must have a clear picture of the limits and possibilities of
such critical approaches to Old English poetry. We must, per-
force, recognize and consider certain crucial problems: the extent
to which 'close reading' of a text, which has become a basic way
of arriving at meaning and poetic value in modern poems, is
applicable to Anglo-Saxon poems in view of the different conventions and traditions determining their composition; the relationship to our modern literary sensibility of the historical knowledge
necessary to the understanding of those conventions and traditions; and the possibility of ever attaining that desideratum of
critical analysis, valid interpretation.

Precedents for this kind of inquiry do exist. For instance, the
first problem has been interestingly raised with respect to later
medieval English poetry by A. C. Spearing, who shows how the
formulaic nature of that poetry, and its composition for oral
delivery, must be considered in any assessment of poems like
Sir Gawain, Troilus and Criseyde, Piers Plowman and *The*

Testament of Cressid.[5] For another, the matter of historical understanding has been approached in one way by B. F. Huppé, who suggests that the only proper mode for interpreting Old English poetry, considering the circumstances of its composition and cultural environment, is the Augustinian *via* of allegoresis, that is, of illuminating dark or enigmatic surface meanings by the spiritual values of Scripture and the expositions thereon of the Church Fathers.[6] Spearing, however, does not touch on Old English poetry, and the high road of Augustinian allegory seems to me less wide for the passage of Old English poems than Huppé will allow. And with regard to the theoretical difficulties involved in the problem of validity in interpretation in connection with Old English poems, practically nothing has been attempted.

In this opening chapter, where I wish to evolve a viable critical methodology, I shall concentrate on the general matters of historical understanding and validity. In subsequent chapters I shall treat, within the framework so evolved, some of the specific conventions of Old English poetry. My procedure will necessitate the recording and criticizing of others' theoretical formulations and practical analyses, as well as the presentation of my own.

We may begin with some brief general remarks on the nature of literary criticism and the directions it has taken in recent times. In a very readable short study of this subject, Graham Hough calls attention to the far-flung empire embraced by literary criticism.[7] Its functions are various, including the editing of texts, literary history, genre studies, interpretation and evaluation; but they are interdependent. One cannot, for example, edit a text without making interpretive judgments, nor can one interpret without having a valid text; seeing a work as a member of a particular literary genre is important for the interpretation of its discrete features, but simultaneously the determination of a text's genre involves a correct understanding of its individual parts. Yet sometimes one, sometimes another function dominates the critical activity of an age. Thus the past half century revolted against the historical antiquarianism and scientific positivism that had dominated nineteenth-century criticism, and it focused its attention upon matters of interpretation and evaluation. Its interests have been primarily aesthetic, emphasizing the formal, the technical, the stylistic aspects of individual poems. There is no need to trace here the development of this New Criticism from the Eliot of *The Sacred Wood* and the early I. A. Richards through the works of men like Cleanth Brooks, W. K. Wimsatt and F. R. Leavis:[8] the modern student of literature will be all too familiar with structural analysis, with the unifying roles of metaphor and symbol, with irony and tension and deliberate ambiguity. For our purposes it is sufficient to observe that a similar critical direction was provided for Old English literature by J. R. R. Tolkien's 1936 British Academy lecture entitled '*Beowulf*: the Monsters and the Critics', an essay in criticism which has become a staple of diet for the student of Anglo-Saxon. Reaction to this aesthetic emphasis has been inevitable, however; the pendulum has swung back again, so that one reviewer of the current critical scene has been able to remark that 'historical studies are silently in vogue while "pure" analysis has a dated air'.[9] Even that silence has recently been breached: in the autumn of 1969 the University of Virginia launched a journal called *New Literary History*. And concurrent with this reawakened historical consciousness has emerged a new form of scientific positivism, in descriptive linguistics.

The new history and the new linguistics challenge the principles and the wisdom of the New Criticism. The former stigmatizes its critical myopia in concentrating its attention on the individual text in isolation from its historical (i.e., contemporary) traditions; the latter observes that it relies too much upon the critic's impressions about the nature of language rather than upon a scientific account of a work's verbal and syntactic structures and their relationship to the norms of the language. The one demands reckoning with the cultural and literary conventions of the past in order to comprehend and evaluate properly any single work of that past; the other calls for an accurate and comprehensive knowledge of the immediate linguistic environment out of which the individual work struggles to assert its unique linguistic identity. D. W. Robertson provides us with a recent example of the call to abandon our modern perspectivism in dealing with literature of the past:[10]

If we are to compose valid criticism of works produced in earlier stylistic periods, we must do so in terms of conventions

4

established at a time contemporary with the works themselves. If we fail to do so, we shall miss the integrity of the works we study, not to mention their significance, frequently profound, for their original audience. . . .
The recognition of valid realities established by earlier generations may lead us at least one small step away from that rancid solipsistic pit into which the major tendencies of post-romantic thought have thrust us.

The argument has much to recommend it. For it is one thing to be attracted to a work of former times, say the Old English *Wanderer*, by what seems to be a timeless and universal theme of loss and transiency applicable to our modern lives; but it is another to write criticism as if the poem *were* a product of our times. Yet it is not so easy, as we shall see, to arrive at a consensus as to the realities of the past which are appropriate and valid for the specific work under analysis.

The linguistic concern in literary studies to see the grammar of a particular work in relation to the grammar of the language as a whole is exemplified in Michael Halliday's recent *cri de coeur*:[11]

A literary text has meaning against the background of the language as a whole, in all its uses; how can its language be understood except as the selection by the individual writer from the total resources at his disposal? Yet all too often the observations about the language of a work of literature bear no relation to any descriptive account of these resources. . . . All literary analysis, if one is at all interested in the special properties of the language of literary texts or of a particular genre, is essentially comparative. This makes it all the more essential to be consistent, accurate and explicit: to base the analysis firmly on a sound, existing description of the language.

Again, there is much truth in this recommendation; and again, as I will suggest later, there are theoretical questions about the relation of total description to meaning and practical difficulties with implementation, especially with regard to Old English.

Halliday and Robertson would in effect respectively deny the validity of intuitive linguistic and modern aesthetic or moral responses to literature of the past. (Halliday is not actually

5

talking about the past: I am extrapolating from his remarks.) They would re-create, rather, the ambience of the contemporary historical audience—culturally, intellectually, critically and linguistically—as the basis upon which to build an enlightened or significant understanding of their literature. That such a re-creation is desirable and even necessary, few would challenge nowadays; and the critic of medieval English poetry is one of the least likely of critical entrepreneurs to ignore either the historical and conventional contexts of his chosen poems, or their linguistic milieux. On occasion it happens that he may be seduced by attractive modern meanings and thematic preoccupations into suggesting unhistorical interpretations which seem 'relevant'. Thus Spearing gives us timely warning, for example, against the temptation to read contemptuous overtones into the Green Knight's use of the word *gyng* when he first addresses Arthur and his court in *Sir Gawain and the Green Knight*: ' "Wher is", he sayd,/"Þe governour of þis gyng?" ' Such a reading, as Spearing observes, has no historical sanction despite the later semantic development of the word as *gang*. And although we today are greatly introspective about the artistic creative process, we must beware of violating historical thematic probability to see in any Old English poem, as one recent critic has been tempted to see in the minor poem 'The Order of the World', 'a poet talking to a prospective poet about poetry and then creating a sample poem which demonstrates the proper subject for poetry....'[12] But historical critics and linguisticians clearly have more in mind than such cautionary observations. It is by a programmatic application to individual poems of historical and linguistic 'systems' that they would have us avoid the Scylla of modern relevance and the Charybdis of linguistic naïveté.

Let us for the moment lay aside the role of linguistic description in criticism and consider the historical caveat. How reliable or viable is any historical 'system'? There would seem to be several limitations. In the first place, we cannot entirely escape from our present or individual perspectives into the historical realities of other voices, other places, however much we may wish to do so. W. K. Wimsatt makes the psychological point that 'our judgments of the past cannot be discontinuous with our experience or insulated from it: to evaluate the past we have to penetrate it with our own intelligence'.[13] Wimsatt is referring here primarily to the critical function of evaluation, of determining the relative merits of this or that piece of literature, but a similar case may be made about the interpretative process. For example, our understanding of the relationship between the so-called 'palinode' to Chaucer's *Troilus and Criseyde* and all that has preceded it in the poem is, first of all, a question of interpretation, though evaluation lags not far behind: is it a superficial, irrelevant, tacked-on, conventional recanting of the courtly-love values the poem has celebrated? is it an ironic negation of those values which it has only pretended to celebrate? is it a juxtaposed second perspective that recognizes the superiority of supramundane values without condemning worldly ones? is it something else again? Literary and cultural historical knowledge will take us only so far towards establishing 'Chaucerian' meaning; thereafter we must resort to our own experience with literature, to our own sensitivity to tone, word-meaning, characterization and structural patterns.

Wimsatt's argument has been advanced a step further by some critics who hold that not only is it impossible to divorce ourselves completely from 'present meaning' in reading a work of the past, but that it is our positive duty to seek out such meanings as are relevant to our modern perspective. A good illustration of this approach in Old English criticism is that of Alain Renoir in his recent study of *Genesis B* as a psychological tragedy of self-deception: [14]

> if Old English poetry cannot be appreciated from the point
> of view of our own time, teachers of English literature
> ought to abandon it with all dispatch and turn it over to the
> linguists and antiquarians. Nor must we forget that a work of
> art may legitimately mean to a later period something it
> never meant to its original audience; in fact, it almost
> necessarily does . . .

One has only to look at the history of Shakespearean stage production to see this principle of 'relevance' in interpretative action: in the academic year in which I finished this book (1970-1), all the presentations I saw of Shakespeare plays in the London theatre (not to mention those of Webster and others), like the justly famous production of *Midsummer Night's Dream* by Peter Brook, did not really distort 'historical meaning': they reinforced it, in their way, by their corresponding stage visualization of certain linguistic and historical details in the plays themselves. Similarly, Renoir is not really renouncing, in his critical visualization, the historical context of *Genesis B*, for he amply suggests that both the poet and his original audience must have been familiar with the common Boethian view of evil being its own punishment—an historical view which he in fact makes the basis of his psychological interpretation.

Can we have it both ways, then? I would argue so, and will present some specific cases in later chapters. Relevance can and must be both historical and modern, focusing upon that aspect of text and context which has a special resonance in our own moral and aesthetic consciousness without, at the same time, falsifying or distorting historical probability.[15] This is not to say, I must hasten to add, that only certain themes and concepts in past literature qualify for our critical attention. Any 'received idea'— that is, theme or concept which has become an accepted part of an age's values—can be aesthetically activated by a poet of talent so that it reacts upon our imaginations. Thus, for example, Wimsatt observes that though the 'normative feudal view of hierarchical relations' between aristocracy and peasantry is artistically ineffective in the Lacy-Margaret denouement of *Friar Bacon and Friar Bungay*, the same historic motif *is* fired and fused imaginatively in Chaucer's 'Clerk's Tale' of Patient Griselda.[16]

A second limitation we may observe in an historical programme for criticism is that all too frequently, in both its contentual and stylistic revelations about the contemporary context in relation to a particular poem, it tends to be unfortunately reductive. That is, by a failure at times to distinguish between the specific thought in an individual poem and the general current of ideas in the cultural and intellectual climate of its time, an insensitive historicism downgrades the literary quality of the best pieces, even as under the New Critical programme the equation of value with technique, of regarding 'subtlety or complexity of arrangement as itself a criterion of literary worth,'[17] often has led to the elevation of the mediocre. Wilbur Sanders cogently makes this point about reductiveness in discussing the critical use of 'sources' to illuminate the meaning of the text. 'Contemporaneity', he says, 'is a misleading criterion of relevance [in such matters] . . .

because it fails to consider the *quality* of the thought involved'; for in dealing with a masterpiece like *Macbeth*, he argues, we are analysing a unique work of literature which should not be whittled down to less than it is by hunting for critical illumination in contemporary thought which only serves to support our original misjudgment of the work's stature.[18] In the realm of Old English literature, where for the most part sources of phrases and ideas are even more open to disputation than in the Renaissance, we must especially beware of treating the ideas and phraseology in different texts as if they were identical, however contemporaneous or even lineally descendant they may be or may seem to be. This is a matter we shall return to shortly in our discussion of the question of validity in interpretation.

A third, and perhaps the most troublesome, feature of the historical approach, one related to its tendency towards reductiveness, is that its practitioners employ what may be called the 'fallacy of homogeneity'. They assume a representativeness or orthodoxy of opinion and thought in the intellectual milieu of an age. They freely use—and abuse—the concept of 'the intended audience', a concept that is the mirror image of 'the biography of the author' to which earlier historical critics paid homage as the key to literary understanding. So entrenched has the power of 'the audience' become in Old English studies that it is difficult to find criticism within the last twenty years, since the publication of Dorothy Whitelock's impressive *The Audience of Beowulf*, that does not resort to the concept. But there must be circularity somewhere in scholars' reconstructions of that silent majority for, *bien entendu*, their interpretations, however disparate they may be, are exactly what the audience would have expected! Even when the critic appeals to what a certain sector of the poet's original audience probably understood, or appeals to the probable response of its most intelligent members, he treads on dangerous ground. After all, modern poems find contradictory readings from presumably equally intelligent modern critics. If it is argued that the Anglo-Saxons were more restricted by their socio-theological and rhetorical conventions than are the writers of today, we might remind ourselves that in another highly conventional era two knowledgeable and literary friends of Sir Philip Sidney could disagree about the substance of his *Arcadia*: Fulke Greville was convinced Sidney intended it as a discourse on the commonwealth, whereas Gabriel Harvey thought it to be about love, wisdom and valour.[19] And Alcuin, we might remind ourselves, need never have been concerned about the monks at Lindisfarne listening to tales of Ingeld if the Anglo-Saxon clerical audience had had the single-minded exegetical perspective which modern historical allegorists propose.

The difficulties of historical criticism may be focused more sharply by examining two recent interpretations of the treasure hoard in *Beowulf*, both of which make their appeals to history. In the first of these, Michael Cherniss reviews the variety of critical opinion about the meaning of treasure in the poem. He suggests that two major views emerge: one group of interpreters sees positive values in *Beowulf*ian treasure, the other believes it to represent the forces of evil or vanity which can tempt even the greatest of heroes (Beowulf) into avaricious behaviour. Cherniss agrees with the former, though he feels they have paid insufficient attention to the fact that treasure in the heroic world consisted not only of rings, gold, precious metals and gems, but also of battle-gear, decorated cups and dishes, and similar ornamental equipment. All such treasures, he argues, 'give moral value to their possessors; . . . they are, in fact, the material manifestations or representations of the proven or inherent worthiness of whoever possesses them'. He documents this assertion from the texts of *The Battle of Maldon* and *Waldere* as well as from that of *Beowulf* itself. The climax of his analysis is his explanation of the puzzling reburial of the dragon's hoard with the dead Beowulf: 'the Geats [by their cowardice] have proven unworthy of the honour and glory which the hoard represents. In the absence of worthy inheritors [Wiglaf having modestly disclaimed credit for his role in the dragon-slaying], the treasure must end on the funeral pyre with its rightful owner, Beowulf . . . [L]ike the treasures of Scyld at the beginning of the poem [it] must also "die" and be buried.'[20]

Quite a different analysis of the hoard emerges in Margaret Goldsmith's *The Mode and Meaning of Beowulf*. Though Mrs Goldsmith acknowledges that treasure in the world of the poem is an appropriate hero's reward, she believes that the hoard 'becomes for the poet a focal symbol for the transience of the material world'. For her the hoard's reburial 'symbolically re-enacts the tragedy of the lost race' whose lone survivor had committed it to the earth: '. . . in the larger perspective [Heorot and the hoard] can be seen to be the images of man's pride and cupidity, the two fundamental sins which tie the carnal man to earth. To their possessors they seem durable; to the Christian audience they are presented as brilliant and destructible, costly and without worth.'[21] In support of this analysis, Mrs Goldsmith cites not only from the text of *Beowulf* but from Scripture and the Church Fathers.

While the two interpretations of the hoard overlap to some extent, they are, with respect to the significance of its reburial, obviously irreconcilable. A couple of observations on this irreconcilability are in order. The first is that both positions are self-confirming. As E. D. Hirsch, Jun., observes,[22]

> when interpreters construe texts differently, the data they use to support their constructions are to some degree sponsored by their constructions . . . . The word patterns and stylistic effects which support one interpretation can become different patterns and effects under a disparate interpretation. The same text can sponsor quite different data (though some of the data will remain constant) and each set of data will very powerfully support the interpretive theory which sponsored it in the first place.

The second observation is that although both analyses use the contemporary historical scene for authentication, they draw upon different parts of that scene: Cherniss resorts to the world of heroic poetry, Mrs Goldsmith to the allegorical mode of patristic exegesis.

The world of heroic poetry, the allegorical mode—such terms lead us into the matter of *genre* and the role of genre in helping to establish interpretational validity. Now, genre studies have a time-honoured place in literary history, as George Watson has recently emphasized: 'when the literary historian identifies the lineage of poems whose pedigrees have fallen into oblivion— when he identifies one of *The Canterbury Tales* as a beast-fable, for instance, and another as a romance of courtly love—he is restoring to the consciousness of the reader knowledge of an indispensable kind'.[23] Such knowledge is useful for criticism in that by classifying a text 'as belonging to a particular genre, the interpreter automatically posits a general horizon for its meaning.

The genre provides a sense of the whole, a notion of typical meaning components', some idea of 'the norms and conventions deposited by previous usages'.[24] In many cases, of course, an author will explicitly inform us about the genre of his work, as Spenser does in his famous letter to Raleigh about *The Faerie Queene*, or as Milton does in his preface to *Samson Agonistes*. And internal evidence, when external is lacking, is often clear enough, as in the specific allegorization of the Old English *Phoenix* or in the riddle questions or exhortations to 'say what I am' in the Exeter Book. The trouble is that for so many poems, including *The Nun's Priest's Tale*, to which Watson was alluding, the simple identification of *one* genre is insufficient for the positing of a horizon of meaning; and when we have a nexus of genres in a poem, or when genre lines are indistinct, how do we make proper decisions about the relative importance of 'typical meaning components'? The notion of a genre itself is, alas, somewhat elusive.

The effect of genre identification upon the interpretation of poems is well illustrated by the various displacements of the 'general horizon of meaning' in the critical history of such poems as *The Wanderer*, *The Seafarer*, *The Wife's Lament*, *The Husband's Message*, *Deor*, *The Ruin* and *Wulf and Eadwacer*. These are the famous elegies of Anglo-Saxon poetry. Their identification as *elegy* occurred in the nineteenth century, probably because they seemed to reflect something of a sense of personal loss in a 'complaint' or *Klage*.[25] And if we read these poems with this expectation in mind, we find a particular kind of meaning in them that has satisfied many critics, and struck a resonant chord in the general reader's mind, down to the present day. Some recent criticism, however, has cast doubt upon this classification as the generic umbrella under which to shelter all these poems. *Deor*, for example, which because of its allusions to Germanic legend has at times in the past been appropriately viewed as an heroic poem as often as elegy, has now been cast by one critic into the genre 'charm' and by another into that of 'begging poem'. *The Husband's Message*, admittedly the least elegiac in tone, has been interpreted by another critic as a prosopopoeic allegory in which neither the usually assumed human agent of the husband nor a surrogate runic stave, but the Holy Rood is the speaker. Those perennial favourites *The Wanderer* and *The Seafarer* have been interpreted now as allegories, now as penitential poems, now as wisdom literature, now as debate—to name but a few of the genre transmogrifications they have undergone. *Wulf and Eadwacer*, the most obscure of these poems, obviously had quite a different horizon of meaning when it was thought to be a riddle (and solved 'Cynewulf') in the nineteenth century than it has now as a presumed psychological-elegiacal love lyric. And a denial of the existence of the genre *Frauenlied*, or song uttered by a woman, in Old English has led some critics to special pleading about the textually-given feminine grammatical gender in the first two lines of *The Wife's Lament*.[26]

A plague on all your horizons, the reader of these poems may well be tempted to exclaim. We seem to be in the realm of the medieval dream world, where the categorizing of a dream as a *somnium coeleste*, *somnium animale* or *somnium naturale*—that is, as the product of divine revelation, psychological trauma or physical stimulus—depends, as Chaucer's Pandarus would have it, upon the interest and inclination of the classifier: whether he be priest, physician or Pertolete. Well, it may not be so bad as all this, but clearly there is a degree of circularity in the identification of genre and the interpretation of parts of a poem, a point I made earlier and shall return to again in a later chapter.

Despite such difficulties in genre identification, E. D. Hirsch, Jun., suggests that herein lies the path to determining interpretational validity. If there is any substance to Hirsch's position, even if it requires some modification, genre can thus be viewed as a pivotal point for both the theoretical problems of interpretation we are concerned with in this chapter: the role of historical criticism and the possibility of achieving validity in our analyses of poems. As will be seen, generic considerations will run like a theme throughout the rest of this book, always in the background even when not specifically mentioned, receiving its full due in the last chapter. But this is to move ahead of ourselves, and we had best return to an examination of Hirsch's hermeneutical argument.

This argument involves establishing a distinction between *meaning* and *significance*. The former, according to Hirsch, is that aspect of the verbal communication which does not change; the latter is that which varies according to the different contexts with which it is correlated: the psychological, the sociological and the like. It is *meaning*, he proposes, which the analytical critic attempts to understand and to communicate through his interpretation; and it is the stability of meaning which allows us to employ a process of validation to verify or to disqualify differing interpretations of the same text. For Hirsch, as I have indicated, the most important criterion for validity is generic appropriateness. He assumes that any critic worth his salt will not attempt a reading beyond that permissible in the norms of the language of the text—that is, he will not ignore what Hirsch labels 'the criterion of legitimacy'; nor will he conveniently overlook any of the significant linguistic components in the text—that is, he will pay heed to 'the criterion of correspondence'. But consideration of genre is the crucial matter: for genre provides the guidelines for the expectations of particulars, even as the visible features of a box, through our familiarity with box-structure, will suggest the box's unseen dimensions and texture. Useful as a starting point in our analyses, Hirsch argues, are the traditional concepts of genre, but we must constantly refine our notion of the 'type' to what he calls 'intrinsic genre', to the smallest class of works of which the text in question is a species. To this end we must inquire not what the language of the text means, but '"What in all probability did the author mean? Is the pattern of emphases I construe the author's pattern?"'[27]

We find ourselves here in the thicket of 'authorial intention', but it is a necessary corollary of Hirsch's distinction between meaning and significance. Hirsch is not, of course, unaware of intentional fallacy, and his proposal is not at all simplistic. He argues that even in anonymous texts—and these are what we must deal with in our Old English criticism—'intention' is discoverable, because the author has embodied it in particular communal linguistic symbols. Whether we can indeed distinguish between meaning and significance, whether 'intention' thus construed is really different from 'what the language of the text means', are subjects for argument beyond the scope of this book.[28] Reviewers of Hirsch's *Validity in Interpretation* have not been slow to raise these and other questions. But I believe an examination of the chief illustration of Hirsch's validating system may help more than theory can to pass judgment upon the effectiveness of his proposal, and to move us further along towards an acceptable and useful critical framework.

Hirsch's example is far removed from Old English poetry. For that very reason it may be salutary, since it will allow the Old English student and critic to examine it with fewer preconceptions and with less critical passion. The poem is Wordsworth's 'A slumber did my spirit seal', and the interpretations Hirsch offers to validate or discredit are those of Cleanth Brooks and F. W. Bateson. It may be convenient to have the poem before us:

> A slumber did my spirit seal;
>   I had no human fears:
> She seemed a thing that could not feel
>   The touch of earthly years.
>
> No motion has she now, no force;
>   She neither hears nor sees;
> Rolled round in earth's diurnal course,
>   With rocks and stones and trees.

The key question in interpreting the poem is what effect the impact of Lucy's death has upon the speaker. A corollary question is, what in particular do the last two lines indicate about this effect? I quote the relevant portions of the two criticisms from Hirsch (p. 228):

> Brooks: [The poet] attempts to suggest something of the lover's agonized shock at the loved one's present lack of motion—his response to her utter and horrible inertness. . . . Part of the effect, of course, resides in the fact that a dead lifelessness is suggested more sharply by an object's being whirled about by something else than by an image in repose. But there are other matters at work here: the sense of the girl's falling back into the clutter of things, companioned by things chained like a tree to a particular spot, or by things completely inanimate like rocks and stones . . . [She] is caught up helplessly into the empty whirl of the earth which measures and makes time. She is touched by and held by earthly time in its most powerful and horrible image.

> Bateson: The final impression the poem leaves is not of two contrasting moods, but of a single mood mounting to a climax in the pantheistic magnificence of the last two lines. . . . The vague living-Lucy of this poem is opposed to the

grander dead-Lucy who has become involved in the sublime processes of nature. We put the poem down satisfied, because its last two lines succeed in effecting a reconciliation between the two philosophies or social attitudes. Lucy is actually more alive now that she is dead, because she is now part of the life of Nature, and not just a human 'thing.'

Here is a disagreement about interpretation every bit as sharp as that between Cherniss and Goldsmith over the hoard in *Beowulf*. And like those interpretations, these too are self-confirming (if we squint hard enough). But when 'two interpretations . . . impose different emphases on similar meaning components, at least one . . . must be wrong. They cannot be reconciled', says Hirsch. How to choose between them? 'We must', he continues, 'posit the author's typical outlook, the typical associations and expectations which form in part the context of his utterance'.[29] Only thus can we arrive at the intrinsic genre and provide our proper horizon of meaning. Brooks has not been concerned with the author's intention but has assumed a 'universal matrix' of human attitudes towards bereavement, Hirsch argues—Robertson's 'rancid solipsistic pit'? Bateson, on the other hand, has 'tried to reconstruct the author's probable attitudes [i.e., his pantheism in 1799] so far as these are relevant in specifying the poem's meaning'. Although Hirsch acknowledges that Bateson has slighted the criterion of correspondence by not paying enough attention to the role of the text's negatives, and although he further admits that typical attitudes are not always applicable to specific cases, he nevertheless validates Bateson's analysis as the more probable.[30]

The probability of Bateson's interpretation seems highly dubious to me, however. Whatever Wordsworth's typical attitudes were at this time, the linguistic data of the text of *this* poem do not seem accurately reflected in Bateson's terminology. Do the last two lines really suggest 'the sublime processes of nature', or that the dead Lucy is 'now part of the life of Nature'? Such descriptive phrases seem, rather, a transference from another Lucy poem, 'Three years she dwelt'. And we notice how quickly *processes* become *life* in this analysis, and how *nature* with a small *n* becomes capitalized and personified! This does not mean that Brooks's reading is automatically to be preferred:

there is no *clutter of things* in the poem that I can see, and the word *chained* to describe the trees goes beyond what the text says or implies; words like *utter* and *horrible* are the critic's, not the poet's. Yet the implications of the precise wording of the first stanza lead to an expectation of a reversal: that the spirit will become un-sealed and the 'I' will awake to human fears. Any interpretation which ignores this syntactic-semantic implication, or which tries to argue it away as Bateson does elsewhere by a somewhat naïve linguistic equation of word-order and meaning in the lines of the two stanzas,[31] cannot be probable.

Of course we do not have to accept either interpretation, and it seems to me that Geoffrey Hartman has come closer to the truth about meaning in this poem when he writes:[32]

> the poet expresses no shock at finding his illusion so
> rigorously betrayed by the fulfillment. . . . Lucy's death . . .
> occurs in the blank between the stanzas. The poem may have
> its structural irony, but the poet's mood is meditative
> beyond irony. The first stanza describes the illusion and
> the second simply speaks its epitaph. . . . It is through
> Lucy's death that Wordsworth learns that nature does
> betray the heart which loves her. Yet the betrayal is not
> absolute; it has its point of comfort. It reveals not
> merely the delusion but also nature's strength in having
> fostered this according to a teleological principle.

This explanation has taken into account the typical attitude in Wordsworth's Lucy poems, and has ranged widely into the history of ideas; but it has also considered the implications of the specific language of *this* poem, and its structure as well. How much more accurate an account of the meaning of the last two lines than either Bateson or Brooks provide is Hartman's 'according to a teleological principle'! Especially if we accept tone as part of meaning, which seems to me essential. Worth noting, too, is Hartman's willingness to accept a discrepancy between structural tone and the speaker's mood without calling into question the poem's integrity. Acceptance of similar discrepancies might well help us resolve some of the interpretive problems in certain Old English poems.

In using genre, then, as a guide to interpretational validity— even when we are dealing with 'intrinsic genre', or with the typicality of expectations of one author, or with a series of poems by one author which *seem* to express a consistent attitude towards the same experience—we must guard against the fallacy of similarity. That is, we must not assume that because there are *some* resemblances between the poem under scrutiny and others by the same author, that all the poems are 'saying the same thing'. This is to err on the subject-matter side even as the fallacy of homogeneity errs with regard to the 'consistency' of an audience.

In Hirsch's use of Wordsworth, it is a presumed ideational similarity among poems on the same subject, the death of Lucy, which has led the critic wrongly, I think, to posit the same intrinsic genre, hence identical expectation of meaning. In Old English criticism this questionable use of thematic resemblance can likewise be found, as in some attempts to force both *The Wanderer* and *The Seafarer*—both poems having as subject matter the insecurity of this world—into the same generic mould of allegory: for whereas the latter can reasonably fill that mould, the former's specific treatment of its subject is not compatible with it, and distortion of meaning results.[33]

Perhaps even more frequently in criticism the concomitant problem of dictional similarity arises. Hirsch has indeed spotted *this* danger, for he counsels 'that two different minds can intend quite different meanings by the same word sequence'; and again, 'nothing is gained by conflating and confusing different "texts" as though they were somehow the same simply because they both use the same word sequence'.[34] For Old English poetry this cautionary counsel is well advised not only when the critic is confronted by formulaic repetition amongst poems, but equally when he is tempted to find dictional similarity, hence ideational identity, between Old English poems and possible Scriptural and exegetical 'sources'. With respect to this admonition, it will be instructive here to examine two illustrations of the uses of similarity in the interpretation of Old English poems before pursuing further the consequences of my criticism of Hirsch's methodology.

The Mode and Meaning of Beowulf will supply my first example. In attempting to demonstrate what she considers to be Beowulf's fallibility in the conduct of his fight with the dragon, Mrs Goldsmith suggests that the hero has this time, in contrast with his behaviour in his previous struggles, abandoned his trust in God. He relies, she argues, solely on his own strength to see him through this crisis; and she cites lines 2540b–1 in support of her belief:

strengo getruwode

anes mannes.   Ne bið swylc earges sið.

(He trusted in the strength of one man. Such is not the way of a coward.)

The following remark indicates the direction her proof will take: 'At this juncture, a man familiar with the Psalms could hardly fail to remember . . . "They that trust in their own strength, and glory in the multitude of their riches" (Ps 48:7).' From this assumption of definitive recognition of similarity, she moves to St Augustine's use of the psalm in his exposition of life as a fight against the Adversary: 'But he conquers in the blow that he strikes who does not presume in his own strength, but in God as protector. . . . If we are with God, we conquer the Devil, but if you should fight alone against the Devil, you will be conquered.' There follow three more pages of quotation from Augustine and Gregory, leading to the interpretation that Beowulf's error was in making no spiritual preparation for this occasion: 'he is already spiritually weakened by the feeling of self-sufficiency which long years of success have bred. Hence he goes into the fight foolishly trusting his own strength, looking neither to man nor to God for help.'[35]

Dictional similarity is here used as the basis for an elaborate interpretational structure. Now I would not deny that Old English poets drew upon associative echoes not only for the enrichment of, but also for giving direction toward, meaning; but we cannot ignore differences in tone and context. We would have to ask, I think, whether the context leading up to lines 2540b–1 suggests that Beowulf really felt self-sufficient, and what the tone of the crucial lines is. Shortly before this passage, the poet has told us that Beowulf's 'spirit was gloomy, wavering, ready for bloody death': 'Him wæs geomor sefa,/wæfre ond wælfus'; and the tone of the hero's 'boasting speech' immediately prior seems more one of resignation to duty than of foolish self-sufficiency. Beowulf's trust in his own strength, then, may well be seen as endeavouring to spare his men's commitment to what the hero knows is an unequal struggle—it is his duty as their leader. (Their duty, in turn, was not to desert him in his need.) All this seems summed up in the poet's comment 'That is not the way of a coward', a comment which Mrs Goldsmith ignores in her interpretation. She likewise takes insufficient account of the second half of the psalm verse she quotes, 'and glory in the multitude of their riches'; for it is surely stretching matters to see Beowulf as such a reveller, even if it is not till after he is mortally wounded that he says he wished to gain the treasure *for his people*. Further, the poet has nowhere indicated that his hero does not trust in God: he is simply silent on that point here, even as he was silent about it in the hero's fight with Grendel's mother. And after the battle, he has Beowulf give thanks, in variational fullness (see chapter 3 on *variation*), to the Almightly *for having allowed him* the power to acquire the gold for his nation:

Ic ðara frætwa	Frean ealles ðanc,	
Wuldurcyninge	wordum secge,	
ecum Dryhtne,	þe ic her on starie,	
ðæs ðe ic moste	minum leodum	
ær swyltdæge	swylc gestrynan.	(ll. 2794–8)

(I for all these treasures which I here gaze upon say thanks with words to the Lord, King of Glory, Eternal Lord, because I have been permitted to gain such for my people before my death day.)

Our interpretations of Old English poems are necessarily based to a considerable extent on comparisons of one sort or another, but if dictional similarity to Scriptural or exegetical sources is to be used convincingly, it must be used cautiously. The second example I wish to adduce demonstrates such discrimination. It is Peter Clemoes's comparison of a passage in *The Seafarer* with one in a tract of Alcuin's, leading to the conclusion that the latter is not just a parallel to, but the probable source of, the former.[36] The poetic verses in question are lines 58–64a, in which the mind or spirit of the speaker leaves his breast to survey sea and land:

Forþon nu min hyge hweorfeð   ofer hreþerlocan,
min modsefa   mid mereflode,

ofer hwæles eþel   hweorfeð wide,
eorþansceatas;   cymeð eft to me
gifre ond grædig,   gielleð anfloga,
hweteð on hwælweg   hreþer unwearnum
ofer holma gelagu.

(Wherefore now my spirit moves beyond the confines of
my breast, my mind with the sea-flood, over the whale's
home, turns widely across the surface of the earth; the
lone-flier returns to me eager and greedy, calls loudly,
urges my heart irresistibly onto the whale-path over the
expanse of the seas.)

The Alcuin tract is *De animae ratione*, the passage in question
that where the ability of the soul or mind, even in sleep, is said to
travel at[37]

such speed that one moment of time it surveys the sky and,
if it wishes, flies across seas, traverses lands and cities, in
short, by thinking, it, of itself, sets before its view all things
it chooses, however far and wide they may be removed. And
yet some people marvel if the divine mind of God keeps all
parts of the universe simultaneously and always present to it
—God's mind which rules all things, everywhere present
and everywhere whole—when the strength and power of the
human mind shut up within a mortal body is so great that it
cannot be restrained . . . from having free power of
thinking without tolerating rest.

Alcuin incorporates a poem in his tract, lines of which are even
closer to those of *The Seafarer*, Clemoes argues. The soul, the
poem says, ennobled by its ability to acknowledge its creator,[38]

. . . mare, . . . terras, coelum . . . pervolat altum,
  Quamvis sit carnis carcere clausa suæ.

(flies across sea, lands and lofty sky, although it is shut in
the prison of its body.)

Clemoes's analysis is worth quoting at some length:[39]

it is highly probable that the *Seafarer* poet's imagination
should have been stimulated by Alcuin's concept of the
mind escaping from the body and flying in thought over sea

and land: Alcuin's poetic statement would have presented it to his mind as a sharply defined thought and the prose statement of it would have impressed him with the idea's significance. Here was exactly the kind of idea to activate a sensibility that is exemplified by the vivid apprehension of the cries of seabirds earlier in the poem. What is more likely than that this poet should actualize *pervolare* as a calling bird in the context of his poem? Both the unique word *anfloga* and the strikingly realistic verb *gielleð* suggest that his imagination was keenly engaged. Alcuin's wording would have given him a powerful nucleus round which to crystallize his portrayal. That he should have been helped associatively by various elements in Christian and Christianized pagan thought is probable too.

Clemoes is just as able in what follows to cite the Fathers as is Mrs Goldsmith, but to more critical purpose. And he is ready to recognize differences between the Old English poem and Alcuin:[40]

for instance, *The Seafarer* does not elevate reason above desire and anger, and the tract has none of *The Seafarer*'s preoccupation with the transitoriness and decay of life in this world. What we can say is that they are in harmony: the statement by the speaker in *The Seafarer* that the direction of his thoughts is as described in lines 58–64a

forþon me hatran sind

Dryhtnes dreamas   þonne þis deade lif
læne on londe

(because the joys of the Lord are dearer to me than this dead life transitory on earth)

depends on the belief that the mind which ranges the world as his does will lead him to God, and this is the point that Alcuin's tract as a whole expounds.

Two points may be made about Clemoes's presentation apropos my argument. First, he, unlike Mrs Goldsmith, goes beyond mere similarities of wording and message to vague Augustinian (or Gregorian) parallels—as might be made between the *Confessions*,

Book x, viii–xxi, dealing with memory (especially viii, say these
lines: 'And in my memory too I meet myself—I recall myself,
what I have done, when and where and in what state of mind I
was when I did it . . . From the same store I can weave into the
past endless new likenesses of things either experienced by me
or believed on the strength of things experienced; and from these
again I can picture actions and events and hopes for the future;
and upon them all I can meditate as if they were present')[41] and
the operation of memory in *The Wanderer*, where the speaker
'sees' his former companions (ll. 51ff.). Clemoes's parallel of the
Seafarer passage and Alcuin is recognizably right because he has
convincingly *analysed* its probabilities instead of simply assuming
a definitive recognition. It is not sufficient for an interpreter to
say, 'Look, here is a similar passage from the Bible or one of the
Fathers', and then build a superstructure of interpretation upon
this precarious foundation. Even in the citation of other Old
English poems as parallels, I think this is an important caveat.
Kaske, for instance, in trying to support his case for *The Husband's Message* being a speech of the Cross says,[42]

> The goal of the journey in 'The Husband's Message' is
> described in the damaged lines 50b–56a in terms of
> treasure and companions, and in lines 61b–63 in terms of
> treasure and banqueting. The Old English *Dream of the
> Rood*, in a passage whose meaning is beyond dispute,
> presents a strikingly similar picture of the heavenly
> kingdom, along with the traditional role of the Cross as
> convoy to it:
>
> . . . .
> ond me þonne gebringe   þær is blis mycel,
> dream on heofonum,   þær is dryhtnes folc
> geseted to symle,   þær is singal blis,
> ond me þonne asette   þær ic syþþan mot
> wunian on wuldre   well mid þam halgum
> dreames brucan,
>
> (And then it will bring me where there is great bliss, joy in
> heaven where there is the Lord's host seated at banquet,
> where there is continual bliss, and it will then set me where
> I may afterwards dwell in glory, along with the holy ones
> partake of joy).

23

As he makes no more than this bald but very positive assertion of dictional relevance, the doubter quite properly turns to the text in question from *The Husband's Message* (Kaske's ll. 50b–6a and 61b–3 are in *ASPR*, ll. 33b–9a and 44b–6):

<pre>
                          siþþan motan
secgum ond gesiþum   s[. . . . .]
næglede beagas;   he genoh hafað
fædan gold [.]s   [. . . . .]
[. . . . .]d elþeode   eþel healde,
fægre foldan   [. . . . .]
[. . . . . .]ra hæleþa
</pre>

(that you two may afterwards [distribute treasure?],
studded arm-rings, to warriors and companions; he has
sufficient of burnished gold . . . holds dwelling in a foreign
land, a fair country . . . of warriors)

<pre>
                     nis him wilna gad,
ne meara ne maðma   ne medodreama,
ænges ofer eorþan   eorlgestreona
</pre>

(he has no lack of desire, neither of horses nor of treasures
nor of mead-joys, no lack of any of human treasures over
the earth).

Are these 'strikingly similar'? It would not seem so: the poet of *The Husband's Message* is talking very concretely about studded rings, burnished gold, horses, treasures, mead-joys and the treasures of men, whereas the poet of *The Dream of the Rood* mentions abstractions: great bliss, joy in heaven, banquet, continual bliss. These sets are hardly equatable!

The second point to be made about Clemoes's presentation in contrast to Mrs Goldsmith's or Kaske's is that he will not push dictional or even contentual similarity further than the text of the poem warrants; and this restraint is important if interpretations are to find general acceptance. Irving makes much the same point in a different context when he says that 'an idea expressed in the Latin prose of a homily is never the same as the idea expressed in Old English verse, unless one ignores style altogether'.[43] Nor, as we have just observed, are averred similarities always more than in the eye of the beholder. As Dogberry happily puts it in *Much Ado About Nothing,* 'Comparisons are odorous'—and insensitive, partial, vague, feeble comparisons of poetic texts with alleged sources or parallels smell more of the single-minded scholar's lamp than of the multifoliate rose of poetic imagination.

We may return now to Hirsch's suggestion for achieving validity in interpretation. It would seem, if the observations I have been making have any force, a vain endeavour to work towards this achievement from the author's intention, from *genre* however widely or narrowly construed, or from the larger contentual or cultural environment of a work, or from dictional similarity—without submitting the knowledge brought from these areas to a close and objective cross-examination from the text itself. Hirsch's theory of expectations, however stimulating and useful, needs modification. In fact, one of its fundamental assumptions, that we must ask not what the text says but what the author means, might better be reversed. For, as John Huntley, in a review essay of Hirsch's book, acutely points out:[44]

> The poetic text, amorphous though it may seem at first,
> at least yields a set of words which individually expand
> possible meanings, and a known syntax which delimits and
> systematizes these possibilities. At the essentially poetic,
> supralinguistic level, a poetic text yields individual images
> and episodes. These, in isolation, expand possible meanings.
> But a text also reveals parallel or antiparallel relationships
> which contract and systematize their bearing on each other.
> At both levels of organization, the more lexical and cultural
> history one knows, the greater seems the suggestive power of
> individual parts; yet the more precisely one construes formal
> relationships, the more severely will burgeoning possibility
> be systematically reduced to limited, therefore determinable,
> actuality.

We may put this idea another way, more in line with the 'horizon of meaning' Hirsch is concerned to discover: the components of poetry—its words, images, themes, genre (in the larger sense)—provide us with sets of expectations whose interaction formally in a text—in syntax, poetic conventions, structure—produce 'intended' and to some extent verifiable meaning.

This is fine so far as it goes, but something significant seems to me left out of account. For the formal relationships also bring sets of expectations with them to a text; and while they narrow the range of meaning of the individual components, they also create new, *ad hoc* meanings by the implications arising from those very relationships. Puns and other forms of ambiguity in meaning, for example, are the creations of just such contextual relationships. A good illustration of this kind of *ad hoc* meaning may be found in the fourth stanza of John Donne's *A Valediction Forbidding Mourning*:

> Dull sublunary lovers' love,
> Whose soul is sense, cannot admit
> Absence, because it doth remove
> Those things which elemented it.

Murray Krieger's comment on the pun here is that[45]

> 'sense' is forced upon us as the root of '*absence*' in letter as well as concept. We are taught what 'absence' really is: a word with a soul of 'sense', with 'sense' the thing 'that elemented it' and thus the thing that 'cannot admit' it since 'absence' involves—in word and concept, in word *as* concept—the deprivation, indeed the elimination of 'sense'.

That is, what forces this new semantic identity upon us is the phonetic similarity of *sense-absence*, a formal relationship established by context.

Krieger's approach to literature and criticism may help clarify further the framework of expectations and implications I am proposing as a model. He says of the literary work itself that it must

> as literature and not another thing, strive to become a self-sufficient system of symbols that comes to terms with itself—in effect, a unique philology, the 'new word' . . . whose definition is provided by the many old words as they together shut off their system. This shutting off compels the submissive and knowledgeable reader towards being utterly contained by the work, despite the fact that its references, taken atomistically, seem to be directed extramurally; despite, that is, the crucial—and obvious—relations between the words in the poem and the words as normally

used in the cultural milieu that surrounds and nourishes the poem, . . . between the forms and devices of the work and the received conventions and disciplines of an historically conditioned medium.

Thus the critic, Krieger concludes,

needs all the knowledge of the world behind the signs that he can discover. This means knowledge of the world outside the poem, literary and real, the poet's and the critic's. That he must distinguish all that was outside from what *is* inside means he must allow the work its right to aspire to its own oneness and integrity . . . although to do so he cannot rest in his knowledge of the signs out of which its oneness can grow but to which it cannot be reduced.[46]

Krieger is perhaps too insistent, even in the case of the most experimental modern poetry, on the linguistic uniqueness of the individual poem; and certainly where Old English poems are concerned the commonality of language and poetic convention makes his assertion about uniqueness seem grossly exaggerated. Nevertheless, his 'contextualist' view of literature and of the critic's proper procedure is salutary; for it goes beyond the New Criticism to embrace past significance as well as present meaning, and it moves in this process from the poem itself to 'history'.[47] It thus avoids the danger of bringing preconceived notions from the culture to the poem, a fault that vitiates much of the so-called historical criticism of medieval literature—or so *it seemeth me*.

Does all this bring us any closer to determinate meaning and to validity in interpretation? I am not sure it does, I must confess, since there are still inescapable problems of focus and choice of relevant context in our criticism.[48] But if we adopt as a critical framework a theory of expectations and implications which enter into and become part of the language of a poem, we can subsume, while simultaneously avoiding their pitfalls, the significant concepts of authorial intention and audience response; and we can utilize comparisons discriminatingly, without entrapping ourselves in the fallacies of homogeneity and similarity. If we respect and make clear in our criticism the various sets of expectations that impinge upon a particular poem, if we are aware of the limitations imposed upon those expectations by formal relationships within a text and of the possible implications those relationships generate, if we work outwards from a poem to its contemporary cultural environment—we are more likely to achieve a larger consensus of agreement about meaning than we will by pursuing 'typical' approaches on the one hand or purely 'internalist' analyses on the other.[49]

Earlier in this chapter I scanted the scientific linguistic approach advocated by Halliday and others as a *sine qua non* in literary criticism. This view includes not only the necessity for a scientific account of the language as a whole, but also such a descriptive account of any poem under analysis. Perhaps the simplest and most engaging response to this 'total' exercise was furnished, *mutatis mutandis*, by A. E. Housman half a century ago in his comment on textual critics:[50]

> A textual critic engaged upon his business is not at all like
> Newton investigating the motions of the planets: he is much
> more like a dog hunting for fleas. If a dog hunted for fleas
> on mathematical principles, basing his researches on
> statistics of area and population, he would never catch
> a flea except by accident. They require to be treated as
> individuals; and every problem which presents itself to the
> textual critic must be regarded as possibly unique.

Such a reply will never, of course, satisfy the true-born linguist, who may justifiably point with pride to the multitudinous and insightful linguistic-literary studies of Roman Jakobson. But the specialists of his heroic size are few indeed, and even in his case I suspect that the valuable critical perceptions do not really emerge from the results of systematic application of linguistic description but are coincident with it, because he is a true-born critic as well as linguist. There are dangers, too, as I. A. Richards and others have noted, even in the methodology. For example,[51]

> probably only some, not all, of the features consciously
> discerned and included in the *account* [of a poem] will be
> actually operative in shaping the *response*. The machinery of
> distinctions used in the account has developed to meet
> general linguistic needs and purposes. It has only in part
> been devised primarily and expressly for the description of

poetic structure. It may therefore distort, may invite attention to features not essential to the poetic process.

I would not pretend that this is a sufficient response to a linguistic programme for literary criticism, nor do I mean to suggest that applications cannot open our eyes to interpretative solutions and values overlooked or distorted by less rigorous and less systematic critical analyses, even as 'historical criticism', despite the difficulties suggested above, is helping to restore a much-needed perspective to interpretive analysis. But we have lingered long enough, for the moment, by theoretical waters.

In the chapters which follow I should like to explore various sets of expectations and their deviations into specific sense in individual passages and poems, and to suggest some implications of meaning they engender in formal relationships. This exploration will by no means be exhaustive, nor will it attempt to use the critical framework developed in this chapter in any systematic way. I would like to suggest through example how we can weigh one set of expectations against others and against implications to arrive at 'reasonable' interpretations. For it is only thus that we can approach an interpretational validity that is, however elusive and ever-receding, surely a desideratum of our critical activity.

2

Expectations and Implications in Diction and Formula

A logical place to commence this exploration of the interpretive process in Old English poetry is with the meanings of words. In our critical endeavours with modern poetry, we assume axiomatically that good poets choose their words with care and use them with precision, whatever compromise they must make in their determinate meaning to meet the formal requirements of their verse.[1] And we take pains to establish the felicity of meanings, both denotational and attitudinal, that their selection of *this* word instead of one of its dictionary synonyms obtains in its immediate syntactical and lexical relationships. The New Criticism in particular, whatever its limitations, has taught us to link key words thematically and structurally across syntactic boundaries, to look for irony and multiplicity of meaning. In analysing the diction of Old English poetry, however, we must acknowledge and respect certain difficulties: our limited knowledge of the lexicon, the formulaic nature of composition, the restrictions placed upon the poet's freedom of word choice by the formal demands of alliteration and metre. An additional difficulty is posed by the theory of oral composition and, whether we accept or reject that theory, by the undeniable fact of recitation for an audience of auditors. These difficulties lead towards the overwhelming question: can we knowledgeably and relevantly, with regard to both historical and present significance, examine words in Old English poems for the precision of meaning and subtlety of effect we find (or sometimes think we find) in the diction of modern poems? Or must our expectations of Anglo-Saxon diction be of a different dimension?

The relation of words to the verbal formula offers a convenient starting point for investigation. The formula has been, and continues to be, amply researched, and I do not propose here to

trace the history of formulaic argument and the various suggestions advanced to define formula and formulaic system in
Homeric, Yugoslavian and Old English poetry.[2] But an examination of certain claims for composition by formula may prove
useful in determining the degree to which we can resort to
nuances of meaning in individual words when we interpret Old
English poems.

The chief significance for critical analysis in the oral composition theory, as distinct from its formulaic element, would seem to
be the idea of the rapidity of composition. For if the scop had
to work quickly, either drawing upon established formulas or
creating new formulas within 'systems', we cannot expect to find
care and precision in word selection. *Beowulf maþelode* in the
a-verse of a line, for example, would almost automatically lead to
the formulaic epithet *bearn Ecgðeowes* in the b-verse; and one
could not consider the pairing to have other than 'formal meaning'
(see chapter 5). Presumably, however, Old English poems that
have found their way into manuscript transcription and have been
considered excellent by generations of critics, even if so considered for different reasons, were not the immediate spontaneous
outpourings of untutored or ungifted singers. From what the
oral theorists themselves suggest about the shaping of an Anglo-
Saxon poem, it may well be, as R. F. Lawrence has proposed,
'that a popular theme, or poem of several related themes, as it is
progressively developed and refined by a succession of oral poets
[or, we might add, by the same singer himself in successive
performances] could achieve a perfection of form and a density of
utterance perhaps even beyond the capacity of written literature'.[3]
Thus, even if a poem like *Beowulf* were to be convincingly
demonstrated as of oral provenience in its extant form, which it
has not been, the case for abandoning standard critical techniques
in analyses of its poetic meanings and values remains unproved.
Further, it is very difficult to prove the oral nature of Old
English formulaic verse; for indisputable written texts use 'oral'
formulas, as many scholars in recent years have observed.[4]

What about the formulaic nature of Old English poetry?
Does this characteristic, accepted as such in one sense or another
by most of the community of Anglo-Saxon scholars, militate
against our praising a scop for having chosen *le mot juste*, and
against its corollaries in critical exegesis and evaluation? An

analysis of R. P. Creed's provocative and frequently-cited essay 'The Making of an Anglo-Saxon Poem'[5] may be instructive in this matter.

Creed focuses attention upon lines 356–9 of *Beowulf*, which depict the door-warden Wulfgar's entrance into Heorot to seek Hrothgar's permission for the entry of Beowulf and his men:

> Hwearf þa hrædlice   þær Hroðgar sæt
> eald ond *a*nhar   mid his eorla gedriht;
> eode ellenrof,   þæt he for eaxlum gestod
> Deniga frean;   cuþe he duguðe þeaw.

(He turned then quickly to where Hrothgar sat, old and grey-haired, with his troop of warriors; the courageous man went so that he stood before the shoulders of [i.e. in front of] the lord of the Danes; he knew the custom of the tried retainers.)

To demonstrate his understanding of the Anglo-Saxon poetic compositional process, Creed recomposes this passage using alternative formulas, arriving at this version:

> Eode þa ofostlice   þær se ealdor sæt
> har and hige-frod   mid his hæleða gedryht;
> eode hilde-deor   þæt he on heorðe gestod
> frean Scieldinga;   cuþe he þæs folces þeaw.

(He went then quickly to where the chieftain sat, grey haired and wise-minded, with his band of heroes; the battle-brave man went so that he stood at the hearth of the lord of the Scyldings; he knew the custom of the people.)

While modestly admitting that the *Beowulf* poet's version is the better, he insists that its superiority is due to its being 'the best of all possible *combinations of formulas*', not to its choice of individual words. The arguments for this contention will bear some scrutiny.

Hwearf þa, Creed claims, is part of a formulaic system useful for getting a person from one place to another, other members of the system being *gewat þa, com þa, eode þa*. The 'singer' (since Creed believes in the oral composition of *Beowulf*, he prefers this term) did not choose the first or second of these alternatives because the former suggests a long journey, the latter new arrival, neither of which is appropriate for the occasion of getting Wulfgar indoors to speak to his lord. So far so good, it seems to me. But there was no semantic reason for choosing *hwearf þa* over *eode þa*, Creed further argues, since 'the singer had no particular need to get Wulfgar from Beowulf to Hrothgar with haste: he *did* need to get him to Hrothgar with alliteration'.[6] But if the scop had decided to use a more general term for the king in the b-verse of the line, he continues, he could just as well have employed *eode þa*, along with a matching alliterative formula for 'quickly'; and thus the alternative combination which Creed creates, *eode þa ofostlice þær se ealdor sæt*.

Now we may observe that the need-for-alliteration argument is not really applicable, since the alliteration of *hwearf* in the line is incidental: all the metre demanded of the poet was the alliteration provided by the chief stressed syllable in the a-verse, *hræd-*; and, interestingly, Creed recognizes this metrical fact several pages later. Further, at the end of his essay, in his note 10, he comments that *eode* is vaguer 'than the singer's more precise suggestion of Wulfgar's turning *away* from Beowulf in order to move *towards* Hrothgar in *hwearf þa*'. So that, it turns out, 'haste' or 'not haste' is irrelevant in the poet's choice of *hwearf*, but rather movement 'away from' and 'towards' is significant—a *semantic* reason anyway for the poet's preference. But we can pursue this further into the stylistic quality of the passage: the poet's use of *hwearf* in the first line of the passage forestalls the needless repetition of *eode* which Creed's version entails. And when we consider *eode* as the poet used it in the third line of the passage, its semantic appropriateness for *its* context becomes evident, as none of the other 'formulaic' options could possibly have been used. In short, the scop chose wisely, even if formulaically. But can one really say that the choice of one word over another is a selection of *formulas?* (The addition of *þa*, pace Creed, hardly renders the combination a formula.) The whole notion of formula threatens to evaporate.[7] It is not, I would maintain, just a combination of formulas that is particularly praiseworthy in the *Beowulf* poet's composition, but the dictional choice itself.

Creed's expressed preference for the *Beowulf* composition over his own shifts its ground in other cases to rhythm. We may

33

look at one of these instances. It is the 'jigging rhythm' of his rhyme-formula *har and hige-frod* that Creed finds objectionable when compared with the *Beowulf* poet's *eald ond anhar*.[8] Once again I would beg to differ. In the first place, I fail to see (or hear) the rhythmic difference perceptible to Creed: both seem to be Type A verses, with Creed's *hige-* having resolved stress (cf. *Beowulf*, l. 2929a, *eald ond egesfull*, which Pope, in his *Rhythm of Beowulf*, lists as Type A, along with *eald ond anhar*: pp. 258, 260). More important, however, is the difference in the semantic burdens of the phrases; for however conventional was the stylistic device of yoking semantically related words in a verse by a copula, *anhar* itself is a *hapax legomenon*, as this is its only appearance in either Anglo-Saxon poetry or prose.[9] Its use with the prosaic *eald* doubly emphasizes Hrothgar's age, contrasting nicely with the vigor of Beowulf and with the herald Wulfgar's rapid movement; and this contrast satisfies the dictional expectations of the passage in a way that Creed's 'hoary and wise-minded' does not. Of some interest is the fact that *hige-frod*, which Creed says he took from *Genesis*, l. 1953, is coupled there with *halig* 'holy' as an epithet for Abraham in his obedience to the Lord, thus suggesting a relevant connection between wisdom and holiness. Since the verse *halig ond hige-frod* does not seem to be repeated elsewhere, it as well as *eald ond anhar* cannot, except by very loose definition, be considered formulas. Both epithets in context reveal, rather, a *combination of words*, whether in a formulaic 'system' or not, that either an individual scop thought particularly appropriate for his one occasion, or a succession of scops found suitable or aesthetically right upon numerous ones.[10]

Other of Creed's so-called formulas might equally be subjected to this kind of scrutiny. His substitution of *on heorðe* in line 3, for example, in place of *for eaxlum* is clearly dictional, not formulaic, as is replacement of *duguðe* in the fourth line by *þæs folces*. But further, these substitutions distort the 'intended' meaning: for the poet is referring to a custom that evidently involved standing *for eaxlum* and not 'on the hearth', and one known to 'tried retainers', not to the people at large. Quite clearly the poet is making a special point about *court* etiquette, not about *folk* custom, and to subscribe to a theory that the choice of words or phrases (or formulas) was here optionally dependent upon the

34

pleasure of alliteration is, in its own way, to resort to the wrench-
ing of language to fit an interpretation which I raised doubts
about in chapter 1.

In the preceding analysis we have seen that simple verbs,
descriptive adjectives and nouns could be used with precision of
meaning by a superior poet within the conventions of formulaic
verse; and in the process I have raised some question about what
is or is not a formula. We may proceed further, however, to ask
whether *bona fide* formulas can also be viewed as possessing an
exactitude of meaning, and even a metaphoric appropriateness
in context, since metaphor is such a staple of poetry. Consider,
for instance, the periphrasis for 'door' at the end of the following
passage describing Grendel's entrance into Heorot, *Beowulf*, ll.
721b–4a:

> Duru sona onarn
> fyrbendum fæst,   syðþan he hire folmum (æthr) an;
> onbræd þa bealohydig,   þa (he ge) bolgen wæs,
> recedes muþan.

(Straightway the door, secured with fire-forged bands,
swung open when he [Grendel] touched it with his hands;
that evil-intentioned one, since he was enraged, tore open
the mouth of the hall.)

Now the phrase *recedes muþ* appears also in *Maxims II*, l. 37a
(I quote ll. 35bff.):

> God sceal on heofenum,
> dæda demend.   Duru sceall on heall,
> rum recedes muþ.   Rand sceal on scylde,
> fæst fingre gebeorh.

(God, the Judge of deeds, is properly in Heaven. The door,
spacious mouth of a building, is properly on the hall. The
boss, firm protection of the fingers, is properly on the shield.)

And a similar phrase occurs in *Genesis A*, l. 1364a, as a kenning
for the door of Noah's Ark:

> Him on hoh beleac   heofonrices weard
> merchuses muþ.

(Behind him, the keeper of the heavenly kingdom sealed
up the mouth of the sea-house.)

The idea of calling a door a 'house's mouth' thus seems conventional, and *recedes muþ(a)* a *bona fide* formula. Nevertheless these and other verses reveal that a poet was under no compulsion to vary *duru* with this formula: he could use it instead of the simplex, as in the *Genesis* verse, or he could dispense with it altogether, as the *Andreas* poet does when he used the *Beowulf* passage as a model (in all probability) to describe Andrew's entrance through God's intervention into the prison where Matthew lay incarcerated:

> Duru sona onarn
>
> þurh handhrine   haliges gastes,
> ond þær in eode,   elnes gemyndig,
> hæle hildedeor.   (*Andreas*, ll. 999b–1002a)

(Straightway the door swung open at the hand-touch of the Holy Spirit, and the brave battle-warrior entered therein, mindful of courage.)

Therefore it seems critically valid to evaluate, if not the originality of the phrasing, the aesthetic qualities *in situ* of the conventional formula.

In context, the *Beowulf* phrase is unquestionably the most poetically meaningful. The gnomic sentence of the Cotton MS. *Maxims* has no wider sphere of collocation or association than itself, except insofar as it is a member of a proprietary series explaining the nature of the divine and human worlds: thus *rum recedes muþ* repeats the conventional pattern of variation in the series (*God . . . dæda demand; Rand . . . fæst fingre gebeorh*) and gives a formal tightness to the passage, but nothing further. (I can see no special advantage in the adjective *rum*, though it was not required for metrical reasons, as the weak form of the noun, *muþa*, could have been employed, even as in the *Beowulf* passage.) The *Genesis* instance seems precious: while 'sea-house' is understandable as a kenning for the Ark, 'mouth' seems irrelevant. But the kenning in *Beowulf* is peculiarly precise and metaphorically apt. The first half of the sentence depicts the door as made fast with fire-forged bands, an image of strength and durability, defying forced entrance; by the time Grendel has finished with it, it is reduced, as it were, to a soft mouth, an easily-penetrated point of entry. In the larger contextual situation, the concept of 'mouth' may be additionally related to Grendel's cannibalistic manner of disposing of his victims, for we are within a few lines to be given a graphic description of the fiend in action:

> bat banlocan,   blod edrum dranc,
> synsnædum swealh;   sona hæfde
> unlyfigendes   eal gefeormod,
> fet ond folma.   (ll. 742–5a)

(he bit into the body, drank the blood from the veins, swallowed him with one gulp after another;[11] straightway he had devoured all of the dead one, [including] feet and hands.)

—though this may be a gratuitous association, which not every listener or reader might make. It thus seems to me immaterial whether 'for all we know, "reccdes muþan" may have been the standard formula for doors entered by monsters; unfortunately the corpus provides us with only one other example, the entry into Heorot by Grendel's mother, but the image is not used there'.[12] Even if, historically, *recedes muþ* had in Old English times become a dead metaphor, like today's 'mouth of a river' or 'eye of a needle', and even if the *Beowulf* poet had not 'intended' to vivify or revivify its metaphoric possibilities, context, from our present aesthetic perspective, allows of such vivification without distorting or falsifying historical meaning, and I see no reason to proscribe it.

But not only *may* we find metaphoric appropriateness in Old English formulas or phrases; in many cases we *must* view them non-literally in order to make legitimate sense of them. In an excellent article, E. G. Stanley has observed that Old English poetic diction is highly figurative: that natural phenomena presented in the poetry are often the products of the moral or mental conceptualizing of the poet rather than 'romantic' well-springs of the poet's psychological or philosophical speculations; and that one must often interpret the diction on a figurative rather than a literal level. As one among many examples, Stanley cites the *morgenlongne dæg* of *Beowulf*, l. 2894: obviously one cannot literally have a 'morning-long day' (though the *sumorlang dæg* of *The Wife's Lament*, l. 37, is another matter). Wishing to evoke a mood and mental state, the *Beowulf* poet has turned to the

Anglo-Saxon traditional association of 'morning' with 'terror without solace': *morgenlongne dæg* is an 'illogical combination that conveys with great economy how the lonely fear of early morning is extended into the day as the band of nobles sat, grieving in their hearts, waiting for the news of Beowulf, his death or safe return'.[13]

Despite these analyses of the *Beowulf* poet's productivity in his use of simple diction, kenning and traditional phraseology, it should be recognized and acknowledged that not all words and phrases are similarly charged, or charged similarly, with meaning in their contexts. D. C. Collins comments of the kennings that

> not only were they ornaments and rhetorical devices with which [the poet] adorned his verse, but by their very nature, and the fact that alliterative verse depended so very largely on noun stress in the line, the poet could hardly avoid their use . . . He depends on them to carry him over pedestrian passages, to fill out a line and to get him out of technical difficulties.

Whallon argues about Old English poetic diction in general that 'once many significant phrases are found in theory or in recurrent practice to provide for prosodic necessity, they are not to be defended for their semantic properties in isolated contexts'.[14] In the *Anglo-Saxon Chronicle* poem on the *Death of Edward*, for example, it would be inadvisable to look for any specificity of meaning in the formulas expressing exile which are applied to the king's movements and deprivation:

> Wæs a bliðemod   bealuleas cyning,
> þeah he lange ær,   lande bereafod,
> wunode wræclastum   wide geond eorðan.   (ll. 15–17)

(The blameless king was ever happy in spirit, though he previously long had dwelt in exile-steps widely over the earth, deprived of his homeland.)

This is a kind of associative usage, like that of *morgenlongne dæg*, but conventional in a pejorative sense, something like a politician's presentation of his proposals 'for the common good'. Nevertheless, it is difficult to establish the 'prosodic necessity' to which Whallon refers, and it is not too much to expect that in an Old English poem which by general accord is felt to be aesthetically superior, even the most frequently repeated phrases and the tritest of kennings may, through the convergence of contextual features, acquire new semantic lustre, as the *Beowulf recedes muþan* does. For as I have argued elsewhere, 'originality in the handling of conventional formulas may be defined as the degree of tension achieved between the inherited body of meanings in which a particular formula participates and the specific meaning of that formula in its individual context'.[15]

So far our exploration of dictional expectations has not had to consider a possible lack of adequate knowledge about the connotations of a word, an inadequacy that can affect our larger interpretation of a passage or even of a whole poem. The comparative method, as Halliday observes in general about literary analysis (see chapter 1), is common and inevitable in Anglo-Saxon dictional studies, and it must help us bridge this paucity of information; for, as cannot be stressed often enough, we have not the intuitive feel for the language and its nuances of meaning that we have with modern English. In a way this comparison of the uses of particular words and formulas in the corpus of the literature as a whole is a small step, though an *ad hoc* one, in the direction Halliday prescribes for the study of poetic language. Whether an adequate description of the language as a whole will ultimately be the saving grace in our assessment of the value of a particular poetic usage is, to my mind, a moot question, and we shall return to this point in chapter 5. Such total information as we can obtain may even, as I hope shortly to demonstrate, be misleading unless utilized carefully, responsibly and sensitively.

The problems of comparative usage may be conveniently approached via F. C. Robinson's recent reminder that in our interpretations we all too frequently take for granted the semantic meanings enshrined in our Old English dictionaries. He observes[16] that a lexicographer sometimes

in assessing the meaning of a word in a given occurrence, . . . slips unawares into the role of literary interpreter, recording a meaning for a word not on the basis of lexicographical evidence but purely because his particular critical interpretation of the passage requires such a meaning. Scholars who then encounter his judgments in the dictionary often fail to distinguish between what is lexicographical fact and what is the dictionary-maker's momentary indulgence in literary criticism.

Among several cases in which he claims interpretation has been misrepresented as fact by the lexicographers, Robinson refers to the famous *lofgeornost* in the last line of *Beowulf*, where the Geatish warriors are mourning their leader's death:

cwædon þæt he wære   wyruldcyning[a]
manna mildust   ond mon(ðw)ærust,
leodum liðost   ond lofgeornost.

(They said that of worldly kings he was the mildest of men and the gentlest, kindest to his people and most eager for praise.)

Of this last word, Robinson says,[17]

Our entire conception of the poet's attitude toward his hero rests to a considerable extent upon our decision whether this term is wholly complimentary in Christian terms (as are the three adjectives preceding and paralleling it) or whether it is a frank acknowledgment of the secular Germanic side of the hero's character. Both *BTD* and *BTS* [the Bosworth-Toller *Dictionary* and *Supplement*] assure us that the word is used here 'in a good sense' meaning 'eager to deserve praise' and *BTS* sets up a special entry for this semantic category. But when the reader notices multiple documentations for the word's use 'in a bad sense' meaning 'ostentatious, boastful' and only the single *Beowulf* occurrence to support the 'good sense' the inevitable question arises. What evidence beyond the lexicographers' benevolent literary interpretation of *Beowulf* warrants the lexicographic authority which the 'good sense' now enjoys? Their interpretation may, of course, be right, but the responsible student must insist upon full access to the evidence for it.

What, indeed, is the evidence? An investigation of *lofgeornost* and its uses is suggestive about comparative methodology in the interpretative process, and thus worth pursuing here.

Robinson is not, as he makes clear, the first to raise a question about the connotations of *lofgeornost*. E. G. Stanley, for one, had earlier come out very strongly for the pejorative sense of the word in *Beowulf*. The crux of his argument is similar to Robinson's, but had best be quoted:[18]

> Perhaps the word *lofgeorn* . . . had a favorable sense of which no example survives, unless it be the use of the superlative at the end of *Beowulf*. In an unfavorable sense the word occurs often. One example will suffice; it is from Ælfric's *Sermo de Memoria Sanctorum*. The implications are ominous:

> se seofoða leahter is iactantia gecweden, þæt is
> ydel gylp on ængliscre spræce, þæt is ðonne se
> man bið lofgeorn and mid licetunge fænð, and deð
> for gylpe gif he hwæt dælan wille. . . .

> (the seventh sin is called *iactantia*, that is, idle boasting in the English tongue, that is, when a man is eager for praise and acts with deceit, and does for boasting [reasons] if he wishes to give aught. . . .)

> Schücking saw in the figure of Beowulf Saint Augustine's *rex iustus*; it seems possible to look upon him rather as Alcuin's *rex perditus*.

The first point I would make is, that though both Robinson and Stanley mention the frequent occurrence of *lofgeorn* in a bad sense, apart from the *Beowulf* and Ælfric passages it actually appears only thrice more, according to *BTD* and *BTS*; and one of these three instances seems to be a transliteration of the Ælfric:

> þe seofoðe sunne is gecweðen *iactancia*, þet is idelgelp on englisch, ðenne mon biþ lofgeorn and mid fieknunge fearð and deþ for gelpe mare þenne for godes luue gif he awiht delan wule. . . .

The other two instances are from a sermon of Wulfstan and from the translation of the *Benedictine Rule*:

> Se ðe wære lofgeorn for idelan weorþscype, weorþe
> se carfull hu he swyðast mæge gecweman his drihtne.

> (He who is eager for praise for the sake of vainglory, let him [rather] be anxious how he may best please his Lord.)

Ne sy nan lofgeorn, ne wilnigende, þæt his dæda halige
gesæde sien, ær hie halige weorðan.

(Let no one be eager for praise, or desirous that his actions
be said to be holy, unless they first are holy.)

A second point is that, of the non-*Beowulf* uses, all appear in
prose rather than poetry, are of the later Anglo-Saxon period
(tenth century or later) and are homiletic or otherwise religious
in nature. As for meaning, in its use in the *Benedictine Rule*,
lofgeorn is possibly emptied of its idea of 'praise' altogether, being
synonymous with *wilnigende*, since the two words are translating
the simple Latin *velle*. In the Wulfstan and Ælfric passages,
the word by itself does not seem necessarily to have a pejorative
meaning, but rather to be a neutral base-word qualified by the
phrase *for idelan weorþscype* in the one case, and by a clarifying
clause in the other, to produce the pejorative sense: if *lofgeorn*
in itself had such a meaning, the qualifying phrase and clause
would seem to have been superfluous. Now, this matter of
semantic interpretation may be open to dispute: it might well be
argued, for instance, that in the Wulfstan sentence and in the
translation of the *Benedictine Rule* (which may be Wulfstan's),
the additional *for idelan weorþscype* and *wilnigiende* are there for
rhythmical rather than semantic purposes, and therefore
lofgeorn is indeed pejorative. But even if *lofgeorn* did mean what
Robinson and Stanley suggest it does in these instances, such a
meaning would, I contend, be irrelevant to the *Beowulf* passage,
other things considered, other expectations weighed, because it is
prosaic, specifically religious and of a later date.

What are the 'other things considered'? For one, the simplices
lof and *georn*, the components of the compound, both have
decidedly favourable meanings in other Anglo-Saxon *poems*.
Georn is used, for example, to praise Azarias, who *dædum georn*,
Dryhten herede 'zealous in his actions, praised the Lord' (*Azarias*,
l. 3), and Boethius, who 'wæs for weorulde wis, weorðmynða
georn (was wise in the way of the world, desirous of honours)'
(*Meters of Boethius*, l. 51). In fact, *weorðmynða georn* in the
Boethius passage is almost exactly parallel to *lofgeorn*, and is
unexceptionably favourable 'in a Christian sense', even though
referring to worldly honours. *Lof*, too, is always used in a good
sense, as, for example, in *The Seafarer*, ll. 72–80, where it refers

to the praise bestowed by both men and angels on one who does 'brave deeds against the devil' before departing from this life. Such simplex meanings ought to be part of our consideration of the evidence in determining the meaning of the compound.[19]

Equally important are the expectations of context. *Lofgeornost* is the fourth superlative of the praise bestowed upon the dead Beowulf by his mourners and, as Mrs Goldsmith justly observes, 'one would not expect the king's followers to review his faults in their lament for him'.[20] Indeed, Kaske goes so far as to see the first three adjectives in the indirect statement of praise as describing 'in a general way traits traditionally associated with *sapientia* in the Vulgate Old Testament: "Est enim in [sapientia] spiritus intelligentiae ... benefaciens, humanus, benignus" (Sap. 7:22–3)', and he sees *lofgeornost* as 'the highest manifestation of Germanic wisdom—the quest for the highest possible good, roughly corresponding to Christian salvation'.[21] Whether Kaske is right to push the interpretation to this point, or whether Mrs Goldsmith is right to see the word, despite her understanding of its literal reference, as ultimately double-edged and tinged with dramatic irony, is to enter upon expectations of genre and upon larger matters of theme and structure, matters which must be put aside till chapter 6. Here I am concerned with dictional expectations, and have endeavoured to show that care must be taken not only in scrutinizing dictionary definitions for the lexicographers' perhaps unwarranted literary importations, as Robinson has warned, but in assuming a monolithic semantic field for the whole province of Old English diction.

The problem of *lofgeornost* seems to me relatively clear-cut. There are occasions, however, when semantic expectations go against the grain of contextual considerations. An illustration of this particular problem may be seen in *The Seafarer*, l. 62a, in the connotations of the formula *gifre ond grædig*. The passage in which this appears was discussed in chapter 1, in connection with Professor Clemoes's comparison of it to a passage in Alcuin. But the connotational difficulties were not raised there. The phrase occurs, it will be recalled, when the spirit or mind of the speaker returns to him after traversing sea and land:

<blockquote>
                    cymeð eft to me
gifre ond grædig,   gielleð anfloga,
</blockquote>

hweteð on hwælweg   hreþer unwearnum
ofer holma gelagu.

Punctuation of the passage is, of course, editorial; and we see here another one of the hazards in the way of interpretation of Old English poems: that punctuation is almost entirely a matter of the editor's sensitivity and his interpretation of Old English style. One could put a full stop after *me*, for example, and take *gifre ond grædig* as an epithet for the *anfloga* which would then be *not* the mind of the speaker in metaphor but a literal bird of some variety, possibly the cuckoo mentioned a few lines earlier in the poem.[22] Or, while equating the *anfloga* with a literal bird, one could put a full stop after *grædig*, in which case the adjectives still refer to the *hyge* or 'mind' of line 58. Or, as Clemoes has plausibly argued, the *anfloga* may be equated with the *hyge*, the adjectives then being applicable to the mind or spirit under both its literal and metaphoric designations. Assuming the probability of Clemoes's analysis, we then must translate with him: 'the solitary flier returns to me filled with eagerness and desire, calls, urges my heart irresistibly onto the whale's path across the expanse of ocean'. This interpretation gives *gifre ond grædig* a favourable meaning, since the transoceanic survey is what prompts the speaker to the joys of the Lord, as lines 64bff. make explicit. But we are faced with a dilemma here, for in other poetic uses of the formula the connotations are strictly unfavourable: the *moldwyrmas* (earthworms) that devour the body in *Soul and Body II*, l. 69; Satan's disciples in *Christ and Satan*, l. 191; and hell itself in *Genesis*, l. 793, are the other designees of this formulaic epithet. There is also one combination in the superlative degree, in *Riddle 84*, l. 30:

fromast and swiþost,
gifrost and grædgost   grundbedd trideþ,

where the riddle object 'water' is pictured as not only as 'most active and strong', but most greedily covering the earth. Further, as individual words, *grædig* seems always to be pejorative in meaning, and *gifre* almost always, though *BTS* gives one undeniable instance of the latter in a good sense, in the prose translation of Boethius: 'Ic heora [læcedomas] eom swiþe gifre ægþer ge to geherenne ge eac to gehealdanne (I am most anxious both to hear and to accept those medicines).'

In this case, then, the weight of lexicographical evidence

seems to come down on the side of an unfavourable connotation as the more probable. The only interpretation I know that attempts to incorporate this sense into an interpretation of the passage is one which sees the *anfloga* separate from the *hyge*, and takes it to be a greedy, devouring valkyrie bringing sickness and death to the speaker.[23] But this interpretation seems much too strained and, with most other critics, I would have to reject it. If this is the case, we must then, in the light of semantic weighting, either see the speaker connotationally condemning his own mind or spirit, which is unlikely, or see the *anfloga* divorced from the *hyge*, with the epithet describing only the *anfloga*—a bird, whose whetting of the speaker's appetite for a journey bodes ill, even as does the cuckoo's speaking with sad voice a few lines earlier. The critics who interpret the *anfloga* as a bird, however, see a favourable meaning in the *gifre ond grædig* epithet! The alternative is to see the poet using the formula in an unaccustomed sense, favourably, against the grain of its conventional meaning. Context, and the weight of Clemoes's argument, cause me to prefer this last possibility until someone proposes a more acceptable interpretation incorporating the unfavourable sense. For in poetry, even Anglo-Saxon poetry, the power of context is stronger than the expectation of word meaning: it is the bending of word meaning or formula connotation to a new suggestiveness through the formal relationships in a text that is one of the prerogatives and glories of the poetic imagination.

Nevertheless, the weight of dictional and formulaic semantic expectations cannot be lightly discarded. An instance where failure to consider sufficiently the semantic expectations of formula usage has led critics to the wrong conclusion (in my estimation) may be instructive. I refer to the identification of the *folces hyrde*, which is a question of referential meaning, near the end of the fragmentary *Battle of Finnsburh*.

Finnsburh is concerned with the resistance of a band of Danes under their leader Hnæf who are attacked treacherously in their hall at night by their Frisian hosts, whose king is Finn. They succeed in holding their own magnificently for five days. The last ten lines (ll. 39–48a) of the fragment are crucial to the argument I wish to present:

ne nefre swanas hwitne medo   sel forgyldan,

ðonne Hnæfe guldan   his hægstealdas.
Hig fuhton fif dagas,   swa hyra nan ne feol,
drihtgesiða,   ac hig ða duru heoldon.
Ða gewat him wund hæleð   on wæg gangan,
sæde þæt his byrne   abrocen wære,
heresceorp unhror,   and eac wæs his helm ðyrel.
Ða hine sona frægn   folces hyrde,
hu ða wigend hyra wunda genæson,
oððe hwæþer ðæra hyssa . . .

(nor ever [have I heard] youths better repaying the
sparkling mead than his young men repaid Hnæf. They
fought five days so that none of them fell [none of those]
retainers, but they held [fast] the doors. Then a wounded
warrior departed on his way [or went away?], said that his
corselet was broken, his battledress useless, and also was his
helmet pierced. Then straightway the guardian of the people
asked him how the warriors were surviving their wounds or
which of the young men. . . .)

The question of moment is, is the *folces hyrde* of line 46b Hnæf or
Finn, and related to this, is the *wund hæleð* of line 43 a Dane or a
Frisian?

In the later nineteenth and earlier twentieth centuries, there
was considerable critical controversy about these identifications.
So much so that by 1914 R. W. Chambers despaired of a solu-
tion: 'It seems impossible,' he wrote, 'to decide who is the
wounded champion of l. 43a or whether the king who enquires is
Hnæf or Finn'.[24] Klaeber a little later adopted the position that
'it appears probable that the wounded man who "goes away" is a
Frisian, and *folces hyrde*, Finn. . . . We may imagine a disabled
Frisian leaving the front of the battle line and being questioned
by his chief as to how the [Danish?] warriors were bearing (or
could bear) their wounds'.[25] Klaeber's 'probability' has been
sanctioned by all other recent editors who comment on the crux,
and the identification has been accepted without question by one
recent commentator in a passing reference.[26] But if we reassess
the various sets of expectations that have entered, or not entered,
into this interpretive decision, I think we must conclude
otherwise.

The expectations and implications that have duly been considered by scholars are those of situation, word meaning and formal relationships of a certain kind. For example, situation: do we not expect the leader who inquires how the wounded are surviving to be out of visual contact with the situation in order to formulate such a question? Word meaning: does not the phrase *on wæg gangan* imply a broad movement away and thus preclude the possible reference to a retreat from the door into the interior of the hall? Formal relationships: since other indirect speeches in the poem are given to the Frisians, and direct ones to the Danes, should we not expect that this indirect question would also be attributed to a Frisian? I have phrased these questions from the point of view of those who have argued for Finn as the referent of *folces hyrde*.[27] There is an additional expectation that has entered into this point of view, an expectation of which I am not sure its upholders are conscious: that of genre. In an heroic poem, we expect the leading antagonists to make an appearance: Hnæf has probably done so in the extant beginning of the poem as the 'sword-young king' who recognizes the night attack for what it is, and he is certainly mentioned in line 40a; but so far as the poem exists, there has been no mention of Finn. This omission, I believe, has unconsciously been put into the balance of evidence by editors and critics. But the poem is fragmentary, and in view of other expectations and implications, the need to include Finn is, I think, gratuitous.[28]

Those who have preferred to see Hnæf as the referent of *folces hyrde* and the *wund hæleð* as a Dane have countered some of the above arguments by suggesting that, situationally, the position of the leader within the hall has not been specified and we have no right to assume he can oversee all the action; furthermore, since a number of Frisians have already been killed in the fighting, the reference here to a wounded warrior would more naturally be to a Dane—and the Danes have been the last-mentioned warriors, anyway—and thus the *hyrde* is Hnæf. Semantically, they argue, that *on wæg gangan* may have been used loosely as a simple opposition to the *duru heoldon* of the previous line, signifying no more than an abandonment of that post; and that *folces hyrde*, literally 'protector of the people', is better as an appellation for the leader of the attacked group than of the attackers.[29] The formal argument of the attribution of speeches has not been scrutinized, perhaps because it appears in disguise as part of Klaeber's introduction to the poem in his edition; but it cannot be definitive, since the assignment of the passage under consideration is crucial.

To the situational-semantic considerations I would add the possibility that the indirect question as to 'how the warriors were surviving their wounds' need not imply a visual lack of knowledge, but may be a form of encouragement to the wounded warrior(s), something like 'How are you doing?' or 'Keep a stiff upper lip, old chap!' And I shall return to the connotations of 'protector of the people' and its applicability to Hnæf or Finn. First, however, there is to be considered an expectation that has surprisingly not been taken into account in the criticism, that is, how this specific formula-epithet is handled on other occasions in Old English poems.

The phrase appears six times apart from the *Finnsburh* instance, five times in *Beowulf*, once in the *Meters of Boethius*:

1 Þa wæs on salum   sinces brytta
  gamolfeax ond guðrof;   geoce gelyfde
  brego Beorht-Dena;   gehyrde on Beowulf
  folces hyrde   fæstrædne geþoht.   (*Beowulf*, ll. 607–10)

(Then the distributor of treasure, grey-haired and battle-brave, was in joy; the chief of the Bright-Danes counted on aid; the *folces hyrde* had heard from Beowulf resolute thought.)

2   Ic on Higelace wat,
  Geata dryhten,   þeah ðe he geong sŷ,
  folces hyrde, . . .   (*Beowulf*, ll. 1830b–2a)

(I [Beowulf] know that, though he is young, [I can count on] Hygelac, lord of the Geats, *folces hyrde*, . . .)

3   Wen ic talige,
  gif þæt gegangeð,   þæt ðe gar nymeð,
  hild heorugrimme   Hreþles eaferan,
  adl oþðe iren   ealdor ðinne,
  folces hyrde, . . .   (*Beowulf*, ll. 1845b–9a)

(I [Hrothgar] expect that if it should come to pass that the spear, sword-grim battle, takes off [in death]

the son of Hrethel, if sickness or iron weapon [takes off]
your lord, *folces hyrde*. ...)

4   þeah ðe hlaford us
þis ellenweorc   ana aðohte
to gefremmanne,   folces hyrde. ...
                          (*Beowulf*, ll. 2642b–4)

(though our lord, *folces hyrde*, thought to accomplish
this deed of courage alone, on our behalf. ...)

5   ða gebeah cyning,
folces hyrde, ...   (*Beowulf*, 2980b–1a)

(then the king [Ongentheow], *folces hyrde*, turned ...)

6 Hwær is eac se wisa   and se weorðgeorna
and se fæstrada   folccs hyrde
se wæs uðwita   ælces ðinges,
cene and cræftig,   ðæm wæs Caton nama?
                (*Meters of Boethius* 10, ll. 48–51)

(Where also is that wise and desirous-of-honour and
resolute *folces hyrde* who was a sage in every thing,
learned and ingenious, who was called Cato?)

What is of some interest is that in all five *Beowulf* passages
folces hyrde is the last component of a two- or three-part variation
(see chapter 3), so that the referent is clearly identified before the
epithet appears. In the *Meters* passage, we have a question rather
than a declarative statement; and though there is no antecedent
for *folces hyrde*, his identity is made absolutely clear in the
relative clause. We may also note that in the collocation in
Genesis, ll. 2316b–17a, 'Ic þæs folces beo / hyrde and healdend
(I will be guardian and keeper of the people)', the referent is
clearly God, who is talking to Abraham; and that in parallel or
'system' phrases like *folces weard* (*Beowulf*, l. 2513a; *Genesis*, l.
2667a) or *folces aldor* (*Elene*, l. 157b; etc.) the referents are likewise clear. But no clarification is possible in the *Finnsburh*
passage, if the reference is to Finn, on account of the intrusive
hu–oððe clauses. From the other uses of the kenning-epithet,
then, it seems unlikely that *folces hyrde* would appear unsuppor-
ted by other designations; and in the *Finnsburh* fragment the only

identifying possibility is the antecedent *Hnæfe* in line 40a. It seems to me improbable that the poet would have brought the powerful king of the Frisians onto the stage of the narrative by the unelaborated kenning, or that his audience would have been prepared for such a reference. Of course it could be argued (as has been suggested to me) that the *Finnsburh* poet was a poor one, anyway, and that we should not expect him to follow the best poetic practice; but then we could argue that in that case he might well have used *on wæg gangan*, which seems the strongest evidence in support of Finn as the referent, sloppily. This way critical madness lies.

There is a semantic emphasis that also sets up an expectation. We are told that the Danes 'fought for five days so that none of them fell'. Having already been informed that Garulf and about him many a good one had fallen (ll. 31–3b) on the Frisian side, surely the language expectation is for an account of how the first Dane fell. If the poet had wished to lead into the entrance of Finn at this point, his focus would have been different: he would have emphasized the Frisians' efforts to breach the defence, not the Danes' ability to hold the doors secure. But there is a further consideration, one which has not been given due weight since Trautmann advanced it in 1903: that the appellation is more suitable to the king of the attacked than of the attackers. Perhaps this oversight is due to a feeling that the formula has been emptied of specific meaning. A glance at the *Beowulf* passages using it, however, reveals that in all but the second the king referred to is, in context, bearing the brunt of an attack; and in the second instance the speaker is referring to Hygelac as a potential succourer of a putative victim of aggression. Likewise, the *Meters* verses refer not to a belligerent but to the wise man Cato. We may add to this observation that kennings in Old English poetry are usually relevant to the meaning important at the moment, rather than to overall thematic or structural strategy.[30] And it is useful to look at an instance where a poet had clearly the option of using this formula but chose otherwise: in *Beowulf*, l. 2357a, interestingly enough, we find that Hygelac, when he is being the aggressor and raiding Frisia, is designated by the epithet *freawine folce* 'friendly lord of the people' rather than by the similarly alliterating formula *folces hyrde*. Accidental? Perhaps, but the total weight of expectational and implicational evidence seems against the attribution of *folces hyrde* to Finn, and rather suggests that Hnæf should be properly mantled in the royal kenning.

The balance between formula and specificity of meaning that we have been examining in connection with *gifre ond grædig* and *folces hyrde* may also be seen in recurring lexical collocations that are not so rigidly bound; that is, where the words associated formulaically are distributed throughout the context of more than a single verse, as in the *Genesis* passage, lines 2316b–17a, mentioned above. A more modern instance may be adduced in the opening lines of Milton's sonnet on his blindness, which partly achieve their effect through the congruity and complementarity of the collocations *light/days/dark* and *world/wide*, which we recognize pleasurably as poetic-linguistic familiars:[31]

> When I consider how my light is spent
> Ere half my days in this dark world and wide.

Both collocations are based upon ordinary semantic affinities and common sound correlations, but they are transformed and infused with specific meaning through syntactic displacement and context. The familiar 'wide world' association assumes here a psychological significance, though its literal meaning is echoed later in the 'Thousands' who 'post o'er land and ocean without rest'; and the familiar *day-light, dark* pattern becomes a complex metaphor for sight–life/blindness–death, the conceptual centre of the sonnet.

An example in Old English analogous to Milton's might be several uses of the 'mod ond mægen (mind and power)' formula. Elene, for example, exhorts the Jews in *Elene*, ll. 1221b–4a:

>   þæt hie weorðeden
> mode ond mægene   þone mæran dæg,
> heortan gehigdum,   in ðam sio halige rod
> gemeted wæs.

(that they should honour with mind and strength, with the thoughts of their hearts, that glorious day on which the Holy Rood was discovered.)

The formula here is not particularly striking, but it does suggest the high value the Anglo-Saxons placed upon the combination of the heart-mind-spirit complex represented by the word *mod* and the physical strength of man. Indeed, this combination, as *sapientia et fortitudo*, has been suggested by Kaske to be a central theme of *Beowulf*.[32] The concept appears in several guises throughout the poem, but the specific collocation of *mod* and *mægen* appears only in Hrothgar's long commendation and exhortation to *Beowulf*, and in his farewell speech to the hero shortly thereafter: 'Eal þu hit geþyldum healdest, / mægen mid modes snyttrum (You will govern it, your strength, steadily with the wisdom of your mind)' (ll. 1705b–6a) and 'þu eart mægenes strang ond on mode frod (You are strong in strength and wise in mind)' (l. 1844). Beowulf is the exceptional hero who combines these desirable attributes, in contrast to other heroes in the poem who lack one or the other. The traditional lexical collocational use here, at these crucial moments, and nowhere else in the poem, highlights Beowulf's magnificence.

Of even greater interest, perhaps, is the use the *Maldon* poet makes of the collocation at the end of his poem (though the real end is missing, of course), when the old retainer Byrhtwold challenges his doomed comrades to even greater heroic endeavours:

> Hige sceal þe heardra,   heorte þe cenre,
> mod sceal þe mare,   þe ure mægen lytlað.

> ([Our] thought must be the harder, heart the keener,
> spirit must be the greater, as our might lessens.)

Though *Maldon* is thematically centred on the concepts represented by *mod* and *mægen*, the only appearance of either of these two common nouns is here, at the climax of the action. The poet has presumably reserved them, with all the force of their traditional association, for a powerful disjunctive coupling (i.e. *mod* in the a-verse and *mægen* in the b-verse) that conceptualizes epigrammatically the point of his narrative, that spiritual courage and wisdom are even more important than physical strength.[33]

If, then, individual words and even conventional epithets could be used with precision, metaphoric aptness and aesthetic effectiveness in Old English poetry, is it possible that under certain circumstances formulas in larger formal patterns or associations could exhibit nuances or extensions of meaning such as we have come to expect in the patterns of modern poetry?

Could, for example, the oft-repeated *Beowulf maþelode, bearn Ecgðeowes* have more than 'formal meaning', which I suggested earlier in this chapter might be its semantic parameter under circumstances of oral composition? An examination of its contextual appearances provides some interesting data. For one thing, *bearn Ecgðeowes* is used only to introduce a formal speech of the hero's with the exception of line 2177, where, at the end of part I of the poem, it introduces a summary of Beowulf's virtues. For another, the epithet is *not* used until the hero replies to Unferth's taunt in line 529: in line 405, for instance, we find instead 'Beowulf maðelode—on him byrne scan (Beowulf spoke—his corselet glistened on him)'. It is also *not* used when Beowulf addresses his own men before his fight with Grendel (1. 676) or at the end of the poem, when he is fighting the dragon and his death is imminent (introductions to his last two speeches, 1. 2510: ... *beotwordum spræc* and 1. 2724: ... *he ofer benne spræc* (he spoke wounded as he was)'. This pattern of uses and non-uses of *bearn Ecgðeowes* seems as if it might be semantically significant, suggesting a *mana* or spiritual power in the identification of the hero as his father's son—a power that is not revealed until his first test, against Unferth, and which leaves him only as the end of his life approaches. One could account for its absence in the introduction to his boasting speech before the Grendel fight by the fact that the poet has used 'Beowulf Geata (Beowulf of the Geats)' in the a-verse, preferring at this point, where the hero's men are most prominent in their tactical support, to identify him with his nation.

A slightly different kind of implication of meaning may be conveniently approached by moving once again outside the sphere of Old English, to an examination of an analysis Spearing provides of a seemingly patterned use of formulas in *Sir Gawain and the Green Knight*. Spearing refers to Savage's suggestion that Gawain's behaviour on the third day in the boudoir may be compared to the fox's in the forest: both resort to trickery, both are undone by it, the fox's physical swerving from Bertilak's thrust taking him into the mouths of the hounds; and Gawain's moral swerving, in his acceptance of the green girdle and saying nothing about it during the 'exchange of winnings', taking him into Bertilak's power.[34] Spearing refers to the diction in which the fox's manœuvre is couched: 'And he schunt for the scharp, and schulde haf arered' (1. 1902), and then to the diction describing Gawain's later action at the Green Chapel when the Green Knight's axe comes hurtling down towards his neck:

And schranke a lytel wyth the schuldres for the scharpe yrne.
That other schalk wyth a schunt the schene wythhaldes.

(ll. 2267–8)

On this diction Spearing comments as follows:[35]

There are similarities in phrasing as well as in idea.
The words *scharp* and *schunt* occur in both passages, and if one were giving the poet the sort of close reading that might be applied to a more recent work, I think one might argue that the similarity was deliberate and rather subtle. . . . This seems convincing, until we remember the formulaic nature of the poem's style . . . it seems that for the poet the idea of evading a cutting edge is almost automatically expressed in a line alliterating on the words *scharp* and *schunt*.

Spearing uses a line from the alliterative *Morte Arthur* to support his observation about the formulaic nature of the verse: 'Bot the schalke for the scharpe he schowntes a littille' (1. 3842), noting the additional use of *schalke* and *littille* here, as in the second *Gawain* passage.

Whether the language here is formulaic or merely collocational is open to question; but the point I am concerned with is that Spearing appears to be discounting the possibility of generated implicational meaning as the result of formal relationships in highly stylized repetition. I would suggest that even if such an implication of meaning were not 'intended' historically, or could not be expected to have been perceived by a listening audience, there is still a possibility for present meaning. Finding implicational meanings in formal relationships is not the same as attributing unhistorical definitions to words, as in the case of *gyng*, which I cited in chapter 1. But matters are not so simple as this: for whereas indeed the fox *schunts* from the *scharp* in line 1902 (and the warrior does likewise in the line from *Morte Arthur*), in the later *Gawain* verse the hero *schranke*, rather, and it is the Green Knight who stays the descending blade *wyth a schunt*. Moreover, *scharpe* and *schunt* are not alliterating 'in a

54

line' but divided between two lines. It almost seems as if the poet were consciously trying to defuse the possibility of an echo here. Associative recall may operate here nevertheless, but our ultimate decision in the matter will have to be made on the grounds of suitability to context, rather than those of formularity: how relevant is a comparision of the fox and Gawain here?

I have dwelt on this *Gawain* analysis at a little length because it presents clearly some of the difficulties involved with formulas, or collocations, and implications of meaning. How many possibilities of formal implication of the *Gawain* kind (if that *is* one!) exist in Old English poems I am not sure. One example that has been mentioned by a few critics is the repetition of *oð ðæt an ongan* in lines 100b and 2210b of *Beowulf*, describing the beginnings of Grendel's and the dragon's depredations; but the concept of 'beginning a hostile action' and the rather unimpressive diction itself are hardly incisive; and there are more than two thousand lines between! An unimpeachable echo, on the other hand, is provided in *Maldon* by Byrhtnoth's reply to the Viking messenger's demand for ransom. The messenger says it will be better for the English if they 'þisne garræs mid gafole forgyldon ... we willaþ mid þam sceattum us to scype gangan (pay for [avert] this rush of spears with tribute ... we will [then] go to our ship with that tribute)' (ll. 32, 40); and Byrhtnoth answers for his people 'Hi willað eow to gafole garas syllan. ... To heanlic me þinceð/þæt ge mid urum sceattum to scype gangon/unbefeoh-tene (They will give spears to you as tribute. ... Too shameful it seems to me to allow you to depart to your ship with our treasure without a fight)' (ll. 46, 55b–7a). This is a deliberate repetition for ironic effect, however, and does not generate further implications of meaning.

Closer to the *Gawain* possibility of thematic-structural implications are the formulaic descriptions which introduce the warriors in *Maldon* who, after Byrhtnoth's death, urge on their companions to the fight:

Offa gemælde,   æscholt asceoc   (l. 230)

(Offa spoke, shook his ash-wood spear)

Leofsunu gemælde   and his linde ahof,
bord to gebeorge;   he þam beorne oncwæð   (ll. 244–5)

(Leofsunu spoke and raised his shield, his shield as a
defence; he spoke to the man)

Dunnere þa cwæþ, daroð acwehte,
unorne ceorl, ofer eall clypode,
bæd þæt beorna gehwylc Byrhtnoð wræce. (ll. 255–7)

(Dunnere then spoke, shook his spear, a humble yeoman,
called out over all, bade each man that he avenge Byrhtnoth.)

Though these speeches, which follow immediately one upon
another, present in their introductions noticeable differences in
diction, they are nevertheless stylized and clearly repetitive; they
are 'intended' to resemble each other. Of the speeches themselves Irving has commented,[36]

> those who criticize the rigid conventionality of the
> retainers' speeches . . . are in one sense missing the point; it
> is the achievement of these men that they become
> conventional. The antique virtues husbanded over the
> centuries in the worn formulas of poetic diction receive new
> life when they become incarnated in living men in a real
> battle.

In the introductions I have quoted, the repetition of diction and
posture implies a unified purpose and determination in the dead
chieftain's comitatus, a sharp contrast to the disorganized and
cowardly flight of Odda's sons. The dictional differences suggest
the individuality of the speakers, whether nobleman or churl; the
formulaic repetition subsumes them in a common cause.

But most interesting for the implications generated by formal
relationships through formulaic repetition are the introductions
to Byrhtnoth's reply to the Viking messenger and to the famous
final exhortation by the old retainer Byrhtwold about the spirit
needing to be the firmer, etc. (see above):

Byrhtnoð maþelode, bord hafenode,
wand wacne æsc, wordum mælde,
yrre and anræd ageaf him andsware (ll. 42–4)

(Byrhtnoth spoke, raised his shield aloft, brandished his
slender ash spear, spoke with words, angry and resolute gave
him answer)

Byrhtwold maþelode,   bord hafenode
(se wæs eald geneat),   æsc acwehte;
he ful baldlice   beornas lærde.   (ll. 309-11)

(Byrhtwold spoke, raised aloft his shield (he was an old
retainer), shook his ash spear; full boldly he exhorted the
warriors.)

Here, with the exception of proper names, we have exact repetition of formulas: *X maþelode, bord hafenode.* Can we infer that the
poet intended a special identification of the two men, that when
the audience hears or reads lines 309-11 it will hark back in its
mind's ear/eye to the image of Byrhtnoth's initial retort, and feel
a rounding out, or finality, in the structure of the poem? These
implications are very tempting from our modern critical perspective; can they be justified historically?

In weighing and weighting our expectations, we must consider
the following points. Did the metrical situation force the poet in
each case to resort to these particular formulas for what he
wanted to say? The use of *maþelode* seems optional, undictated by
alliterative or rhythmic necessity: the poet could have used
gemælde, as he did in lines 230 and 244 in introducing Offa's and
Leofsunu's speeches; and he does in fact employ this verb,
minus its *ge-* prefix, in variation with *maþelode* in the Byrhtnoth
introduction. Of interest is that whereas *(ge)mælan* is used on five
occasions in *Maldon*, there are only the two occurrences of
maþelian. This seems more than coincidental.

The use of *bord hafenode* is somewhat different. The act of
raising a shield or brandishing a spear seems to have been a
formal indication of impending speech, as all five passages
suggest,[37] and the alliterative requirement for the off-verse (a
word beginning with *b*) was constraining. The poet might,
however, have created a Type E verse such as *beaduwæpen ahof*
(cf. *meodosetla ofteah, Beowulf*, l. 5), consonant with the *æsc* and
daroð shaken by Leofsunu and Dunnere; or he might have used
the tried and true *bearn Xes* formula in one or the other of these
instances, as in our *Beowulf maþelode, bearn Ecgðeowes*—he
actually does employ this epithet in introducing Ælfwine as
bearn Ælfrices in line 209. But the only uses of *bord hafenode* in the
extant corpus of Old English poetry are these two in *Maldon*—
and the only other use of *hafenian* at all is in the verse *wæpen*

hafenade, Beowulf, l. 1573. Again, it looks as if this were more than coincidence.

Another counter that must be weighed, however, is the fragmentary condition of the poem: both beginning and end are missing, and it is therefore speculative to talk about a structural completion intimated by the repeated formulas. Still, most commentators feel that it is not very likely that much has been lost at either end of the poem, and I am inclined to agree with them.

One final consideration might be whether a listening audience would be likely to catch such a formulaic echo separated by 267 lines. On this point we might note the unusual use of *homoeoteleuton* (or repetition of ending) linking *maþelode* and *hafenode,* a sound pattern which could well attract the attention of an audience more accustomed to oral recitation and listening than we, even after such a lapse in time. Even if this point is not historically valid, present meaning in the repetitive echo would not be precluded. There is also the striking fact that whereas Offa, Leofsunu and Dunnere are depicted as either raising a shield or shaking a weapon, Byrhtnoth and Byrhtwold both raise their shields *and* shake their spears. That is, the actions of the last two are both defensive and offensive in nature. On balance, then, I am inclined to believe in the implications of meaning generated by the formulaic echo in these two passages which envelop the speeches and actions of the English, and which make their own stylistic contribution to the heroic ethos of the *Battle of Maldon.*

How far is it legitimate to push this kind of implication? Can we, for example, see in the fact that, when the Geats in *Beowulf* arrive at the mere where the hero will grapple with Grendel's mother, they 'on þam holmclife hafelan metton (on that seacliff found the head [of Æschere])', and some two hundred lines later, when they leave the mere with the victorious Beowulf, they 'from þam holmclife hafelan bæron (from that seacliff bore the head [of Grendel])'—can we see in this repetition of formula an echo which suggests that Grendel's head is payment in kind for Æschere's? Perhaps, but it would have been more satisfactory, for this meaning, if the latter were the mother's head, since she, and not Grendel, had killed Hrothgar's advisor. The subtleties of interpretation begin to grow apace, and we run the danger that the critic's imagination may become a surrogate for either historical or present meaning. We shall have to look carefully at several varieties of subtlety in the following chapters. It will be well, however, to spend some time first exploring a formal feature of Old English verse that has been mentioned on several occasions in the first two chapters, the feature known as *variation*. For it, like diction and formula, presents its own interpretational difficulties, and even its dimensions and qualities have not been adequately formulated.

3

The Uses of Variation

As the case of *folces hyrde* illustrated in the previous chapter, an examination of the uses of variation may pay unexpected dividends in helping to establish referential meaning. The phenomenon called *variation* deserves, however, special study in its own right, as it is probably the most distinctive as well as pervasive stylistic feature in Old English poetry.[1] Unlike metre and alliteration, which are mandatory formal requirements in the poetry, variation is an optional formal feature; that is, there seems to be no discoverable (or as-yet-discovered) 'rules' which determine its appearance or non-appearance. Yet an Old English poem without variation would be as unthinkable as a more modern poem without metaphor, which is likewise an optional feature. A great difficulty with handling it critically, however, is that it is not always easy to distinguish it from other Old English stylistic phenomena, nor do critics readily agree upon its characteristics and limitation.

In the largest sense of using different words to say the same thing in order to avoid repetition, variation is not restricted to Old English poetry, or to Old English at all, but is common to verse and prose of all times and places. In an interesting essay in which he begins with the rhetorical fault that H. W. and F. G. Fowler dubbed 'elegant variation', W. K. Wimsatt goes on to show the literary properties and proprieties of 'non-elegant' variation.[2] He distinguishes two types, which H. W. Fowler had lumped together in *Modern English Usage*. The first is demonstrated by Fowler's example: 'They spend a few weeks longer in their winter *home* than in their summer *habitat*'. This, as Wimsatt explains, is 'where several physically separable things (a southern part of the earth and a northern) are denoted under slightly different aspects (home and habitat), while the context indicates that the things are really thought of under one aspect (call it either home or habitat)'. The second type is illustrated by Fowler's sentence 'Dr Tulloch was for a time *Dr Boyd's* assistant, and knew the *popular preacher* very intimately, and the picture he gives of the *genial essayist* is a very engaging one.' In this case, 'under different aspects only one thing is denoted'. Wimsatt suggests that the latter type is not nearly so reprehensible as the former, though the particular example is horrifying enough. Indeed, it is the type of variation that is put to good and often excellent use in literature, where 'every rift is to be packed with ore'; and Wimsatt is not slow to perceive such excellent use in *Beowulf*. Among other passages from the poem, he cites lines 1906–19 in John Lesslie Hall's translation:

> The *sea-boat* resounded,
> The wind o'er the waters the *wave-floater* nowise
> Kept from its journey; the *sea-goer* traveled,
> The *foamy-necked vessel* floated forth o'er the currents,
> The *well-fashioned vessel* o'er the ways of the ocean . . .
> The *wave-goer* hastened . . .
> He bound to the bank the *broad-bosomed vessel*
> Fast in its fetters, lest the force of the waters
> Should be able to injure the *ocean-wood winsome*.

The italicized terms denote Beowulf's ship as he and his men, their mission accomplished, sail back to Geatland from Hrothgar's now-cleansed Denmark. Wimsatt's comment on this passage is as follows:[3]

> There are places in *Beowulf* where one might attribute a
> variation to metrical or alliterative necessity. But surely not
> here in these eight ways of naming the boat. . . . He was
> eager to tell about it, as much about it as possible
> while telling what it did. Not only did it go, but it was a
> wave-floater and well fashioned and foamy necked. An
> opportunity for such interesting predictions came each
> time the boat was denoted. So it was well to denote it many
> times, to repeat the fact that it went. . . . Nay, the going
> itself has interesting aspects. The boat traveled, it floated,
> it hastened. . . . One of the most constant characters
> of the poem is the incrustation of ideas around single
> objects. An extreme example, in several propositions,
> like that of the boat, is felt as only a concentration
> of what occurs more casually on every page.

I have quoted Wimsatt at some length for both positive and negative reasons: because he captures quite well the effect and effectiveness of kennings in *Beowulf*, the periphrases for simple substantives which are such an essential part of Old English variation, and because this general type of what he is calling variation is *not* what Old English critics usually mean when they refer to this formal feature of Old English or other Old Germanic verse. In the passage cited, for example, only the kenning for boat in lines 1908b–10 would probably, for syntactic reasons, be recognized as part of a variation:

> sægenga for,
> fleat famigheals   forð ofer yðe,
> bundenstefna   ofer brimstreamas.

This brings us to the question of definition and description of Old English variation; but before turning to this matter, we may look at one further observation Wimsatt has made that has some relevance, though it has not been particularly noticed or noted, for Old English poetry.

Wimsatt quotes a passage from Conrad's *Heart of Darkness* which describes a French warship shelling the African coast:

> A *small* flame would dart and vanish, a *little* white smoke would disappear, a *tiny* projectile would give a *feeble* screech.

He comments[4] as follows on the appropriateness of the adjectives he has italicized to the nouns they are describing:

> Here is a kind of variation which is demanded by the context. . . . The different things must be named and each must be small or weak in its own way . . . [but] there need not be any clear or explicit propriety in the difference in words. . . . 'Feeble' indicates exactly the way in which a 'screech' is small, and . . . would not do so well for 'projectile'. But it might do for 'flame'. And 'small' might do for 'projectile' and 'little' might do for 'flame'. But taken in a series, applied to these different objects, these different words for 'small' do suggest accurate application and complete relevance. . . . A difference in the sound of words, a difference in their range of meaning, implicitly means the right difference.

This is a shrewd and perceptive insight into one of the ways in which words project semantically. Now, I think one can find this kind of variation, with substantives or verbs rather than adjectives, providing a kind of tonal unity in passages of Old English verse, too. For example, when the speaker of *The Seafarer* describes the sounds of different birds which are, for him, but poor substitutes for those of men, he says:

> Hwilum ylfete *song*
> dyde ic me to gomene,   ganetes *hleoþor*
> ond huilpan *sweg*   fore hleahtor wera,
> mæw *singende*   fore medodrince.   (ll. 19b–22)

(At times the song of the wild swan I took for my pleasure, the cry of the gannet and the sound of the curlew instead of the laughter of men, the seagull crying instead of [the conviviality accompanying] mead-drinking.)

How appropriate the particular words for the birds' cries, *song*, *sweg* and *singende*, may be is immaterial: overall, they recreate the relevant variety for context, sufficient to contrast this kind of sound from that of men's merriment. Another instance may be observed in *Beowulf*, ll. 3171–2, where the mourners utter their distress over their king's demise:

> woldon (care) *cwiðan*   [ond] kyning *mænan*,
> wordgyd *wrecan*   ond ymb w(er) *sprecan*.

(They wished to utter their grief and mourn their king, recite a dirge and speak about the man.)

Whether the various words for 'speak' are precise in each instance is not the point, but rather the unifying effect they have upon the concepts of king/man, the speakers' sorrows and the song of lamentation itself; in effect this kind of variation in this context prompts us to Yeats's question at the close of 'Among School Children', 'How can we know the dancer from the dance?'

Let us now turn to the more specialized application of the term *variation* in Old English literary criticism. I should first like to confront the problem of definition and description, then try to assess some of the implications and expectations of meaning in this structural-stylistic technique. Before proceeding, however, it might be well to remark that though Wimsatt's perception of variation is quite clearly from a modern perspective, we should not be misled into thinking that the Old English critic's perspective is conversely *echt-historisch*. There is no treatise on the subject in Old English or in Medieval Latin, and the only possible reference to the technique—and a questionable one—is in *Beowulf*, l. 874a: 'secg eft ongan/sið Beowulfes snyttrum styrian,/ond on sped wrecan spel gerade,/*wordum wrixlan* (the man undertook in turn to recite cunningly the venture of Beowulf, to utter skillfully an apt tale, to vary with words [?])'. This reference is questionable, since the phrase *wordum wrixlan* occurs also at *Beowulf*, l. 366a, where it can only mean 'exchange words with someone'. Despite the absence of critical historical evidence, our attempts at discussion aim to recover an Anglo-Saxon point of view, though we cannot escape a certain predilection of the here and now.

Critics would not quarrel, I think, with the general definition advanced by Arthur Brodeur, that variation is a 'double or multiple statement of the same concept or idea in different words, with a more or less perceptible shift in stress'.[5] It is not so easy in practice, however, to determine whether the 'different words' apparently in apposition to a given word really *are* restating the same concept, or whether instead they are providing an enumeration or a progression. Identity of reference is particularly difficult with actions or states of mind, but even with identifiable objects it is not always easy to be sure. And with clauses in apposition, the Old English paratactic style in poetry—its tendency to use a coordinate rather than a subordinate syntactic structure—often leaves doubt as to whether or not we have true apposition between the clauses, and thus restatement, or whether we have in effect a clausal subordination of one sort or another. Further, there is disagreement among critics as to whether the restatements need be grammatically parallel to constitute a variation.[6] I would argue that some kind of parallelism is necessary for effective recognition by listener or reader, so that the implications of the form can be measured on the pulse, so to speak, even as phonetic parallelism (i.e. rhyme) functions to enforce notice of semantic links. But though the majority of instances of variation involve grammatical parallelism, I believe there are passages where rhetorical devices provide an effective appositive substitute, as I shall try to illustrate later. Still another problem, adumbrated in my critique of Wimsatt's *Beowulf* example, is whether the words or groups of words sharing the common referent need 'occur within a single clause (or, in the instance of sentence variation, within contiguous clauses)'.[7] We shall have to make final judgment in all such matters by examining specific cases in which critics have alleged variation to exist.

With the difficulties of definition thus abstractly stated, we can move to descriptions and illustrations of the several types of variation employed by Old English poets. It will be convenient to use the terminology adopted by Fred C. Robinson in his unpublished thesis: *variation* for the total construction; *components* for the various members of the total construction; *variatum* for the first component; and *varians* for the second and subsequent components. The number of components may be two, three, four or five, and the number of parts of speech involved may vary from one word to a whole sentence. As Brodeur has observed, 'All content-words lend themselves to variation, and the figure may assume many forms.'[8] Among the forms he lists are simple substantive words like these pairs for 'ship' and 'treasure' in *Beowulf*, ll. 294b–5a and 80b–1a respectively: *flotan~nacan, beagas~sinc;* substantive compounds in variation with such simplices or in variation with compounds, like *byrne~searonet* 'corselet' and *Gar-Dena~þeodcyninga* 'Spear-Danes~kings of the people' in *Beowulf*, ll. 405b–6a and 1a–2a; adjectival variation like *guðwerigne~aldorleasne* 'battle-weary~lifeless' in *Beowulf*, ll. 1586a–7a; adjective-noun combinations like *geomor sefa~murnende mod* 'sorrowing spirit' in *Beowulf*, ll. 49b–50a; adverbial variation, including phrases, like *ellor~of earde* 'elsewhere~from the earth' in *Beowulf*, ll. 55b–6a; and others, including verb and clausal variation, like this pair for 'they defended the treasure' from *Beowulf*, ll. 1204b–5a: *sinc ealgode~wælreaf werede.*

The varians of a single word may be two words (or phrases) in coordination, as in *Brunanburh*, ll. 10b–12a:

> *Hettend* crungun,
>
> *Sceotta leoda   and scipflotan*
> fæge feollan.

(The enemies fell, the Scots people and sailors fell doomed.)

Here the verb is also varied, so that we have overall clausal variation. As this example demonstrates, the varians may be separated from its variatum by an intervening word or words (here *crungun*). Robinson comments, with respect to this stylistic practice, that the most popular single metrical-syntactical pattern of variation in *Beowulf* consists of variatum (usually preceded by minor sentence elements) in the a-verse, infinitive plus auxiliary in the b-verse, and varians in the succeeding a-verse. *Beowulf*, ll. 961–2a illustrates the pattern nicely:

þæt ðu *hine selfne*   geseon moste,
feond on frætewum . . .

(that you might see him himself, the enemy in his trappings.)

Often, of course, the variation does take the form of two or more successive appositives, as in the opening lines of *Brunanburh:* 'Æthelstan cyning, eorla dryhten, / beorna beahgifa (Aethelstan the king, lord of warriors, ring-giver to men)'.

Semantically, the components of a variation conventionally show the same referent under different aspects or with different attributions, as in the last example. On occasion such a semantically conceived variation is given more focus or productive meaning, as in *Elene*, ll. 460–1:

þæt he Crist wære,   cyning on roderum,
soð sunu meotudes,   sawla nergend. . . .

[that he was Christ, king in the heavens, true Son of God, Saviour of souls.)

Here the different aspects of the referent 'Christ', as represented by the threefold varians, are surely meant to indicate the Trinity. A variation may also have a semantic order or progression, moving from the general to the specific, as in *Beowulf*, ll. 39–40a: 'hildewæpnum ond heaðowædum, / billum ond byrnum (battle-weapons and battle-garments, swords and corselets)'; or from the specific to the general, as in *Beowulf*, ll. 1158b–9a: '*to Denum* feredon, / læddon *to leodum* (they brought her to the Danes, led her to her people)'. And when multiple variation is used, there may be a sense of climax along with increasing specificity, as in *Beowulf*, ll. 1380–2: *feo ~ealdgestreonum ~wundini golde* 'wealth ~

ancient treasure ⁓ twisted gold'. But I am not proposing to be exhaustive in categorizing the kinds of possible variation, and I think the description I have provided is sufficient to suggest the wide variety of forms in strict grammatical parallelism that this stylistic feature affords.[9]

What is of greater interest are those cases where identity of referents is disputable, because implications of meaning become involved. In its simplest form the problem can be seen with a series of three or more substantives, where the reader or hearer must select either variation or enumeration to be the 'meaning'. Take the following two examples:

> se þe moras heold,
> fen ond fæsten . . .   (*Beowulf*, ll. 103b–4a)
> land ealgodon,
> hord and hamas.   (*Brunanburh*, ll. 9b–10a)

Of the former, Brodeur says, 'the three substantives do not stand in variation: the territory inhabited by Grendel contained both moors and fen'. In the latter, Bolton sees a twofold variation in a 'bifurcated pattern . . . the appositive to the simplex *land* is the duplex *hord and hamas*'.[10] I think both these observations are mistaken. 'Moors' consist of both marshy and firm ground, and surely *fen ond fæsten* is a varians of *moras* in which *fen* signifies 'marshy area' and *fæsten* 'firm ground'. On the other hand, in the *Brunanburh* verses, although 'homes' might be considered part of 'land' in a most general way, it is extremely doubtful that 'treasure' can be so conceived. In this case I think we have an enumeration: 'they protected land [and] treasure and homes'— three things vital to society and in need of protection from the incursions of the Viking and Scots forces. There is something of a contrast, I believe, between this passage in *Brunanburh* and another at the end, which compares the actions of Aethelstan and his brother with those of the original Angles and Saxons who came to England: in the chronologically earlier military victory the 'English' only *eard begeaton* (I give an analysis of this passage below). There is an implication of meaning in the contrast: whereas the invading Angles and Saxons were coming to found a society and only 'seized the land', Aethelstan and Eanmund were defending a prosperous establishment with its treasure and homes—which, of course, is historically true.

Of even greater interest are lines 221–3a of *Beowulf*, where the hero and men approach the shores of Denmark on their mission of mercy to Hrothgar:

> ... ða liðende   land gesawon,
> brimclifu blican,   beorgas steape,
> side sænæssas.

(then the sailors saw land, seacliffs shining, steep hills, broad seacliffs.)

Brodeur would consider the components of this passage as 'parallelism without variation: the poet is enumerating the various features of the Danish coast-line as the Geats raise it in view: "steep hills" and "broad promontories" are distinct elements of the landscape'.[11] But Robinson, arguing with this interpretation, remarks:[12]

> Brodeur seems to mean that as the men approach Denmark, first the dark line of the land is dimly perceived, then the glint of the sheared cliff-sides, then high hills (behind the cliffs?) and finally, the broad tongues of land protruding into the sea. But the sequence of the last three items is hardly satisfying. Also *clif* and *næs* are almost surely synonyms ... and the *steape* modifying *beorgas* seems to repeat once more the same image. I, therefore, take this passage as a four-part variation in which the general term *land* is varied by three more precise terms for 'land fronting the sea'. These three terms contrast with each other only in so far as they suggest different aspects of the same referent—a suggestion achieved largely through the three words which depend upon the nouns: *steape, side, blican*. ... This is almost surely right, for as [the variations in lines 571–72 and 1911–13] show, the poet's usual procedure is to supply a variation for the shore-line, not a consecutive list of typographical features as they are descried.

That we have variation here I think is indisputable; but Brodeur is not totally mistaken, for there are implications for meaning in this variation for the shore-line which accord with his interpretation. What the poet is doing here, I suggest, is subtly indicating the ship's approach to land: for the first thing the sailors would see is an amorphous 'land'; as they came nearer, the landscape would begin to shape itself into the 'sea-cliffs shining'; and when nearer yet, the steepness of those very harbour cliffs would first become apparent, then their breadth. If I am correct in this analysis, we have a logical order of perception of the same elements of the landscape as the sailors reach their destination; and the *Beowulf* poet has indicated not only the objects of sight but movement and shift of perspective simultaneously in this seemingly-simple variation. Caroline Brady has argued that in such a passage as *Beowulf*, ll. 3132b-3, where the Geatish warriors shove the dead dragon over the cliff into the sea,

> leton weg niman,
> flod fæðmian   frætwa hyrde,

(they let the wave take, the flood embrace the guardian of the treasure)

the noun *weg* refers to the swell of the wave and the verb *niman* to its reaching up to receive the falling body, whereas the varians *flod fæðmian* envisages the horizontally moving water encircling the body; and Robinson gives other examples of this kind of variation indicating 'consecutive actions' with both infinite and finite verbs.[13] My point about the 'cliffs' passage is similar, but goes a step further in suggesting this implication of meaning by the use of variation *without* employing verbs of movement; that is, a sense of movement is created, a shift in perspective obtained, without explicit statement or the employment of other syntactic means.

That such an implication is not an isolated occurrence but always a possibility with variation if the context is not only congenial to it but focuses attention upon it—and thus an expectation or horizon of meaning—can be illustrated by other passages. A good one occurs in *Brunanburh*, when the poet remarks that neither Constantine nor Anlaf nor their Scots and Viking forces could laughingly boast

> þæt heo *beaduweorca*   beteran wurdun
> on campstede   *cumbolgehnastes,*
> *garmittinge,*   *gumena gemotes,*
> *wæpengewrixles* . . .

(ll. 48-51a)

(that they were better in that battle-place in battle-deeds, in the clash of banners, in the meeting of spears, in the coming-together of men, in the exchange of weapons.)

Beaduweorca (gen. pl.), like *land* in the *Beowulf* selection, may well be considered the variatum, a general term varied more specifically four times by different genitive compounds (one of these being, rather, a genitive phrase) with the referent 'meeting': *-gehnastes, -mittinge, gemotes, -gewrixles*. (That 'deeds' is not quite the same thing as 'meeting' poses a bit of a problem, but context makes abundantly clear that the 'meetings' are the 'deeds'; I discuss this point further below.) But the varians-series, moving as it does from the clash of banners to the encounter of spears to the meeting of men to the trading of weapon-blows, suggests the progress of battle as in a tapestry, with the opposing forces coming closer and closer together till finally they meet in hand-to-hand combat. It could be argued, I realize, that *garmittinge* and *wæpengewrixles* are really indistinguishable, but I think the general sense of the movement of the series would imprint upon the latter, the general term 'weapons', the notion of swords.

This same implication, incidentally, may be present in the clausal variation of *Brunanburh*, ll. 5b–6a: 'bordweal clufan, / heowan heaþolinde (they clove the shield-wall, hewed the battle-shields)'. Here too there is no explicit suggestion that the forces are closing in, but the verbal movement from 'phalanx' to individual 'shields', framed by the chiastic arrangement of the grammatical elements in the subject-verb/verb-subject pattern, may serve to move the action from a mass attack to a man-to-man situation. The same action is accorded the Hebrews as they cut a path through the Assyrians in *Judith*, ll. 301–4a, but in reverse order and without chiasmus: 'linde heowon, / scildburh scæron (they hewed the shields, sheared through the shield-defence)'. Perhaps in this reverse order we can see individual efforts leading to a mass rout. Mass movement is further suggested through variation in *Judith*, ll. 162ff.

Wið þæs fæstengeates   folc onette,
weras wif somod,   wornum ond heapum,
ðreatum ond ðrymmum   þrungon ond urnon
ongean ða þeodnes mægð   þusendmælum,
ealde ge geonge.

(Towards the fortress-gate the people hastened, men and
women together, in swarms and crowds, in troops and
throngs surged and ran towards the maiden of the Lord in
thousands, both young and old.)

In this passage, in addition to the specific movement denoted by
the verbs *þrungon* and *urnon*, the substantives used adverbially
in variation, *wornum ond heapum~ðreatum ond ðrymmum~
þusendmælum*, suggest the pell-mell rush, as well as the vast
numbers of the Hebrews, as the people flock to the city's gate
to see the triumphant return of the heroine.

Variation makes possible other kinds of shifts in perspective in
Old English poems. *Judith* again affords a convenient illustration.
It has frequently been observed that Holofernes is presented now
as a Germanic chieftain, now as an embodiment of evil; but it has
not been noticed, I think, that variation is a key stylistic feature in
yoking these disparate presentations, as in the following cases:

Swa *se inwidda*   ofer ealne dæg
dryhtguma sine   drencte mid wine,
swiðmod sinces brytta . . .   (ll. 28–30a)

(Thus the evil one, the proud-minded giver of treasure,
the whole day long drenched his warrior-band with wine.)

                             þæt *se bealofulla*
mihte wlitan þurh,   *wigena baldor*.   (ll. 48b–9)

(so that the evil one, the prince of warriors, might look
through [the curtain].)

þæt *se beorna brego*   ond seo beorhte mægð
in ðam wlitegan træfe   wæron ætsomne,
Iudith seo æðele   ond *se galmoda*. . . .   (ll. 254–6)

([they thought] that the chief of men and the bright maid
were together in the beautiful pavilion, Judith the noble
and the licentious one.)

What these variations achieve is a simultaneous view of Holofernes from his own and his men's heroic perspective, and from a
Christian moralistic one identified with the heroine. Interestingly
enough, Holofernes' warriors also participate in a shift in moral
perspective through variation: near the beginning of the extant poem, they attend his feast as his 'weagesiðas, / bealde

71

byrnwiggende (woe-companions, bold corsleted warriors)' (ll. 16b–17a), and they receive the proffered stoups of wine as 'fæge, / rofe rondwiggende (doomed, brave shield-warriors)' (ll. 19b–20a). The word *weagesiðas* has been something of a semantic crux, it should be noted: Gordon translates it as 'companions who do evil' and Timmer as 'companions who suffer misery'. Both meanings are well attested in other contexts. Ringler endorses a dual interpretation here, seeing deliberate ironic ambiguity: he suggests that Holofernes' men are his present comrades in crime, but they will before long become his comrades in suffering the pangs of Hell.[14] Whether there is ironic ambiguity present in this passage is moot (on the whole matter of ambiguity and word play, see the next chapter): the parallel of lines 19b–20a suggests that Timmer's is the correct interpretation and that the Christian perspective in the variation reveals the warriors as doomed to misery in their association with Holofernes. Perhaps we might compare these uses of variation for shifts in moral perspective with Homer's use of simile to give 'the reader a double point of view by which the poem communicates an idea of two antithetical worlds, one at peace, the other at war'.[15]

In the above exegeses, a number of subtle and not-so-subtle difficulties concerning the limits of variation have been glossed over. Some of these will repay examination. Are we to consider, for example, the first part of the compounds with the terms for 'meeting' in *Brunanburh*, ll. 49–51a components of the variation? Banners, spears, men (a genitive modifier rather than an element of a compound, but equivalent thereto) and weapons do *not* have the same referents (though the last might, as I indicated in the earlier discussion, be considered a generalized form of the second), but they can hardly be culled from the variation. They are all more specific aspects of *beadu-*, and their separate identities as components of warfare are subsumed in context by the generic relationship. Thus there can be no question of their role in the variation, though simultaneously, as I have tried to show, their specific referents imply the progress of the battle. A more obvious case is the *beodgeneatas ~ eaxlgestellan* variation of *Beowulf*, ll. 1713–14: the 'table-companions' of the variatum are quite clearly the same men as the 'shoulder-companions' of the varians, even though 'table' and 'shoulder' are hardly identical referentially.

But if elements of compounds with different referents are 'felt on the pulse' as participating in the variation with those parts of the compounds which clearly *are* in variation, what about adjective or genitive noun modifiers? Can we deny them equal participation? Here we enter upon ground less firm. Brodeur, for example (pp. 43, 280), will have none of this, and in such appositive sequences as *side scyldas~rondas regnhearde* 'broad shields~very hard shields' and *swyn ealgylden~eofor irenheard* 'all-golden boar~iron-hard boar' (*Beowulf*, ll. 325b–6a, 1111b–1112a), he would deny the adjectives a role in the variations. This distinction between non-identical parts of nominal compounds and non-identical descriptive adjectives seems to me dubious insofar as stylistic effect and meaning in context are concerned; and we may clarify the problem, I think, with an even more subtle example. When Beowulf and his men are returning from Denmark, they sail until they

... Geata clifu   ongiton mcahton,
cuþe næssas ...   (ll. 1911–12a)

(could spy the Geats' cliffs, the well-known nesses.)

Now, *clifu* and *næssas* are obviously in variation, but 'Geats'' and 'well-known' do not, out of context, have the same referent; but surely the cliffs in this passage are well-known because they *are* the Geats' and are *not* foreign soil! The genitive noun modifier and the adjective, though normally indicating different referents, are thus related semantically in this particular case and, I would suggest, the relationship is made stronger by the implication of identity inherent in the technique of parallel variation.

Robinson (p. 29, note 2) would accept this point with reference to the broad and wondrously-hard shields and the golden and iron boar-figures; i.e., he, unlike Brodeur, will accept the adjectives as part of the variations. Neither he nor Brodeur (pp. 9–10, note 15, and p. 274 respectively) will, however, allow the different prepositional phrases in *Beowulf*, ll. 210b–11a to be part of the variation in these lines:

                    flota wæs on yðum,
bat under beorge.

(the ship was on the waves, the boat under the cliff.)

73

These verses occur as Beowulf and his band move on their journey from Hygelac's court to the harbour where their ship lies waiting to transport them to Denmark. *Bat* varies *flota* without question, but 'on the waves' and 'under the cliff' have different referents. Still, it is not only the same ship, but its position remains unchanged, and the prepositional phrases are referring to the same location. What is happening here, I think, is that the implication of movement in variation (see above in connection with *Beowulf*, ll. 221–3a) is being channelled into a changing perspective, as Beowulf's men first sight the boat from the promontory, where they would see it *on ȳðum*, and then view it from the level of the water itself, where it would appear in their line of sight as *under beorge*. Thus the warriors' movement from the top of the cliff to the water's edge is implicitly indicated by the apparently 'motionless' variation, and the next sentence tells explicitly how they entered the ship: 'Beornas gearwe / on stefn stigon (the ready warriors climbed on the prow)'.

Where does one draw the line, then, when there is formal parallelism and part of the expression is clearly in variation? I propose that though such elements as the adjectives, parts of compounds and prepositional phrases are not identical in their referents, that the syntactic parallelism plus the variational quality of the rest of the expression effectively *does* equate, or at least link, the disparate elements: the shields' broadness co-exists with their hardness, the table companions are indeed the same warriors who stand shoulder-to-shoulder in time of war, the cliffs are well-known because they are their very own Geatish ones, and the boat's being beneath the cliff indicates that, in addition to the difference in perspective, it is equally on the waves.

Verbal variation can also lead to the question of inclusion or exclusion. An interesting example occurs in *Beowulf*, ll. 129b–31, where Hrothgar's grief over Grendel's initial attacks is expressed:

> Mære þeoden,
> æþeling ærgod, unbliðe sæt,
> þolode ðryðswyð, þegnsorge dreah.

(The famous prince, the noble one virtuous of old, sat unhappy, the mighty one suffered, endured sorrow for his thanes.)

On this passage, Brodeur comments as follows (p. 49):

> *Mære þeoden—æþeling ærgod* constitute a combination of adjective and substantive variation; in line 131 there is verb variation (*þolode—dreah*); the adjective *ðryðswyð*, used substantively, varies *mære þeoden—æþeling ærgod*. But semantically there is a third element in the verb-variation: *unbliðe sæt*. Without the adjective, the verb *sæt* would be too colorless to participate in a variation of verbs meaning 'suffer' and 'endure'; but 'sat unhappy' is, in all ways except pure structure, a sound variation of them.

This is an excellent observation insofar as it catches something of the full play of variation in the passage; but more, I think, can be said. For it seems that while allowing the adjective *unbliðe* to constitute part of, and indeed be necessary to, the verbal variation (we might compare this with such a common variation as *andswarode~wordhord unleac* 'he answered, unlocked his word-hoard'), Brodeur is satisfied to consider *dreah* without its object *þegnsorge* as a varians. If we consider the noun object to be part of its constituency, however, the passage takes on some significant contours of meaning: the verbal variation moves from under-statement (*unbliðe sæt*) to strong statement of suffering in *þolode* to an intensive kind of specific suffering in 'he suffered sorrow for his thanes'. Yet concurrently, the variations for 'Hrothgar' intensify from 'famous prince' to 'prince good-of-old' (or 'immeasurably good') to 'the very powerful one', *ðryðswyð* being all the more notable for its being an adjective used sub-stantivally. Thus we get something of the theological-rhetorical *communicatio idiomatum* used in *The Dream of the Rood*, where the God-man duality of Christ is forcefully expressed in such verses as 'Genamon hie þær ælmihtigne God (they lay hold there on Almighty God)' (l. 60b) and 'gesetton ðæron sigora waldend (they laid therein [in the tomb] the Lord of Victories)' (l. 67a).[16] (We might notice in passing that the emotional intensity of this *Beowulf* passage is heightened not only by this imaginative use of variation, but by the sound pattern as well: the *th* sounds, either internal to the words or not part of the alliterative pattern in lines 129b–30: *þeoden, æþeling, unbliðe*, become both alliterative and non-alliterative in the last line, reinforced by the voiced dental: *þolode, ðryðswyð, þegnsorge dreah*.)

This section on Hrothgar's grief for his devoured thanes, with its substantive and verbal variations, leads us in one way back to the more general type of variation which Wimsatt observed. Nevertheless, it is still tighter in form, with marked parallelism and chiasmus. Further, the semantic situation or action in which the variational words or phrases are embedded is the same, despite the intensification and paradoxical effect of 'the king suffered'. And this has been the case in all the variations I have so far adduced: where any change in the action has been involved, it has been only by the *implications* of the variations. Can we feel, however, that there is a *bona fide* variation of the kind associated particularly with Old English and other ancient Germanic poetry when there is clearly repetition or restatement of the substantive, but just as clearly a progression of action in the predicate?

Brunanburh, ll. 13b–17a, offer a case in point:

> siðþan sunne up
> on morgentid,   mære tungol,
> glad ofer grundas,   Godes condel beorht,
> eces Drihtnes,   oð sio æþele gesceaft
> sah to setle.

(since the sun [rose] up in the morning-time, the glorious star, glided over the lands, the bright candle of God, the eternal Lord, until that noble creation sank to its rest.)

There are several restatements of the 'sun' here, but curiously enough Paetzel, in his definitive study of variation, lists only *sunne~mære tungol~Godes condel beorht* as constituting the variation.[17] He excludes *sio æþele gesceaft* probably (although he gives no reason) because he felt that unlike the first three components, it occurs in a separate clause indicating a change of movement. Bolton, on the other hand, in his study of the variations in *Brunanburh*, includes this last item because, as he says, it is 'linked by the forceful *siðþan . . . oð* correlation' and because the 'grammatical techniques support the appearance of apposition: *glad ofer grundas* and *sah to setle* not only share parallel subjects, but parallel structure of verb and preposition+noun'.[18] Both Paetzel and Bolton seem to have acknowledged only two actions here, the sun's gliding over the earth and its sinking to rest; but there is really a threefold action, three clauses, the first being a statement of the sun's rising: *siðþan sunne up / on morgentid;* this is elliptical, but such elliptical expressions, the verb of movement being omitted, are common enough in Old English poetry. If Paetzel had recognized the ellipsis, presumably he would have reduced his variation by one member (though the punctuation poses something of a problem); but I am inclined to believe Bolton is correct in seeing the tightness of the passage producing the effect of variation in the nouns, despite the shifts in action.[19] In fact, one might see even the progressive actions of rising, gliding and sinking being given an intensive unity by the noun variations, a sort of unified sweeping motion across the sky, analogous with the sweeping action of the English as they put the invaders to flight, hewing them from behind 'ondlangne dæg (the endlong day)'.

In connection with this 'sun' passage, we might also look at the end of *Brunanburh*, where the victory of the two noble kinsmen is compared with that of their forefathers when they first seized the island:

	siþþan eastan hider
Engle and Seaxe	up becoman,
ofer brad brimu	Brytene sohtan,
wlance wigsmiþas	Wealas ofercoman,
eorlas arhwate	eard begeatan.

(since hither from the east the Angles and Saxons came up, sought Britain over the broad seas, proud war-smiths conquered the Welsh, brave warriors seized the land.)

These lines offer a variety of possibilities for punctuation: that which I have indicated suggests a reading where the first two clauses are in variation (though the second lacks a subject, *ofer brad brimu* varies *eastan*, *Brytene* varies *hider* . . . *up* and *sohtan* varies *becoman*) and the last two are likewise. Of course, we shall probably wish to take *Engle and Seaxe* as varied by *wlance wigsmiþas* and *eorlas arhwate*, cutting across the two clausal groups of variations; and, as Bolton remarks, the four verbs are suggestive of variation in their identical positionings, the last three having additionally identically placed objects. The verbs are not identical in meaning, however; they indicate, rather, a progression of arrival, fighting for possession and settling in, a progression similar to that of the sun's in the earlier passage. The tightness of this movement gained by the variations and the grammatical parallelisms also establishes a sense of a unified sweeping action. If we note additionally that we have here the only other *siþþan*-clause in the poem, it is not too fanciful to see a meaningful relationship between the movement of the sun in the earlier passage and this movement, a relationship suggestive of progression and circularity, kinesis and stasis, in historical events, so that the victory of the royal brothers in 937 A.D. is given a retrospective quality associated with their forebears and, simultaneously, a glorious, even celestial dignity associated with the sun. Whether, as Bolton claims, the poet is merely looking at the victories *sub specie eternitatis*, and that the 'form of the poem . . . shows that its praise is [really] for God in his heroes',[20] seems to me questionable in terms of the context and text of the poem.

Another direction we may pursue away from our firm central conception of variation leads towards clausal variation without exact parallelism. In *Beowulf*, ll. 1655–7a, for example, the hero, speaking of his difficult struggle at the bottom of the mere with Grendel's mother, says,

> Ic þæt unsofte   ealdre gedigde,
> wigge under wætere,   weorce geneþde
> earfoðlice.

> (Not easily did I survive that with my life, battle under the water, with difficulty did I come away from that piece of work.)

Robinson, in his discussion of adverbial variation, will not, unlike Brodeur, allow that *unsofte* and *earfoðlice* stand in this relationship because, he says, each modifies a different verb and because 'there is no effect of variational restatement at all'.[21] This seems a curious view of the two clauses involved, where parts appear very effectively to vary each other in chiastic arrangement (if we ignore the proleptic *þæt: unsofte ⁓earfoðlice*, *ealdre gedigde ⁓geneþde, wigge under wætere ⁓weorce*. I would see this as clausal variation, the double statement by Beowulf serving as a reflection of the difficulty he experienced in surviving the struggle.

78

Less tight yet is a passage in *The Phoenix*, ll. 34b–41a, which
Leslie cites as an example of what he calls *conceptual* variation:

Wæstmas ne dreosað,

beorhte blede,   ac þa beamas a
grene stondað,   swa him god bibead.
Wintres ond sumeres   wudu bið gelice
bledum gehongen;   næfre brosniað
leaf under lyfte,   ne him lig sceþeð
æfre to ealdre,   ærþon edwenden
worulde geweorðe.

(Fruits do not decay, the bright fruits, but the trees stand
ever green as God commanded them. Winter and summer
the wood is similarly hung with fruit; never does leaf decay
under the sky, nor shall flame harm it ever and ever until
change [Doomsday] comes to the world.)

This is, of course, a description of the earthly paradise, based on
the Latin poem of Lactantius, *De ave phoenice*. Leslie sees
variation in the passage in rhetorical terms:[22]

> A negative statement is followed by a positive one; then
> follows another positive variant, followed by a negative one.
> It is notable that we find nothing of this configuration in the
> Latin source, the poem by Lactantius, which simply has:
> 'Here is the grove of the Sun, a holy wood thickly planted
> with trees, green with the glory of never-failing foliage'.

But there is more to this 'conceptual' variation than Leslie has
indicated by calling attention to the rhetorical chiasmus. The
variation has three elements: (1) the fruit not decaying; (2) the
trees standing green while the world endures; (3) the command
of God that they do so. The contiguous sentence provides a
conceptual varians for each variatum, in the same order, thus
cutting across the rhetorical chiasmus. (I do not think it is
stretching matters to see the *ne*-clause of the varians as equivalent to *swa him god bibead*.) Though we do not have grammatical
parallelism here, then, the rhetorical and conceptual arrangements of parts does, I feel, constitute a variation which emphasizes the enduring fruits and verdant richness of the Phoenix's
Edenic abode.

The *Beowulf* poet used this looser, though still recognizable, kind of variation to mark momentous occasions in his heroic story, two of which are worth some analysis. When the hero returns from his underwater exploit against Grendel's mother, he bears with him the hilt of the magical sword with which he killed the she-monster. To celebrate the occasion of the end of the reign of terror, he gives the hilt to Hrothgar. The poet comments:

Ða wæs gylden hilt   gamelum rince,
harum hildfruman   on hand gyfen,
enta ærgeweorc;   hit on æht gehwearf
æfter deofla hryre   Denigea frêan,
wundorsmiþa geweorc;   ond þa þas worold ofgeaf
gromheort guma,   Godes andsaca,
morðres scyldig,   ond his modor eac,
on geweald gehwearf   woroldcyninga
ðæm selestan   be sæm tweonum
ðara þe on Scedenigge   sceattas dælde.   (ll. 1677–86)

(Then the golden hilt was given into the hand of the old man, the ancient war-chieftain—the ancient work of giants; after the fall of devils, it, the work of wonder-smiths, passed into the possession of the lord of the Danes; and when the grim-hearted man, God's adversary, guilty of murder, and his mother also, gave up this world, it passed into the power of the best of worldly kings between the seas, of those who share out treasure in Scandinavia.)

There are here four major components in what is a triple variation: (1) the hilt; (2) the king; (3) the former owners' death; (4) the action of taking possession—though the hilt itself, which has its own varians in the first variation (*enta geweorc*), is only implied in the third, and the monster's decease is only suggested by the *Ða* of the first. Verbal repetition and grammatical parallelism bind the several parts together: *enta geweorc ⁓ wundorsmiþa geweorc; wæs ... on hand gyfen ⁓ on æht gehwearf ⁓ on geweald gehwearf; gamelum rince ⁓ harum hildfruman ⁓ Denigean frean.* But the fall of the king's adversaries is expressed first as the simple adverb *Ða*, then in the phrase *æfter deofles hryre*, then in a long clausal expansion in *þa þas worold ofgeaf | gromheort guma, Godes andsaca, | morðres scyldig, ond his modor eac.* And the last varians for 'king' expands Hrothgar's goodness clausally outward over the whole Scandinavian region.

Grammatical transformation of variational components may perhaps be seen at their most inventive, even pyrotechnical, in *Beowulf*, ll. 2824b–35, in which the death of the dragon is described:

```
                        Bona swylce læg,
egeslic eorðdraca       ealdre bereafod,
bealwe gebæded.         Beahhordum leng
wyrm wohbogen           wealdan ne moste,
ac him irenna       ccga furnamon,
hearde heaðoscearpe        homera lafe,
þæt se widfloga         wundum stille
hreas on hrusan         hordærne neah.
Nalles æfter lyfte      lacende hwearf
middelnihtum,           maðmæhta wlonc
ansyn ywde,         ac he eorðan gefeoll
for ðæs hildfruman         hondgeweorce.
```

([Beowulf's] slayer likewise lay dead, terrible earth-dragon bereft of life, overcome by violence. No longer was the coiled dragon permitted to rule the ringhoard, but [=for][23] iron blades had taken him off, hard, battle-sharp leaving [forging] of hammers, so that the wide-flier, stilled by wounds, fell to the earth near the treasure-house. Not at all did he wheel flying through the air in the middle of the nights, make an appearance exulting in the possession of his treasures, but he fell to earth through the handiwork of the battle-chieftain.)

The variation covers the second and third sentences of the above passage. Though parallelism in words or word-groups is for the most part absent here, we do have similar clause patterns, each part of the sequent sentences expressing the identical ideational relationship: 'the dragon couldn't do something, for he had been killed'. As in the verses on the passing of the sword-hilt, there are four components of the experience repeated in each sentence: (1) the dragon's ownership of the treasure; (2) the drag-on's aeronautical prowess; (3) the power of battle that caused his death; (4) his actual 'fall'. Only in the fourth instance do we find a rough, if inverted, verbal parallelism, in *hreas on hrusan* ∼

eorðan gefeoll. Despite this looseness, however, the sequence must surely be felt as a variation, and must have been so felt by the Anglo-Saxon audience. And it is precisely in the differing emphases secured by its non-parallel members that its poetic puissance lies. These emphases are the products of different grammatical structures, some of which occupy only one verse and are coincident with syntactic frames, others of which extend up to two whole lines. Thus, the first element in the variatum series places great stress on the dragon's guardianship of the treasure through a complete clause: *Beahhordum leng | wyrm wohbogen wealdan ne moste,* and even greater emphasis on the sword that took him off: *him irenna ecga fornamon, | hearde heaðoscearpe homera lafe.* Least attention is paid to the beast's flying proclivity, the single compound noun *widfloga.* But the first element in the varians expands this last and least-emphasized component of the variatum into a complete clause: *Nalles æfter lyfte lacende hwearf middelnihtum;* the treasure-relationship, on the other hand, is reduced to a genitive noun depending upon an adjective: *maðmæhta wlonc;* and the sword's derring-do finds expression in the varians in a two-verse prepositional phrase where it is only hinted at as part of the hero's *hondgeweorc.* The poet has been like a jeweller, turning the several facets of his gem to the light so that each may sparkle in its turn; and it would not be amiss, I think, to compare this description with that of the death of the dragon in Book I, Canto xi, of *The Faerie Queene*:[24]

> So downe he fell, and forth his life did breath,
> That vanisht into smoke and cloudes swift;
> So downe he fell, that th'earth him underneath
> Did grone, as feeble so great load to lift;
> So downe he fell, as an huge rocky clift,
> Whose false foundacion waves have washt away,
> With dreadfull poyse is from the mayneland rift,
> And, rolling downe, great Neptune doth dismay;
> So downe he fell, and like an heaped mountaine lay.

The repetitions and 'variations' of the fall in Spenser are designed to effect some of the same sense of momentousness of the occasion as are the *Beowulf* poet's uses of variation.

Further individual instances of productive variation would not be difficult to find, but enough has been indicated in this chapter of the several directions of emphasis, intensification and tonal unity it may provide, as well as some of the expectations of meaning inherent in the stylistic device. This is not to say that every instance of variation in Old English poetry serves some thematic need: in an orally based mode of poetry, variation may often be its own justification, even as rhyme may be in another mode. In interpreting variations, the critic must weigh thematic probabilities against the purely stylistic need or pleasure *per se* afforded by the convention.

In the above discussion, I have not at all explored possible formal uses of variation in individual poems. Robinson, for example, suggests that variation is formally used in *Beowulf* to underscore periodic structure in scenes of little suspense, to mark structural and rhetorical divisions, to effectuate transitions. Bolton would find five complex variations in *Brunanburh* as marking major structural divisions of that poem. I am not entirely convinced by these allegations, but they are worth further investigation. But whatever the structural uses of variation may be, the technique at its most elaborate, as in the passing on of the golden sword hilt or the death of the dragon, serves to enlarge the world of meaning of a poem. In a way it serves a function similar to that of the epic simile, of which Ruth Wallerstein has written,[25]

> In the large and leisurely movement of the epic poem, with
> its broad picture of life, the extended simile, which begins
> in a luminous description of the object figured and then
> moves on to complete its own beautiful scene before
> returning to the narrative, is an element of great organic
> beauty in that it helps to create that ample background
> scene and that sense of a whole world which are so necessary
> to the manifold life of the epic.

4

The Play of
Sound and Sense

Variation, especially as defined and limited in the preceding chapter, is a stylistic feature significant in Old English verse and one which has received its fair share of critical attention. It is not, however, prominent in later Old English poetry. From the discussion of its nature and implications of meaning in different contexts, I should like to turn to a basic characteristic of that later poetry which has, until recently, scarcely been observed in the earlier poetry and which perhaps deserves closer attention as a *bona fide* expectation in our interpretation of Old English poems.

I refer to what Empson called, 'in an extended sense', *ambiguity*: 'any verbal nuance, however slight, which gives room for alternative reactions to the same piece of language'.[1] I find the term, as Empson uses it and as it has come to be employed in much modern criticism, both too broad and too narrow, however, and prefer to speak of the play of sound and sense, a designation that seems to me more flexible and accurate for subsuming the variety of give-and-take between the phonological and semantic resources of words in which poetry delights. That variety can best be shown, I think, if we limit the concept of ambiguity to those situations in which, when a single word is used, two or more possibilities from its semantic range are, by force of context, made operative in the meaning of a passage. We may then additionally consider such other plays of sound and sense as puns (paronomasia) and *double entendre*, the repetition of the same word with different meanings, the use of sound similarities to underline antithetical meanings, metaphoric word play, onomastic (i.e., proper name) word play and so forth—though admittedly these categories inevitably overlap. All of the sound-sense interrelationships we shall consider in this chapter will be of the informal kind; discussion of formal play in the metrical requirements of the alliterative line will be reserved for chapter 5.

Possibly the failure of Anglo-Saxon critics to explore very much the play of sound and sense in Old English poetry, as Fred Robinson suggests, has been the belief that word play was foreign to the Anglo-Saxon temperament. If so, he continues, 'the basis for this assumption is hard to determine'; for at least 'paronomasia was a favorite device among the writers most familiar to the Anglo-Saxons, and the OE writers themselves discussed and used puns both in their vernacular and in their Latin writings'.[2] The Old Testament and St Augustine, for example, use paronomasia, and Bede, as might be expected, discusses it in his Latin treatise on schemes and tropes. Aldhelm employs the rhetorical figure in his *Ænigmata*. Byrhtferth, in his vernacular compendium of scientific information known as *Byrhtferth's Manual*, has a section on it; and though his illustrations are only from Latin and Hebrew, he manages to decorate his own prose occasionally: 'ond ic hopige þæt cherubin se mæra ætwesan wylle, ond of þam upplican weofode mid his gyldenan *tange* þære gledan spearcan to minre *tungan* gebringan (and I hope that the glorious angel will be present, and from the divine altar bring a spark of that fire with his golden *tongs* to my *tongue*)'.

The student of Anglo-Saxon literature and language will not be unaware of the future Pope Gregory's punning remarks on seeing the fair-haired Anglo-Saxon slave boys in the Roman marketplace: his 'angelizing' of *Angles*, affixing *-lulia* to *Ælla* and splitting *Deire* into *de ira* for the salvation of their souls. This sort of word play was not, as it might seem from our modern perspective, simply a bit of pious facetiousness, for[3]

> the process of reasoning behind the three puns is based on Gregory's assumption that verbal similarities tell us something about the essential nature of the thing named. . . . The fact that [the Angles] are heathen and the fact that they are angelic are both 'true' facts simultaneously, though they are contradictory facts. So long as they remain heathen, the pun contains a paradox; by their conversion the temporal paradox will be resolved with the realization of the eternal promise inherent in their names.

This kind of serious word play was used to good effect by the homilist Wulfstan to emphasize through ironic antithesis his oratorical lessons:[4]

La, for hwy þonne bið hit swa, buton forðam þe se mann byð þonne *beswicen* ond deofol ah ða saule butan he *geswice* ond ðe deoppor gebete þa misdæde? Of deofle ne cymð ænig oþer bot buton þonne he hæfð þæs mannes sawle *beswicen*, þonne *geswicð* he þære dare þe he þam menn elles ær mid derede, ond, witod, se þe his broces bote secð, buton to Gode sylfum ond to his halgum ond to rihtlæcum, he dryhð deofles *willan* and Godes *unwillan*.

(Lo, why then is this so except that the man is then ensnared and the devil will have his soul unless he cease and deeply atone for the misdeed? From the devil never comes any help except that when he has ensnared the soul of the man, then he ceases the injury with which he formerly harmed him, and, certainly, he who seeks help for his woes except from God himself and his saints and the true physician, he does the will of the devil and God's displeasure.)

The play between *beswicen* and *geswice* (*geswicð*) and *willan* and *unwillan* neatly points up the folly of resorting to heathen practices.

Such evidence would seem to favour the proposition that Old English poets were likely to have indulged their poetic fancy in the play of sound and sense to achieve a richness of texture and meaning in their poems. And there are obvious examples of their indulgence with which we may begin. We may then proceed to less obvious and to even doubtful cases of various kinds, suggesting the limitations we must place upon our critical selves in pursuit of this fancy, lest we become too much of-the-land-busy in our zeal to find interpretational enrichment.

The Exeter Book *Riddles* are a natural place to expect that kind of sound-sense play called *double entendre*. That play may be 'innocent', as when we are told of the bookworm that

Stæl-giest ne wæs
wihte þy gleawra,   þe he þam wordum swealg.

(The stealing-visitor was not a whit the wiser by having swallowed those words.)

Or it may be salacious, as in those riddles whose answers are 'key', 'onion' or 'ornamented shirt'. Paull Baum translates the last of these as follows:[5]

Often a goodly damsel,   a lady, locked me
close in a chest.   Sometimes with her hands
she took me out   and gave me to her lord,
a fine chieftain,   as he commanded her.
Then he thrust his head   well inside me,
up from below,   into the narrow part.
If the strength prevailed   of him who received me,
adorned as I was,   something or other rough
was due to fill me.   Guess what I mean.

On another level, the play of sound and sense can be similar to that in the Wulfstan homily, though without irony, as in the famous 'swan' riddle:

Hrægl min *swigað*,   þonne ic hrusan trede,
oþþe þa wic buge,   oþþe wado drefe.
. . . .   Frætwe mine
swogað hlude   ond swinsiað,
torhte singað,   þonne ic getenge ne beom
flode ond foldan   ferende gæst.

(My garment *is silent* when I tread the earth or inhabit the dwelling or stir up the waters. My adornments *sound* loudly and make melody, sing brightly, when I am not near water and land, [am] a travelling spirit.)

Here the phonetically similar but semantically antithetical words *swigað* and *swogað* point up the central paradox of the riddle, the silence of the bird's feathers when not flying and the (folkloristic) singing noise they make in its flight. Or the play of sound may completely dominate the meaning, as C. L. Wrenn implies when he says[6] of the riddle on the making of a harp, that it

is an astonishing instance of suggesting the quality of the musical instrument by choosing repetitive sounds only very loosely related to meaning:

Corfen, sworfen, cyrred, þyrred,
bunden, wunden, blæced, wæced,
frætwed, geatwed, feorran læded
to durum dryhta.   (*Riddle 28*, ll. 4–7)

(Cut and curved, turned round and dried, bound and
twisted, bleached, softened, adorned and ornamented,
brought afar to the dwellings of noble warriors.)

A different kind of play emphasizes sense over sound: it
repeats the *same* word within a limited context so as to counterpoint two or more different meanings of that word. George
Herbert plays upon the word *rest* in 'The Pulley' in this way:

When almost all was out, God made a stay,
Perceiving that, alone of all his treasure,
  Rest in the bottom lay.

'For if I should', said He,
'Bestow this jewel also on my creature,
He would adore My gifts instead of Me,
And *rest* in nature, not the God of nature;
  So both should losers be.

'Yet let him keep the *rest*,
But keep then with repining *restlessness*'.

The Herbert illustration is baroque in its ringing of changes, and
I doubt whether anything so elaborate can be found in Old
English poetry. But the selfsame technique can easily be validated
in *The Seafarer*, where different word repetitions cohere into a
pattern of meaning for the poem. For example, in lines 41b and
43a, *dryhten* is repeated with two different referents, an earthly
lord and God:

                         ne him his *dryhten* to þæs hold,
þæt he a his sæfore   sorge næbbe,
to hwon hine *dryhten*   gedon wille.

([There is no man] whose *lord* is so dear to him that he will
never have a care as to what the *Lord* will assign him [i.e.,
his fate] on his sea journey.)

Somewhat later in the poem, in lines 64b–88, the words *dream*, *blæd* and *duguð* are similarly used in two distinct senses, with reference to heavenly joys and consortium on the one hand, and with references to departed social communion on the other. The speaker, reaffirming his decision to embark upon his voyage, will do so

> forþon me hatran sind
> dryhtnes *dreamas*   þonne þis deade lif,
> læne on londe.

(because dearer to me arc the joys of the Lord than this dead life, transitory on earth.)

It is best for a man, he says, to fight against the devil to achieve 'ecan lifes *blæd*, / *dream* mid *dugeþum* (the glory of eternal life, joy among the [heavenly] hosts)'. These *dreamas*, this *blæd*, are of the divine variety, and the *duguð* is the host of angelic comrades. But immediately following this last phrase, the speaker reminisces in elegiac mood about the days that have departed:

> Dagas sind gewitene,
> ealle onmedlan   eorþan rices. . . .
> Gedroren is þeos *duguð* eal,   *dreamas* sind gewitene,
> wuniað þa wacran   ond þas woruld healdaþ,
> brucað þurh bisgo.   *Blæd* is gehnæged.

(The days have departed, all the pomp of earth's kingdom. . . . This host has all fallen, joys have departed, the weaker live on and possess this world, possess it with toil. Glory is laid low.)

It would seem more than coincidental that the poet has used the same words he had previously employed in connection with eternal values to describe transient earthly ones. Here is purposeful word play reinforced in this very passage by the use of *lof* 'praise' in a corresponding earthly-heavenly duality (cf. my remarks in chapter 2 in connection with *lofgeornost*). The pattern thus established serves to emphasize, it seems to me, an ambivalence of feeling in the emotional or tonal quality of the poem: it is certainly the speaker's recognition of the transience of earthly life that urges him to seek the security 'hwær we ham agen . . . in þa ecan eadignesse, / þær is lif gelong in lufan dryhtnes (where we may possess our home . . . in the eternal bliss where there is the source of life in the love of the Lord), (ll. 117b–21), but the repetitive use of the same words with earthly referents suggests that he is still wistful in his backward glance at a departed golden age. It is wrong, I think, for us to ignore or to twist this aspect of the poem's meaning to bring, as some critics would insist, tonal unity into harmony with its intellectual direction (cf. my remarks in chapter 1 on Hartman's interpretation of Wordsworth).

From these varieties of sound-sense interaction, let us turn to ambiguity proper, as I defined it earlier in this chapter, where a single word, without repetition, contributes several of its meanings, even possibly antithetical ones, to the sense of its passage. In modern poetry, perhaps the most notorious example of ambiguity appears in Hopkins's 'Windhover':

> Brute beauty and valour and act, oh, air, pride, plume, here
> Buckle!

Though some critics have in the past argued that only one of the several meanings of *buckle* is appropriate here (different critics arguing for different ones!), I think it would generally be agreed nowadays that context suggests 'fasten', 'equip for battle', 'engage' and 'crumble' are all part of the complexity of meaning in Hopkins's poem.

Perhaps the best case to date that has been made for an Anglo-Saxon poet's use of ambiguity proper is M. J. Swanton's in his recent study of *The Dream of the Rood*.[7] The word is *fah* (*fag*), a rather difficult word in many contexts as two words, *fag* and *fah*, had coalesced in Old English pronunciation and spelling, so that the graphic form ending in *g* or *h* is no indication of which word was intended. The basic meanings are (1) decorated, shining; and by extension (blood) stained; and (2) hostile; and by extension guilty, outlawed. These distinct meanings occur, for instance, within twenty-five lines of each other in *Beowulf*: the second in a reference to Cain (l. 1263b), 'he þa fag gewat, / morþre gemearcod mandream fleon, / westen warode (he departed then outlawed, marked by murder, fleeing human joys, inhabited the wasteland)'; the first in an image of battle (l. 1286a), 'heoru bunden, hamere geþruen, / sweord swate fah swin ofer helme / ecgum dyhtig andweard scireð (when the bound blade, forged by the hammer, the sword stained with blood and doughty in its edges shears through the boar image above the opposing helmet)'. But in *The Dream of the Rood* Swanton suggests that in line 13, 'Syllic wæs se sigebeam, ond ic synnum fah (Wondrous was that tree of victory, and I *fah* with sins)', the different meanings 'stained' and 'proscribed' are both relevant to the context. The physical brightness and the moral virtues of the Cross are both being contrasted, he argues, with the condition of the sinner-dreamer who is not only stained with the darkness of his sins but proscribed from salvation by them. This duality of meaning in *fah* thus combines the physical and abstract qualities which are highlighted antithetically in the poet's handling of the Cross throughout the poem. This is an attractive reading, and one which seems wholly justified as a legitimate expectation.

Among other illustrations of the same kind of physical-abstract duality in the poem, Swanton adduces *wealdes treow*, line 17b: 'gimmas hæfdon / biwrigene weorðlice wealdes treow (gems had worthily bedecked the tree of the forest)'. Although this is frequently emended for metrical reasons to *wealdendes treow* (thus *ASPR* II—cf. *hælendes treow*, l. 25), Swanton would keep the manuscript reading and allow the two meanings of *weald*, 'forest' and 'power', to operate: the Cross is a 'tree of the forest' in anticipation of its own story of being hewn 'holtes on ende' (from the edge of the forest)' (l. 29b) and later being *geweorðode . . . ofer holtwudu* (l. 91; MS. *holmwudu*, however), and it is a 'tree of power' in its salvational role 'honored above (all) trees of the forest'. There is also the possibility that *wealdendes* is implied by sound and context, so that the meaning 'tree of the Ruler', anticipating Christ's mounting of the Cross later in the poem, contributes further to the textural richness of the passage. All this seems reasonable in context, for, as Swanton remarks,[8]

> the paradoxical matter of the Cross is especially sensible to such linguistic obliquity and ambiguity is structural to the poet's conception. The symbol is defined first in that interlocking of physical and abstract aspects that illustrates its tropological role, and to this is added a third, chronological dimension referring either backwards or forwards in the length of the poem.

The critic must be careful, however, that he does not allow the profusion of senses to extend beyond the formal confines of syntax and immediate context (see Huntley's remarks, chapter 1). Empson himself is guilty of such indiscrimination when, for example he examines the word *stremes* in the following speech of Troilus:

> What that I mene, O swete herte dere?
> Quod Troilus. O goodly fresshe free,
> That with the stremes of your eyen clere
> You wolde frendly sometimes on me see . . .
>
> (Troilus and Criseyde, iii. 126–9)

Troilus is here responding to Criseyde's question, in their first love scene, as to the *fyn* of his intention. 'Stremes', says Empson, 'has the straightforward meaning of "beams of light" (*Compleynte unto Pite*, line 94)'. But, he continues,[9]

> The N.E.D. does not give this meaning, but shows *stremes* as already a hyperbolical commonplace use for blood and tears, or 'beams of sweet influence', like those of the Pleiades. Thus after *fresh* and *free*, there is some implication of a stream (Naiads) that he can drink of and wash in, cleansing and refreshing, so that one glance of her eyes recovers him as by crossing a stream you break the spells of black magic, or the scent by which the hounds of your enemies are tracking you down; and the ready tears of her sympathy are implied faintly, as in the background.

This streaming patter is nonsense, of course, for Empson has historically mis-taken the meanings of *fresshe* and *free* and consequently constructed an ambiguity that is irrelevant to the Troilus passage.

Several recent 'findings' of ambiguity in Old English poems seem similarly misdirected. Paul Taylor, for instance, commits this critical indiscretion when he says he is 'inclined to recognize purposeful ambiguity in the formula *ealdor-leasne* (l. 3003) to describe the Geats after Beowulf's death. Beowulf is now life-less (*ealdorleas*), his people are lordless (*ealdorleas*), and, being lordless, they are in threat of losing their own lives in the approaching hostilities.'[10] Now, it is true that the surface form *ealdorleas* had come to have a semantic range embracing both 'lordless' and 'lifeless', but to abstract the word from its sentence, as Taylor does, to find both meanings relevant in its single usage *within* the sentence, is to deny what the text says (or what the poet 'intended'). For verse 3003a occurs towards the end of the Messenger's speech, when he is predicting that the Swedes will soon attack the Geats 'syððan hie gefricgeað frean userne / ealdorleasne (after they learn our lord to be lifeless)'. The masculine singular accusative ending -*ne* and the syntax and context make abundantly clear the limitations placed upon the semantic possibilities in this passage; to see the meaning 'lordless' here in application to the Geats, uncritically opens the door to the semantic world of Humpty-Dumpty.

Another case of this kind is presented by Mrs Osborn when she argues that *earmlic* in *Beowulf*, l. 807a, means both 'wretched' and 'by means of an arm', since the homonyms *earm* 'miserable' and *earm* 'arm' exist in Old English.[11] The immediate context may seem favourable, from a modern perspective, to such an interpretation: the poet has just said that Beowulf's men cannot harm Grendel with their swords because 'he had put a charm on victory-weapons, on each of edges'. Then follows,

> Scolde his aldorgedal
> on ðæm dæge   þysses lifes
> *earmlic* wurðan,   ond se ellorgæst
> on feonda geweald   feor siðian.

(His separation from life was destined on that day of this life to be *earmlic*, and the alien spirit to travel far into the possession of devils.)

Though the abrupt juxtaposition of 'swords couldn't harm him' and 'his separation from life was to be *earmlic*' might tempt the modern exegete to supply such a meaning as 'arm-ly' along with the meaning 'wretched', there is no such word in Old English. Further, the semantic force of -*lic* was probably much stronger in Old English than its modern counterpart -*ly;* and even were it not, the tone of such a pun in context seems *infra dig*. We must, I think, reject such an interpretation, and all interpretations not consonant with historical or grammatical 'reality'.

Related to the phenomenon of ambiguity is a play of sound and sense which I have, in a recent article, dubbed *phonological ellipsis.* In this situation, a word by its sound evokes, through force of context, a similar-sounding but semantically unrelated word whose meaning is necessary, or adds depth to, a passage. In E. E. Cummings's poem 'A man who had fallen among thieves', for example, the solid and stolid townspeople who stare at the passed-out drunk are thus depicted:

> whereon a dozen staunch and leal
> citizens did graze at pause . . .

The metaphor is bovine, and we are not explicitly told that the citizens are looking at the drunk, but the word *graze* in this context suggests *gaze*—and the latter is necessary to fulfill the literal meaning of the lines ('whereon . . . did [gaze]').[12]

A page or two ago, in discussing ambiguity in *Dream of the Rood*, I mentioned that Swanton sees *weald* suggesting *wealdend* in the phrase *wealdes treow*. If this is acceptable, it might be considered an instance of such phonological ellipsis. More certain, though still doubtful, would be the reference to Grendel in the notorious phrase *healðegnes hete* of line 142a, where 'hall-thane' might suggest 'hell-thane' (*helðegn*), a likely meaning since the monster *has* been granted a lineage among the denizens of hell even as he roams at will in Hrothgar's hall. Mrs Osborn makes several attempts in this direction. She finds, for instance, that the *Beowulf* poet gives an ambiguous hint of the judgment of Heaven on his hero when, at his funeral pyre, '*Heofon rece swealg* (Heaven swallowed the smoke)'. She sees *rece* as evoking *rice* 'ruler' (i.e., Beowulf), implying the hero's Christian salvation: 'the word-play is made almost inescapable', she says, 'by the frequency in Christian contexts of the compound *heofon-rice* "the heavenly kingdom"'.[13] Well, no. Such an interpretation ignores the literal meaning of 'swallowed', draws a red herring across the path with *heofon-rice* (since it calls for *rice* to mean 'ruler' whereas in the compound it means 'kingdom'), and introduces a most un-Christian sign of grace in the image of the 'swallowing', literally or figuratively, of a man. Mrs Osborn's other suggestions along these lines are equally untenable, and I think we must be extremely careful in postulating this kind of sound-sense play in the poetry of a language whose nuances are so tentatively known to us as are those of Old English.

I should like, therefore, to consider a more rewarding kind of poetic play, one we may broadly label 'metaphoric'. Personification can be considered a marginal case of this kind, and Isaacs has well demonstrated the prevalence of such animation in *Beowulf*.[14] Of greater interest for our purposes here is the possibility of synesthesia, though as Robinson points out, lexicographical entries often obscure what may well have been the poets' 'intentions' to produce such concomitant sensation in their imagery. He observes, for example, that in *Beowulf*, ll. 1160b–2a, the sounds of revelry are described in these terms:

> Gamen eft astah,
> beorhtode bencsweg,   byrelas sealdon
> win of wunderfatum.

> (Mirth once again ascended, the bench-sound
> *beorhtode*, the cup-bearer poured wine from the
> wondrous vessels.)

He notes that though the dictionaries list many instances of *beorhtian* meaning 'brighten' in the visual sense, they shift to a meaning 'sound clearly' when recording this one instance. But, he continues, 'the force of this description ... lies in the synaesthetic representation of the convivial sounds "glittering" through the hall as the wine streams out of the bright chalices'.[15] His other illustration is the notorious crux *dennode* in *Brunanburh*, l. 12b: 'feld dennode / secga swate (the field *dennode* with the blood of warriors)'. There are many conjectures about this word and its etymology:[16]

> One of the least strained interpretations is the view that it represents the common verb *dynade* 'resounded', but this reading, of course, presupposes a remarkable synaesthetic image, 'the field resounded with the blood of men'. Before rejecting this interpretation as too bizarre, however, careful attention should be given to the battlescene described in ll. 28,357ff. of Layamon's *Brut*:

> > feldes beoueden eke;
> > gurren þa stanes   mid þan blod-streme,

> 'the fields also trembled; the stones resound with the streams of blood.' Our own sense of the limits of synaesthetic imagery may not have been that of the

earlier writers, and we should remember this when evaluating the dictionaries' numerous *ad hoc* entries which implicitly deny synaesthetic effects in OE poetry.

Although Robinson has not proved his point about the prevalence of synaesthesia in Old English poetry through these two cases, which are still arguable, he has been suggestive of a small area of interpretation which bears further investigation. Rather than explore this area here, however, I should like to examine a related kind of metaphorical word play which has also been lexicographically obscured. I wish to examine a passage in the Old English *Judith* in some detail, taking a close look at B. F. Huppé's recent analysis of it. The discussion will help clarify some further proscriptions, as well as prescriptions, I have been advocating in the interpretation of Old English poems.

Holofernes, 'the wicked one', having summoned his men to a feast, plies them with drink over the course of the whole day:

> Swa se inwidda   ofer ealne dæg
> dryhtguman sine   drencte mid wine,
> swiðmod sinces brytta,   oðþæt hie on swiman lagon,
> oferdrencte his duguðe ealle,   swylce hie wæron deaðe
>   geslegene,
> agotene goda gehwylces.   (ll. 28–32a)

Of this passage, Huppé comments that[17]

> the actions of Holofernes filling his men with wine [is] an action likened to his drowning of them. First, Holofernes, *se inwidda* (28) 'drenched (*drencte*) in wine/the lords of his retinue . . . until they lay in a stupor;/he drowned (*oferdrencte*) his attendants all, as if dropped in death they were/emptied of any lingering good' (29–32). The structure of repetition underscores the metaphoric likening of the stupor of drunkenness to death by drowning. In effect Holofernes' feast creates in his men the simulacrum of the death which they—and he—will undergo.

There is no question that Huppé is right in asserting that the stupor produced by the drinking creates an image of the Assyrians' approaching death: the poet himself makes this explicit in his simile 'as if they had been slain by death' (l. 31b).

But is Holofernes' vinous hospitality indeed 'likened to his drowning' of his men? And if it is, can we truly say that such a death is a 'simulacrum' of their deaths to come, which are rather by beheading in the case of the chieftain, and by battle in the case of his men? Where does Huppé find this concept of death by drowning, and his warrant for translating *oferdrencte* as 'drowned'?

His next paragraph, while purporting to go beyond the 'obvious metaphoric implications' of the key verbs, reveals the basis for his interpretation—and a certain circularity in his argument:[18]

Oferdrencan appears only in *Judith*, and the uncompounded form, *drencan*, appears only in *Judith* and the Psalms, 59.3, 68.21, 106.17. In the first two occurrences in the Psalms, the verb has the meaning 'drenched', 'made to drink', but in the last occurrence, by metaphoric extension, it means 'die', translating *et appropinquaverunt usque ad portas mortis*. The Old English translator's use of 'drencan' with referent 'to die' can be explained. Psalm 105 speaks of the Egyptian captivity and in verse 11 tells of God's drowning of the Egyptian host, and *heora feondas flod adrencte*; similarly in the Old English translation of Judith 5.31 [*sic*], [God] *adrencte hi ealle*, and in Ælfric's paraphrase, line 108, *Ac god hine adrencte*. It must clearly be such a referent that the Old English translator had in mind when in the next psalm, 106, he translated verse 17, *et appropinquaverunt usque ad portas mortis*, *þæt hy wið deaða drencyde wæron* [*sic*]. The possibility that the *Judith* poet had a similar metaphoric referent for the word *drencan* is suggested by the earlier reference to the drowning of the Egyptians in *Judith* [*sic*] and the cross reference in the Vulgate of Psalms 105 and 106 to Judith 13.21. Since Holofernes was indeed offering his men the drink of bitter death, *poculum mortis*, the analogue with the Pharoah [*sic*] would have been suggested. Holofernes, like the Pharoah [*sic*] leading his men into the Red Sea, drowned his men in their iniquities. Their stupefaction is the prelude to their death, literally and spiritually, for after their day (28) they will die emptied of all good (32), when their dark night comes (34).

I have presented Huppé's argument on this passage in full, for it is a curious one when examined closely, especially when its factual assertions are checked. It shows, I think, how reasonable expectations can be drowned in pumping external cultural knowledge into a text instead of allowing textual meaning to flow out. It shows how erroneous expectations established by such critical pump-priming can lead the analyst, consciously or unconsciously, to misreading of the text, falsification of facts and, thus, to misinterpretation. There is indeed metaphorical word play in the *Judith* passage, but, as I shall attempt to demonstrate, it is not that which Huppé claims to have discovered.

First of all, *oferdrencan* does not appear 'only in *Judith*', despite Huppé's bald statement: *BTD* cite some half-dozen examples of its occurrence, all of them meaning 'to inebriate' or, literally, 'over-drench'! Second, we may note that the cases Huppé cites of Old English translations of the drowning of the Egyptian host in the Red Sea crossing use *adrencan*, not *oferdrencan* or *drencan*; additionally we may observe that, *pace* Huppé, *drencan* occurs in several places other than *Judith* and the Psalms, in *Leechdoms* for one (see *BTS*). Third, there is the strange use of *drencyde* in the translation of Psalm cvi.17, which seems to be Huppé's chief piece of analogical evidence. Let us look at this evidence more closely.

The Vulgate reads

omnem escam abominata est anima eorum
et adpropinquaverunt usque ad portas mortis.

The *Paris Psalter* turns these verses into Old English as

Hi onhysctan æghwylcne mete,
mode mægen heora, oð unmihte
þæt hy wið deaða duru drencyde wæran.

(They shunned all food, bodily strength of their spirit,
until in weakness they were drawn towards death's door.)

Now, *BTD* give the meaning *submergere* for *drencyde* here, but this seems a little odd. Perhaps not so odd if one omits *duru* from the Old English translation (Lat. *portas*), as Huppé does when he says that verse 17 was translated '*þæt hy wið deaða drencyde wæron*'! Such a meaning does not make much sense in context,

98

however, and to say that 'it must clearly be such a referent' to the drowning of the Egyptian host 'that the Old English translator had in mind' in the translation of Psalm cvi is to assume a seer's clarity of vision. In more humble vein, I wonder whether it is not more likely that the Old English translator nodded and misread *adpropinquaverunt* as a form of *propinare* 'to give to drink'? Or possibly, with his need for an alliterative *d* word in his b-verse, the Old English poet decided to use the word more loosely with the general sense of 'drawn under', as I have translated it above, with the idea that 'death's door' is, after all, below. At any rate, whatever *drencyde* means in this passage, it cannot 'by metaphoric extension' mean 'to die'—it must be taken with its adverbial phrase 'towards death's door' and it is the whole phrase that approaches the concept of dying, not the verb *solus*.

Huppé's principal witness to his metaphorical interpretation, then, seems to be as 'drenched' and visually distorted as Holofernes' warriors. But the distortion does not end here. We must travel several steps further along this tortuous analytical path in this interpretive lesson. For when Huppé says that 'the possibility that the *Judith* poet had a similar metaphoric referent for the word *drencan* is suggested by the earlier reference to the drowning of the Egyptians in *Judith*', he is confusing different texts: there is no such reference in the Old English poem *Judith*, and if we look carefully above in his paragraph we see that he is actually referring to Ælfric's Old English paraphrase. (His reference to Judith 5.31 must be a printer's error for 5.13: *ita aquis coopertus est ut non remanent vel unus qui factum posteris nuntieret*, for there is no Judith 5.31. Moreover, I cannot discover what text he is referring to by 'the Old English translation of Judith' apart from Ælfric's and the poem.) Finally, we may note that it is *oferdrencte* which Huppé translates as 'drowned', not *drencte*: he has conflated all three verbs in his discussion, *drencan*, *adrencan* and *oferdrencan*. This is something like treating Modern English *muse*, *amuse* and *bemuse* as if they were one and the same word. I am afraid this will never do as a model for interpretative validity.

Not only does it go metaphorically astray in its determination to see Holofernes in the light of the Egyptian Pharaoh, but it fails to see what is actually at work metaphorically in the passage. It offers no comment at all on the verb *ageotan* (*agotene*), which *does* give us a clue, I think, as to what the poet was aesthetically intending. Huppé translates the adjectival past participle as 'emptied', but Timmer in his edition is more on the right track when he notes that there is 'a figurative use of *ageotan* "to pour out"'; but Timmer then throws away this observation by continuing 'so that the past participle, used with the gen., means "empty of"'.[19] Dobbie in his edition of *Beowulf and Judith* comes closer when he remarks that 'the verb regularly means "to pour out, to shed" usually with reference to blood, as in Genesis 984, Andreas 1449, Guthlac 522, etc.'; and, following Sweet and Cook, he concludes that 'it is likely that "to drain" is the meaning which was in the poet's mind . . .'.[20] Dobbie nevertheless does not indicate *why* this meaning might have been 'in the poet's mind', and still feels the exact significance here is uncertain. My understanding must surely be obvious by now: we have in this passage a neat antithetical play on words: Holofernes has 'overdrenched' or 'poured into' his men so much wine that they, in turn, are 'poured out' of any good or virtue. Further metaphoric overtones relate to the shedding of blood—theirs—before long, as in the other instances Dobbie cites. Thus their stupor indeed becomes a simulacrum of their imminent deaths.

I have laboured the above discussion because I think it affords us, as critics and students of Old English literature, both positive and negative example. We must work from the poem itself outwards and submit our cultural knowledge to the text's rein; we must treat individual word meanings with respect and not ignore affixes, for example, as if they had no semantic significance; we must not treat different texts cavalierly as if they were one and the same; and we must be more alert to the possibility of metaphoric word play among the implications to be found in Old English verse.

Still another kind of word play in Old English has recently been urged by Robinson in another essay: an onomastic one. He convincingly argues and illustrates the penchant for serious etymological word play on *names* in both the Latin material known to the Anglo-Saxon writers and in the writings of the Anglo-Saxons themselves. Not only does Robinson, on the basis of this assumption, provide credible solutions to several cruxes in different poems by resorting to the exegetical glosses on biblical names, but he shows the large impact that the play on names had on structure and theme in certain poems: how the Old

English name-meaning of *Guthlac* 'reward of battle', for example, shapes 'the very theme and conception of [*Guthlac A*] to a considerable degree'.[21] That is, an Anglo-Saxon poet, like his Latin predecessors and contemporaries, could not only use fictional names, but might 'be expected to construct a dramatic situation or shade a character sketch in such a way as to bring alive some poignant etymological meaning in a proper name received from tradition'.[22] In concluding his admirable treatise, Robinson highlights the differences between Anglo-Saxon onomastics and those of writers of our own time:[23]

> Their precedents . . . were the sacral etymologies of the Bible, the commentaries of the Fathers, the exuberant interpretations of Isidore and the Irish writings, all of which encouraged a learned searching out of etymological significance in names received from tradition. Our own precedents, by contrast, are the explicit, moralizing names of late medieval drama and the comic sobriquets of Congreve or Dickens. On the whole, their tradition was subtle, learned, and artful, while ours tends to be spontaneous and obvious.

Despite this difference in onomastic outlooks, the Old English poets could also employ fictitious names for their contextual purposes. Most critics agree that *Unferth* in *Beowulf* is one. The name and character of Hrothgar's *þyle* have, however, led to considerable controversy, and since the name occurs at one point in what seems to be a play of sound and sense, this seems a good place to re-evaluate our interpretations not only of the literal significance of his name, but of his role in the poem. For not only dictionary definitions benefit from re-examination, but also critical remarks and accepted 'facts' of scholarship that have come to be taken for granted. In the process of this re-evaluation, we shall see once again how our horizon of expectations can, for better or for worse, direct our critical perceptions.

We may look first at the etymology of the name *Unferth*. Though it appears in its four occurrences in *Beowulf* as *Hunferð*, editors and critics generally accept Rieger's suggestion that the *h* should be dropped for alliterative reasons: the scribe or 'one of his forebears simply did not understand the name and changed it to a more familiar form' since 'Hunfrid, and variants, was a fairly common Anglo-Saxon and Middle English name'.[24] Although this emendation seems to be a fairly safe one, we cannot entirely discount the possibility of vowel/*h* alliteration, and we must recognize that this is a first step onto speculative grounds. When it comes to analyzing the segments of the name, we become even more speculative, despite the general critical consensus. Two significant options are open for the prefix *un-*: it may be the negative particle, or it may be an intensive as in *unhar* 'very old', *Beowulf*, l. 357 (though this is often emended to *anhar*); and *Hun-* might offer still another option, as we shall see shortly. 'About the second theme, *-ferth*', writes Morton Bloomfield, 'there can be little room for disagreement. It is obviously a metathesized form of *frith* (peace) which occurs in many Germanic names both as a first and second element'.[25] We must, however, scrutinize more carefully this onomastic 'fact'. First, what about the orthography? True, *-frid* (*-fred*, *-ferd*) occurs commonly in Germanic names, but in *Old English* the word *friđ*, in its many occurrences singly and in compounds, including *unfriđ*, never appears metathesized (i.e., as *-ferđ*), so far as I can ascertain. Further, if it were metathesized in our unique case, should not its form be *-firđ* rather than *-ferđ*? Further yet, while the scribe of the Cotton Vitellius MS. might add an *h* to the *un-* as the more common form in names (though we actually find the name *Unferth* as a variant of *Hunferth* in MS. E of the *Old English Chronicle*, A.D. 744), if he were changing the name to a more familiar form, surely *Hunfriđ* would have been his choice? It seems to me more likely, or at least possible, that the scribe indeed had *Unferđ* or *Hunferđ* in his exemplar.

Shifting our ground now to the semantic side of the name, we may infer that one reason critics have been prone to accept *-ferđ* here as a metathesized *-friđ* is Klaeber's vigorous note to the name, 'Hardly *Unfer(h)đ*, "nonsense"'.[26] But would a negation of *fer(h)đ*, assuming for the moment that *un-* is correct and is, moreover, the negative particle, necessarily mean 'nonsense'? *Fer(h)đ* (and forms both with and without the medial *h* are well attested) means 'spirit, mind, soul, heart'. Is it not more likely that its contrary would mean 'absence of spirit or heart' even as *unfriđ* means 'absence of peace'? And suppose *un-* was, rather, the intensive particle, as Forssner categorically states it is relative to the Old Germanic names *Unfrid*, *Unfred*, and *Umfred*?[27] Then the name might well signify 'having great spirit or heart'. But, critics will exclaim, this is the very antithesis of the character of the *Beowulf*ian *þyle*: not only dare he not meet Grendel in this instance, but we are told he has played his brothers false in battle! We shall look at his character in a moment, for analysis of this sort must move back and forth between smaller and larger perspectives; but I should like to bring the apparent play on words involving his name into the picture first.

Mrs Osborn has recently suggested that the poet has played on the name in lines 1165b–7a:

> Swylce þær *Unferþ* þyle
> æt fotum sæt frean Scyldinga;   gehwylc hiora ferhþe
>   treowde,
> þæt he hæfde mod micel.

(Likewise there Unferth the thyle sat at the feet of the lord of the Scyldings; each of them [i.e., Hrothgar and Hrothulf] trusted in his spirit, that he had great courage.)

Here, says Mrs Osborn 'the poet himself . . . provides an etymological gloss which cannot be ignored'.[28] But several interpretations of the *Unferþ-ferhþe* sequence are possible. One could argue that there is no relationship between the name and the word, that the poet would have substituted something else for the latter if he had felt the former semantically related to it. Or the statement that Hrothgar and Hrothulf trusted in Unferth's *ferhþ*, which seems to be synonymous with *mod micel* (or almost synonymous), could be seen reflecting positively upon the meaning of the thyle's name. Or one could find irony in such a reflection, with *Unferth* meaning 'absence of great spirit'. On this last point, let us hold a decision on the meaning of the prefix *un-* in abeyance while we retrace our steps once more, this time to the contextual basis for the general acceptance of the name as signifying 'mar-peace'.

It would be possible to see the two references to Unferth's having killed his brothers, once in Beowulf's taunt and once by the poet, and his implied future treachery in Heorot,[29] as sufficient testimony to the suitability of the sobriquet 'mar-peace'. But one action is prior to, and the other subsequent to, Unferth's part as a character in the poem; and these are not, in actuality, the basis critics build upon for this interpretation. Rather, it is in his major role as challenger to Beowulf at the feast in Heorot that they see his disturbance of the peace. H. B. Woolf's comment is typical: Unferth's name, he says, 'is descriptive of its bearer, an aptronym, for it becomes apparent that Unferth is the very negation of peace once he commences to speak'.[30] Sisam's remark follows a similar line: 'His name *Un-friþ* means "strife" and at his first appearance, when he serves to introduce the adventure with Breca, he picks a quarrel with Beowulf'.[31] It is true that he 'picks a quarrel' with the hero, but is this the same as a 'negation of peace'? No one in the Danish court seems particularly disturbed—at least we are not told of any such reaction—and what follows Unferth's 'unbinding of a battle-rune' (l. 501a) is simply a taunting of Beowulf, to the effect that a boy should not undertake a man's job. Beowulf's rejoinder hits back in kind: first at the drunkenness of Unferth who, the poet had already said, spoke besottedly out of jealousy; then, after setting the record straight about the swimming match with Breca, at Unferth's lack of courage (ll. 590-4):

> Secge ic þe to soðe,   sunu Ecglafes,
> þæt næfre Gre[n]del swa fela   gryra gefremede,
> atol æglæca   ealdre þinum,
> hynðo on Heorote,   gif þin hige wære,
> sefa swa searogrim,   swa þu self talast.

(I tell you truly, son of Ecglaf, that never would Grendel, the terrible monster, have performed such terrible deeds against your lord, injuries in Heorot, if your spirit, your mind, were so formidable as you yourself consider [it to be].)

The nouns *hige* and *sefa* are synonyms of *fer(h)ð*. And Unferth's *fer(h)ð*, his having *mod micel* under all other circumstances, is requisite for his being a proper foil to Beowulf.

There have been several critical efforts recently to reduce the *þyle*, via glossarial equivalents, from 'spokesman, orator' to '*scurra*' or 'court jester', and to deny that place at the king's feet indicates an honourable position.[32] Though ingeniously argued, these critiques, it seems to me, fail to satisfy narrative expectations. What fame or honour would accrue to the hero by his besting the court fool? Or why would such a man be concerned that another be thought braver than he? Or why would such a man have a very famous sword? The poet himself indicates the *þyle*'s prowess when he lends his sword Hrunting to Beowulf:

> Huru ne gemunde   mago Ecglafes
> eafoþes cræftig,   þæt he ær gespræc
> wine druncen,   þa he þæs wæpnes onlah
> selran sweordfrecan;   selfa ne dorste
> under yða gewin   aldre geneþan,
> drihtscype dreogan;   þær he dome forleas,
> ellenmærðum.   (ll. 1465–71a)

(Indeed the son of Ecglaf, powerful of strength, did not remember what he had previously said when drunk with wine, when he lent the weapon to the better sword-fighter; he dared not himself risk his life beneath the turmoil of waves, put his valour to the test; he lost glory thereby, fame for courage.)

Unferth is 'powerful in strength'; his lending of his sword to a 'better sword-fighter' implies that he is no slouch himself; and he could not 'lose' his 'glory, fame for courage' if he did not possess some of it. (On this last point, we might compare lines 2860-1, where Wiglaf gives answer to the men who had fled to the woods when the dragon snorted out of his barrow—men, it will be remembered, who had been the pick of Beowulf's army, chosen for this last venture: 'Þa wæs æt ðam geong*an* grim andswaru/ eðbegete þam ðe ær his elne *forleas* (Then was a grim answer easily forthcoming from the young man to him who earlier had lost his courage)'.) Surely Sisam is right in this matter when, despite his belief that the name *Unferth* equals *Un-frith*, he says,[33]

> the part he plays must be eminent: he is Hrothgar's
> *þyle* 'spokesman', with a place of honour at the king's feet
> (cf. 500). Beowulf calls him 'far-famed' (*widcuð* 1489).
> He owns the sword Hrunting that has never failed in
> battle, and so provides the incident of its generous loan and
> return. . . . He must be an active champion, not an old man
> like Hrothgar or Æschere: otherwise Beowulf's taunt that
> he had not stopped Grendel's raids would be ineffective.

It is as a man of courage, though lesser than the hero's, that Unferth fulfills his part in the poem, not as a breaker of the peace, especially since there is no such breach, really, even at the feast in Heorot.

All these circumstances incline me to favour a root *-fer(h)ð*,— to accept a play of sound and sense in the *Unferð-ferhþe* sequence of lines 1165–6—rather than *-frið* as the etymological basis of Unferth's name and character. Even if Unferth was an historical figure and not a fictitious character created specifically for this poetic role, this would hold good—compare Robinson's remarks on *Guthlac A*, above. There is, however, one piece of evidence against this theory that *-ferð* = *-fer(h)ð*, which brings in still a further factor which must be considered in the interpretation of Old English poems. Though the alternation of spelling with or without an *h* is common in Old English generally, the only examples in *Beowulf* of *ferhð* spelled without the medial *h* appear in lines 2785a and 2863a: *collenferð* and *sarigferð*. Both of these, it happens, are in the second scribe's portion of the manuscript (which begins at line 1939b), and the former of these two words appears in the first scribe's portion, line 1806a, *with* an *h*. *Ferhð* and its several compounds, moreover, occur in twelve other places in the first scribe's part, always with an *h*. Unferth's name appears on all its four occasions in that part. Clearly the matter of scribal practice must be weighed in the balance of expectations in the interpretation of poems. But the fact that *Unferð* is a proper name might account for this divergence of practice, since as a name it would lack the *h*. This possibility, plus the other evidence I have adduced, seems to me to weight the scale in favour of the explanation I have been proposing. If, then, Unferth's name does not represent a variant of *-frið* and is to be most significant in context, the *un-* prefix might better be taken as the intensive particle rather than the negative (or we may even retain the manuscript *Hun-* = 'giant')[34], and whatever irony inheres lies in the *þyle*'s failure to live fully up to his name in the crucial conflicts with the Grendel clan. The reading of *un-* as a negative, however, in no way would affect my central thesis.

I have tried, in the above analysis, to bring as many sets of expectations to bear upon the name and function of Unferth as I feel reasonably relevant to the purpose. At the least they should indicate that larger interpretations of Unferth's role based upon his being Mr Mar-peace have a precarious foundation. Perhaps the best and most widely accepted of these is Morton Bloomfield's attempt[35] to see a Prudentian kind of Christian allegory as the poet's 'intention' in introducing the figure into *Beowulf*:

> If he conceived of Beowulf as the *rex justus* or ideal king, the defeat of discord in the person of Unferth is demanded. If the ethic of the poem is based on *ordinata concordia*, *discordia* must be overthrown. Prudentius tells the story of how Discord wounds Concord and is killed by Faith. Beowulf, however, defeats his antagonist, not by force, but by example, and Unferth hands over his sword, the symbol of his might. Without trying to reduce the relation of Beowulf to Unferth to the purely allegorical level of Faith or Concord versus Discord, I do urge that such concepts were in the poet's mind as he dealt with what was perhaps a well-known story and that by giving the enemy the name of Unferth he wished to suggest this overhanging meaning (not necessarily as in Prudentius) to his readers. The story was colored by the allegorical pattern.

Bloomfield himself is prudentially aware of the large discrepancies between his allegorical model and his heroic analogue, and his paragraph is a model of cautious critical persuasion. Nevertheless, it is ultimately unconvincing: for one thing, Unferth is not properly Beowulf's antagonist, in the sense that Discord is Faith's; for another, his 'handing over his sword' is a *lending*, on a different occasion from that in which he is bested in the verbal exchange with the hero, the occasion of Beowulf's dive into the mere to fight Grendel's mother. I suspect that if Bloomfield had not been so convinced to begin with that *Unferð* meant 'mar-peace', he would not have allowed himself to be led down the primrose path of this interpretive garden.[36]

With this somewhat lengthly disquisition on the name and character of Unferth, we may pass on to different considerations, to another set of expectations in Old English poetry. I think it is clear, however, that the play of sound and sense *did* exist in that poetry. Moreover, it could fulfill a serious intellectual and aesthetic role in individual poems, as we have seen in *The Seafarer* and *The Dream of the Rood*. Its possibilities, of which I have treated but a few, should therefore be considered more actively in our interpretations. Yet, as I think the course of this chapter shows, it is difficult to deal with certainty in such matters, and we should be humble in our linguistic naïveté. In particular we should not allow the associations of our modern perspectivism to lead us astray, beyond the confines of the formal relationships of the text or the historical facts of grammar and semantics. If we do so, we run the risk of moving away from, rather than towards, interpretational validity.

5

Verse Form, Syntax and Meaning

A relatively new approach to the critical exegesis of literary texts, as we saw in the first chapter, derives from modern linguistic analysis. Linguists interested in such texts have generally been concerned with establishing models of description, with seeing the grammar of a literary work as part of the grammar of the whole language. When a particular text has been their target, they have usually sought to describe as fully as possible its syntactic, phonemic or morphological structures without recourse to semantics; and their concern has been to show how such structures, especially the grammatical, differ from those in normal usage. Until recently it has been the rare linguist who has tried to correlate, or who has succeeded in correlating, his grammatical description with fruitful literary analysis.[1] There is an inherent difficulty in making such a correlation, since the formal features of grammar would seem to have no semantic values—they do, of course, show possession, or linking, or substantivity, or number, etc.—but serve chiefly to direct the listener's or reader's attention toward including or excluding certain semantic possibilities inherent in the words and images embedded in and embodying forth that form. (The surface structure of grammatical elements, i.e., word order and surface grammaticality, may suggest different emphases, and thus meaning differences, by producing different intonation patterns: cf. 'John didn't argue with Bill about money' with 'John didn't argue about money with Bill', where not-*money* and not-*Bill* are the respective semantic focal points.)[2] The formal features of verse structure likewise would seem to have no semantic values: recurrent sound patterns like rhyme and alliteration serve chiefly harmonic, perhaps emphatic ends; and stress patterns give prominence, for semantic consideration, to certain words, much as word order may provide different semantic foci.

Nevertheless, syntax and verse form can contribute more than superficial direction to a text's meaning. They can, for one thing, provide a kind of 'formal meaning' that may be helpful, even necessary, for interpretation. It is essential, as we have seen, to understand *variation* in Old English poetic practice, and to be able to distinguish instances of it from enumerations and progressions. In another area, M. B. Emeneau makes the interesting observation[3] that in interpreting the oral poems of the Todas it is necessary to recognize verse-pairing as *de rigueur*, whether or not one member of the pair is relevant to the particular context:

> Frequently . . . only one of the paired related entries is in point. The technique, however, requires that both members of the pair be sung. The meaning of the irrelevant member . . . is then not informational, nor even comment on the situation. At times it may be thought metaphorical, but there are many instances where this is impossible. Then it must be said that there is esthetic value (or meaning) merely in the paired, formulaic occurrence of the song-unit, whether relevant or irrelevant.

One might question such an equation of 'esthetic value' with 'meaning'; but the case is even clearer when, for example, J. B. Bessinger comments that in *The Battle of Maldon* we cannot assume an historical reason, and hence a literal referential meaning, in the poetic account of the Vikings crossing the river.

> Wodon þa wælwulfas, for wætere ne murnon,
> wicinga werod; west ofer Pantan
> ofer scir wæter scyldas wegon,
> lidmen to lande linde bæron. (ll. 96–9)

> (Then the slaughterous wolves, the band of Vikings, gave no heed to the water; westwards over the Pante over the shining water they bore their shields; the seamen carried their shields onto the land.)

The Vikings, says Bessinger,[4]

> do not advance north or east or south over the stream (although along the winding approaches of the river close to

its estuary there must have been places at which they actually could have found a crossing in one or more of these directions); they advance westward because the poet is causing them to advance in formulas and sets of formulas tuned, as we might say, to the key of *w-*; or to put the matter less fancifully, because he was reluctant or unable to interrupt, for a line or two more, his aurally intoxicating development of an alliterative pattern based upon that bilabial semivowel.

Further, even though there are no necessary correspondences between form and meaning, formal features of both verse and syntax can reinforce the semantic level or generate implications of meaning in ways similar to those discussed in previous chapters. Beyond this, the pleasurable effects of verse and syntactic features cannot be ignored if we are to perceive the full complement of meaning in a poem. For, as Winifred Nowottny has commented about syntax,[5]

> however little it is noted by the reader, [it] is the ground-work of the poet's art. Often it supports a poetic edifice elaborated by many other poetic means and the reader is content to believe that these other means are the cause of his pleasure, but when a passage relies chiefly on its especially compelling and artful syntax to make its effect, the reader and the critics, who never expect syntax to be more than 'a harmless, necessary drudge' holding open the door while the pageantry of words sweeps through, will be at a loss to understand why the passage affects them as it does and at a loss to do critical justice to its art.

Though alliteration and other metrical features by their very nature attract greater attention to themselves, somewhat the same may be said about our recognition or lack of recognition of their exact role in poetic meaning. It will be my purpose in this chapter to explore some particular examples of the relationship between syntax, metre and meaning in the interpretation of Old English poems, as well as to discuss further matters of expecta-tion and implication with respect to these formal features.

First, however, we must consider the general problem of expectations and the concept of *normal usage*. Halliday, it will be recalled (chapter 1), believes that any study of the language of a poem cannot properly be undertaken except against the backdrop of our knowledge of the language as a whole; and this idea, *mutatis mutandis*, emerges in Old English studies in reference to our inescapable lack of *Sprachgefühl* for the nuances of Old English meaning, especially poetic meaning. Of course there is an element of truth in all this, but the implication that if only we knew all about the normal operations of syntax or the normal semantic range and collocability of individual words we would be able to solve the interpretational problems posed by individual words and phrases and poems, will not bear scrutiny: Keats's 'Beauty is truth, truth beauty' will continue to disturb critical repose no matter how much more we discover about normal Romantic use of language, or about Keats's own tastes in the matter. Coupled with the concept of normality is that of *deviation* in poetry, and several modes of syntactic analysis have tried to explain syntactic deviation in the poems of people like John Donne, Dylan Thomas, and E. E. Cummings, for example, by establishing 'grammars' that relate the deviations to the norms through one 'rule' or another.[6]

Old English poetry was much more conventionalized, and thus presumably more predictable, in the expectations of meaning harnessed by its formal features; and we have used this predictability on several occasions in this book to help with interpretational problems. Deviation also plays a role in this poetry, however. The normal syntactic placing of particles, especially of possessive pronouns and articles, and the normal stress and alliterative patterns of Old English verse have, for example, recently been used by Lydia Fakundiny to show how deviation from the norm not only emphasizes the words in question but generates implications of meaning. She shows that prose 'overwhelmingly' uses these words proclitically, that is, before the substantives they modify, so that such usage may be considered the standard or norm by which their various poetic displacements in syntax and metre may be judged. She further observes that a standard feature of Old English verse form is that substantives take precedence in stress over particles.[7] Now, when the first norm is kept and the second violated, we have such instances as *Beowulf*, ll. 557b–8b: 'heaþoræs fornam / mihtig meredeor þurh *mine* hand (the rush of battle destroyed the mighty sea-beast through *my* hand)', and *Exodus*, ll. 261b–3a, where Moses tells his people how 'mihtig drihten þurh *mine* hand' encompassed the destruction of Pharaoh's army. On these Miss Fakundiny comments that though frequently when a possessive pronoun leads its noun in alliteration the reason may be convenience or formulaic tradition, in these instances 'the alliterative pairing of "mihtig" and "mine" strengthens the possessive pronoun', so that the particle becomes metrically dominant in a rhetorically significant context.[8] When the second rule is observed (about substantives taking precedence in stress over particles) and the first is violated (about the proclitic use of particles), we have such a passage as *Beowulf*, ll. 1703b–7a:

> Blæd is aræred
> geond widwegas,   wine min Beowulf,
> ðin ofer þeoda gehwylce.   Eal þu hit geþyldum healdest,
> mægen mid modes snyttrum.   Ic þe sceal *mine* gelæstan
> freode, swa wit furðum spræcon.

(Thy glory is raised up throughout the wide ways, my friend Beowulf, over all nations. You will contain it all steadily, strength with wisdom of mind. I shall fulfill our friendship, as we spoke further.)

Miss Fakundiny remarks:[9]

Beowulf's far-reaching fame is powerfully asserted here through the widely separated phrase 'blæd . . ./ /. . . / . . ./ /ðin' which seems almost to distend itself in order to encompass its meaning. The metrical stress on *ðin* underlines its importance and effects the transition from the normal two-beat verse to the hypermetric series in such a way that sense and rhythm are perfectly co-ordinated. The other displaced pronoun *mine* draws attention to itself in the alliterative scheme, so that reciprocation is established between Beowulf's fame, 'blæd . . . ðin', (resulting from his brave services to Hrothgar) and the king's friendship, 'mine . . . freode'.

This strikes me as all well and good, but that identification of the norm and its violation in formal features does not necessarily lead to acceptable or valid interpretation of meaning may be seen in still another example Miss Fakundiny offers, this time of a stressed demonstrative. After his killing of Grendel's mother, Beowulf promises Hrothgar that he and his troop of men may sleep henceforth without sorrow in Heorot,

> þæt þu him ondrædan ne þearft,
> þeoden Scyldinga,   on þa healfe,
> aldorbealu eorlum,   swa þu ær dydest.   (ll. 1674b–6)

(that you need not fear for them, prince of the Scyldings, from *that* quarter, death to your warriors as you formerly did.)

'The terrifying monsters are now beyond the power of frightening anyone; they can now be designated almost contemptuously as "*that* quarter", a horror that is nameless not because it is unspeakably great but because it is nearly forgotten.'[10] So Miss Fakundiny. But it seems to me, with the great hilt-passing scene about to appear, that this is not right. Certainly the *þa* is emphasized metrically and rhetorically, but it suggests, rather, that Beowulf is saying to Hrothgar that he need not fear hostility from *that* quarter, i.e., the monsters, and implying that there is still the possibility of internal hostility, or the conflict of men against men, as his report to Hygelac, foreseeing the Ingeld business, would indicate. Thus once again I would contend that context, which by now may be defined as the nucleus of expectations other than those of the feature being interpreted, is significant in ascertaining valid meaning.

It is not only the concept of normal usage and deviation from it which must be considered when assessing the interpretive role of verse form and syntax in a poem: there is also the play of patterns against each other *within* the poem, in a sense the establishment of norm and deviation of the poem, or of a segment of the poem, itself.[11] Browning's 'My Last Duchess', for example, though using rhymed couplets, makes its norm, through careful placing of the caesura and the use of enjambment, the de-emphasis of both rhyme and couplet, as in its opening lines:

> That's my last Duchess painted on the wall,
> Looking as if she were alive. I call
> That piece a wonder, now: Frà Pandolf's hands
> Worked busily a day, and there she stands.

This de-emphasis of the expectation of the verse form produces a conversational tone, implying the speaker's tight control over his emotions and over the situation. But when the speaker arrives at that part of his narrative where his indignation is aroused by his re-telling of his wife's 'democratic' favours, the normal pattern of the rhymed couplet asserts itself, the rhymes become prominent despite caesura and enjambment, suggesting the emotional pitch to which his thoughts drive him:

> Sir, 'twas all one! My favour at her breast,
> The dropping of the daylight in the West,
> The bough of cherries some officious fool
> Broke in the orchard for her, the white mule
> She rode with round the terrace—all and each
> Would draw from her alike the approving speech,
> Or blush, at least.

This concept of the poem as providing its own 'grammar', so to speak, of self-supplied norm and deviation, is used to advantage by Randolph Quirk when he turns his attention to the dragon's hoard in *Beowulf* in his interesting essay on the range of meanings generated by the lexical-grammatical-alliterative collocations in Old English verse.[12] Quirk suggests that in the second part of *Beowulf*, words for 'treasure' are given connotations in context by their being collocated with 'unfavourable' words in the verse line. He cites, for example, the linking of *deoremaðmas* 'precious treasure' with *deað* 'death' in line 2236, of *lytel fæc* 'short time' with *longgestreona* 'ancient treasure' in line 2240; and the syntactical linking of *hæpen* 'heathen' with *gold*. In lines 2414 and 2536, *gold* goes with *guð* 'battle', in lines 2419 and 3018 with *geomor* 'sad', in 3012 with *grim*. *Feoh* 'fee' collocates with *fyren* 'crime' in line 2441, and *beahhord* 'ringhoard' with *bealu* 'destruction' in line 2826. And *Hord* alliterates with *hatode* 'hated' in line 2319. These alliterative and syntactic collocations, Quirk feels, undermine the heroic values of gold that had been the established norm in the first part of the poem, established by collocation as well as by societal values, implying its ultimate comparative worthlessness, a worthlessness made explicit in ll. 3011b–21a:

> ac þær is maðma hord,
> gold unrime   grimme gecea(po)d,

ond nu æt siðestan   sylfes feore
beagas (geboh) te;   þa sceall brond fretan,
æled þeccean,—   nalles eorl wegan
maððum to gemyndum,   ne mægð scyne
habban on healse   hringweorðunge,
ac sceal geomormod,   golde bereafod
oft nalles æne   elland tredan,
nu se herewisa   hleahtor alegde,
gamen ond gleodream.

(but there is a treasure hoard, countless gold grimly purchased, and rings bought finally with his own life; these shall the fire devour, the flame consume,—not at all shall a warrior bear treasure as a memento, nor the beautiful maiden have on her neck a ring ornament, but she shall, sad-minded, bereft of gold, many a time tread a foreign land now that the battle-leader has laid aside laughter, sport and mirth.)

Quirk's analysis through metre and syntax would thus seem to furnish us with another set of expectations to weigh in the balance in the interpretational differences between Mrs Goldsmith and Michael Cherniss (chapter 1): the former, it will be remembered, sees gold as a symbol of transience and also of cupidity; the latter as a symbol of men's intrinsic worth. But Quirk's evidence, like Miss Fakundiny's on *þa*, can bear a somewhat different interpretation if taken in full context. For the gold that Quirk is referring to in the latter half of the poem is the treasure *hoard*, and this is not the same as gold *per se*. I think his evidence can be read to see the poet not condemning all gold ultimately, but only hoarded gold or treasure. And this has been the poet's sense of values throughout! One of the earliest scenes in the poem suggests the power for good, in the heroic ethos, of giving, when Beowulf I, the son of Scyld, is praised for distributing treasure while still young. And this ideal of generosity is upheld on other occasions. Condemned throughout is niggardliness, a condemnation reaching its Christian climax in Hrothgar's homily; but Hrothgar himself gives lavishly of treasure and talks about giving more to Beowulf in his very last speech to the hero. Thus, I think, the hoard should not be equated with earthly treasures vs. heavenly—when it is reburied, the poet comments on the *hoard* being useless to men as ever it had been (l. 3168). Surely he had the opportunity here to make perfectly clear his 'intention' of total condemnation of all gold, had he so desired.

With such a preliminary consideration of norms and deviations, we may now examine at greater length a famous poetic passage for the light syntax and other formal features throw, *in context*, upon meaning. The passage is a long sentence in *The Wanderer*, which begins at line 19:

Swa ic modsefan	minne sceolde,	
oft earmcearig,	eðle bidæled,	20
freomægum feor	feterum sælan,	
siþþan geara iu	goldwine minne	
hrusan heolster biwrah,	ond ic hean þonan	
wod wintercearig	ofer waþema gebind,	
sohte sele dreorig	sinces bryttan,	25
hwær ic feor oþþe neah	findan meahte	
þone þe in meoduhealle	minne myne wisse,	
oþþe mec freondleasne	frefran wolde,	
wenian mid wynnum.		

(So I, often full of sorrows, separated from my native land, far from friendly kinsmen, had to shut my mind in fetters, since many years ago the darkness of earth covered my gold-friend, and I wretched thence travelled full of the cares of winter over the frozen waves, sought drearily the hall of a giver of treasure, where I far or near might find one who in the meadhall might know my thought, or would comfort me friendless, entertain me with joys.)

Even before we can proceed with this sentence, however, we should make note of certain textual problems, problems not atypical in the study of Old English poems. In line 22, for example, I read with Krapp–Dobbie (*ASPR* III), *goldwine minne* where the MS. has *mine*; but though they retain MS. *heolstre* in line 23, I emend to *heolster*. I follow Bliss–Dunning[13] in emending MS. *mine wisse*, line 27, to *minne myne wisse*; and I adopt the universally accepted editorial emendation of MS. *freondlease* to *freondleasne* in line 28. Finally, I follow Leslie[14] and Bliss–Dunning in emending MS. *weman* to *wenian* in line 29. We have not previously dealt with textual emendation and its relation to criticism, but as questions of syntax or metre are involved in four of the five instances, this seems an appropriate place to raise, at least briefly, matters so basic to the interpretation of Old English poems.

The change of *weman* to *wenian* is a concession to semantics: 'allure me with delights' simply seems a bit far-fetched in context. Since the Exeter Book scribe did make other *m* for *ni* copying mistakes, since the phrase *wenede to wiste* appears in line 36 where the speaker remembers 'how his gold-friend entertained him at feasting in his youth' and since *The Wanderer* is full of verbal repetition (a 'norm' for this poem?), the weight of expectations seems in favour of this emendation.[15] The emendation *freondleasne* is demanded by syntax, since the word can only, in context, modify *mec*, and therefore ought to be masculine singular accusative in form. MS. *mine wisse*, on the other hand, poses serious metrical as well as syntactic and semantic problems, which Bliss–Dunning's emendation, argued fully in their introduction (pp. 61–5), tries to take into account. Their arguments utilize both the concepts of normality—or at least of other Old English poetic usage—and of a semantic pattern they see *in the poem*.

It might be well to emphasize here that, the corpus of the poetry and prose being relatively small in size, textual and analytical critics are often glad to find even *one* parallel syntactic or semantic instance to support their interpretation, let alone a 'norm'! Going further, we may note that statistically there is very little difference between one example and none. Thus Bliss–Dunning, after presenting and rejecting the various extant meanings Bruce Mitchell has ferreted out for the conjunction *swa*[16] in connection with lines 41ff.:

> þinceð him on mode   þæt he his mondryhten
> clyppe and cysse   and on cneo lecge
> honda and heafod   *swa* he hwilum ær
> in geardagum   giefstolas breac

(it appears to his mind that he embraces and kisses his liege-lord, and lays hands and head on his knee *swa* he enjoyed favours from the throne formerly in bygone days)—

can properly say that though usage of *swa* meaning 'as when' here 'would be unique', but 'literary considerations must outweigh linguistic arguments' (pp. 112–13). In advancing this proposition, Bliss–Dunning are making an important point about the relation between textual, syntactic and literary concerns which bring us, in a way, back to the historical versus present meaning considerations raised in the first chapter. This is a point they make on several occasions, including the emendation to the singular *goldwine minne* in line 22, rather than accepting the syntactically possible MS. plural:

> a decision must be made on literary rather than linguistic grounds. In line 22 the emendation to *minne* (a plausible emendation, since the scribe has made mistakes involving *n* in lines 14, 59, 89, and 102) seems desirable in the light of the meaning of the following line; though the wanderer may have lost more than one lord, he is not likely to have buried more than one (p. 108).

I think this 'literary' argument correlates with the larger context rather than with just the next line, however, since I would emend, as I have indicated above, *heolstre* to *heolster*, so that it is the darkness of earth that covered his lord; and even Bliss–Dunning consider as a possible translation *without* emendation, assuming *hrusan* to be a late form for *hruse* (by levelling of endings), 'since long ago earth covered my lord in darkness' (p. 108).

Bliss–Dunning's 'literary considerations' are obviously predicated upon their own inescapable present aesthetic perspective; there is also some circularity in their linguistic-literary choice relationship. But significantly, they have laid out the historical choices: they are aware of, and let their readers know, what the score is in their weighing and weighting of expectations.

I have been dealing with some basic principles of textual and analytical criticism in the last few paragraphs, principles that must be taken into account before, or at least simultaneously with, the 'higher criticism' of a poem. I should like now to return to the interpretation of the *Wanderer* sentence, emphasizing the contribution that syntax makes to its meaning. That sentence is one of the more complex in Old English poetry, possessing an undeniable majesty and sweep which bears the listener or reader with the speaker from an earlier action in the past to a later action in the past, from a mood of despair to one of some hope, however frustrated that hope may have been. What are the specific syntactic features that carry its narrative and emotive burden?

The sentence consists of a main clause (ll. 19–21) and a subordinate clause beginning *siþþan geara iu.* . . . . The subordinate clause contains within it coordination, *ond ic hean þonan* . . .; and within that coordinating element there is further subordination with *hwær ic feor oþþe neah* . . ., relative subordination within that adverbial clause in *þone þe in meoduhealle* . . ., and finally coordination within that relative subordination in *oþþe mec freondleasne.* . . . This complex of clauses, like a set of Chinese boxes nesting one inside the other, is in itself, apart from emotive words, a vital element in conveying the sense of movement and frustration felt by the speaker. We may notice how the subject of the main clause is *ic,* and that the speaker continues to speak of himself as the subject of the action in the *ond ic hean* and the *hwær ic feor* clauses; but that in the last two clauses the speaker becomes the object of the action, in *minne myne wisse* and *mec freondleasne frefran wolde.* This syntactic inversion seems to mirror the change in the speaker's outlook on his actions: from his past dependence on his own behaviour, his relying on himself alone for his existence in his exiled state, to that devoutly-to-be-wished-for state wherein he can depend upon another, have a lord to care for him. In a very real sense, this formal, syntactic arrangement here anticipates the later happy dream of submissive dependence upon his former lord, and the rude awakening to the reality of independent insecurity that will ultimately lead to the statement at the end of the poem about the only real security lying in God.

As I interpret the sentence, there is only one clause where the speaker is not subject or object of the action; this occurs, fittingly, at the pivotal point in the action, the break between the former life of joy within the comitatus and the beginning of the frustrated searching for the establishment of a new lord-thane relationship: *siþþan geara iu goldwine minne | hrusan heolster biwrah* (see above on the emendation to *heolster*). That is, the death of the speaker's lord is presented objectively as 'the darkness of earth covered my gold-friend'. This 'darkness' as subject of the action, hiding the twin prized values of gold and friendship, in its way foreshadows the central theme of the poem, the transience of all earthly values. We may note that this pivotal accident of nature or war, the death of the speaker's lord, is emphasized further syntactically by the placing of the verb *biwrah* at the end of the a-verse. Although such final position was normal for the verb in a subordinate clause, this word order was not mandatory in Old English syntax; the *Wanderer* poet himself uses subject-verb-object order in the *þeah þe* clause in lines 2b–5a.[17] This placement of *biwrah* is the first of nine such in the poem, only four of the nine not being auxiliaries. Contrast this rarity of end-placed verbs in the a-verse of *The Wanderer* with the frequency of such placement in *The Seafarer*, where there are twenty-two occurrences, only one of which may even be considered to be an auxiliary. Here is a good example of the poem setting up its own norm, its own 'grammar' as it were, and using deviation therefrom for meaningful emphasis.

Clustered with the verb *biwrah* at the centre of the sentence's action are two other finite verb forms, *wod* and *sohte*, both appearing as the first word and the first stress in the succeeding a-verses (again such word order is rare in *The Wanderer*). This verbal emphasis, by finite form and position as well as by stress and alliteration, contributes to the sense of motion, to what I have called the sweep of the sentence. As something of a contrast to this 'actional' mode, the verb in the main clause consists of an auxiliary and an infinitive; in addition, two whole lines separate *sceolde* from *sælan*, and while separations of this kind are common in Old English poetry, lengthy ones like this are not. The ideational referent here is a mental or spiritual one, and the difficulty of keeping to the heroic code which demands one keep one's mouth shut in such circumstances is, I think, suggested by this deviational suspended verbal phrase. Finally, in connection with the verbs, we may remark that the only variation in the sentence which is dependent upon a prior word is the infinitive *wenian* in the last clause, varying *frefran* and dependent on *wolde*—a variational lingering that seems highly appropriate to the thoughts of consolation it calls up in the mind of the speaker.

If the sentence's sweep is partially conveyed by the finite verb forms, it is also suggested by the very succession of clauses that contribute to its linguistic complexity. What about the sentence's majesty? Old English poetry, with its repetitions, its variations, its envelope patterns, is notoriously balanced and stately; but the sentence under consideration goes further in this direction than most. Consider, for example, its adjectives and adjective phrases. First, there is the triple modification of the subject *ic* in lines 20–1a: *oft earmcearig, eðle bidæled, | freomægum feor*. The wretched state of mind (adjective) is ideationally the *effect* of the deprivation of native land (participle with dative complement) and of kinsmen (adjective with dative complement), though positionally it is parallel to them. This triple modification is reinforced in the subordinate clause's second co-ordinating element, describing the speaker's actions to find a new lord; but this time there are three adjectives: *hean, wintercearig* and *dreorig* (all referring to the state of mind), and they occupy only parts of half-lines. In the last clause of the sentence there is but one modifying adjective: *freondleasne* (referring to the deprivation of companions), a modification that reinforces the threefold repetitions of the earlier segments of the sentence, but which by its very singularity allows the hope that the last clause implies to filter through. The threefold modification of *earmcearig, eðle bidæled, | freomægum feor*, representing the state of mind, the deprivation of land, and the alienation from kinsmen, is also reflected in the larger structure of the sentence: lines 19–21 emphasize state of mind, lines 23b–5 stress movement into a new land, and lines 26ff. reinforce the idea of absence from kinsmen in their concentrating on the search for comfort in the understanding and benevolence of a hypothetical new liege-lord.

This analysis of the *Wanderer* sentence suggests how a kind of formal meaning may operate in a poem. For a further exploration of the expectations of formal meaning, I should now like to turn to a longer passage, a passage which shows even more clearly how a poem sets up its own norms and counterpoints formal pattern with formal pattern to generate implications of meaning. The passage is the famous one of Grendel's approach to and entrance into Heorot in *Beowulf*, ll. 702b–36a, which has been described as a 'hair-raising depiction of death on the march'.[18] Renoir has applied the term 'cinematographic' to its brilliant use of visual details and alternation of point of view between the exterior and the interior of the hall.[19] But the lines themselves had best be placed before us:

> Com on wanre niht
> scriðan sceadugenga.   Sceotend swæfon,

þa þæt hornreced   healdan scoldon,
ealle buton anum.   Þæt wæs yldum cuþ,   705
þæt hie ne moste,   þa Metod nolde,
se s[c]ynscaþa   under sceadu bregdan;—
ac he wæccende   wraþum on andan
bad bolgenmod   beadwa geþinges.
   Ða com of more   under misthleoþum   710
Grendel gongan,   Godes yrre bær;
mynte se manscaða   manna cynnes
sumne besyrwan   in sele þam hean.
Wod under wolcnum   to þæs þe he winreced,
goldsele gumena   gearwost wisse   715
fættum fahne.   Ne wæs þæt forma sið,
þæt he Hroþgares   ham gesohte;
næfre he on aldordagum   ær ne siþðan
heardran hæle,   healðegnas fand!
Com þa to reccde   rinc siðian   720
dreamum bedæled.   Duru sona onarn
fyrbendum fæst,   syþðan he hire folmum (æthr)an;
onbræd þa bealohydig,   ða (he ge) bolgen wæs,
recedes muþan.   Raþe æfter þon
on fagne flor   feond treddodc,   725
eode yrremod;   him of eagum stod
ligge gelicost   leoht unfæger.
Geseah he in recede   rinca manige,
swefan sibbegedriht   samod ætgædere,
magorinca heap.   Þa his mod ahlog;   730
mynte þæt he gedælde,   ær þon dæg cwome,
atol aglæca   anra gehwylces
lif wið lice,   þa him alumpen wæs
wistfylle wen.   Ne wæs þæt wyrd þa gen,
þæt he ma moste   manna cynnes   735
ðicgean ofer þa niht.

(In the black night the walker in darkness came gliding.
The warriors slept, who were supposed to guard that gabled
house, all except one. That was known to men, that when
God did not wish it, that hostile injurer might not draw
them under the shadows;—but he [Beowulf], watching in
anger against foes, awaited the outcome of the fight enraged

in his heart. Then from the moor under the mist-hills came Grendel striding—he bore God's wrath; the evil ravager intended to ensnare one of the race of men in that high hall. He moved beneath the clouds to where he most readily knew the wine-hall, the gold-hall of men shining with gold ornaments, [to be]. That was not the first time he had sought Hrothgar's home; never in his life-days did he find harder luck, [hardier] hall-thanes! The warrior came journeying to the hall, deprived of joys. The door straightway gave way, [even though] fast with fire-forged bands, when he touched it with his hands; the evil-intending one, being enraged, tore open the mouth of the hall. At once thereafter the foe stepped onto the shining floor, advanced angry-minded; from his eyes stood forth a horrible light, most like to flame. He saw in the hall many a warrior, a band of kinsmen asleep all together, a company of warriors. Then his spirit exulted; he intended to separate, ere day should come, that dreadful monster, from each of them life from the body, since an expectation of a huge feast had befallen him. It was not his fate at that time that he should feast on more of the race of men beyond that night.)

In the lines preceding this passage, Beowulf and his men have taken possession of Heorot for the night; and the poet has assured the audience that although the warriors felt they would never see their homeland again, God, through the strength of the hero alone, would enable them to overcome their enemy. The passage in question seems to me to fall into four distinct sections: the first three are marked by the varied *com* verses (ll. 702, 710, 720), the last by *geseah* (l. 728a). The first section arranges the prospective antagonists: Grendel, Beowulf, and Beowulf's men; the second focuses exclusively on Grendel's movements and motivations; the third brings Grendel to the door of Heorot and thence onto the floor of the hall itself; and the fourth emphasizes what Grendel sees and his great expectations therefrom. Each phase has its own particular character and special poetic emphasis.

The disposition scene is a brilliant tableau. The three forces that are soon to be brought into collision in combat are presented here as separated, each with its own attitude and behaviour toward the impending event. The walker in darkness is on the march, his murderous intention implicit in his association with night and darkness; the warriors are sleeping, believing that the monster will not have the power to harm them if God so wills; Beowulf is watching, enraged and anticipating the outcome of battle. These differences are rendered poetically effective by the syntactical, metrical and rhetorical patterns in which they are rooted.

The first contrast is conceptually between the striding Grendel and the sleeping 'shooters', a contrast reinforced by the complete syntactic break (i.e., a full stop, a period) in the middle of line 703; by the chiastic arrangement (abba pattern) of verb-noun-noun-verb; and by the complementary infinitive *scriðan*, which suggests 'durative' action as opposed to the preterite plural *swæfon*, depicting the warriors' *in*action. At the same time, the metrical-alliterative pattern and the chiasmus link the *sceadugenga* and the *sceotend*, satisfying the lexical expectation of the line, intimating that the *sceotend* are indeed the objective, even if not the syntactic object of Grendel's movement. The second contrast is between the sleeping band and Beowulf, conveyed at first by the dangling appositional phrase *ealle buton anum*, separated from *sceotend* by line 704, in which a subordinate clause mentions the duty of the men to guard the hall. But even more striking are the syntactic differences in lines 705b–9, which portray the different states of mind of the men and their chieftain. The comitatus's reliance on God's will is expressed periphrastically via a proleptic *þæt* in a pseudo-passive principal clause *þæt wæs yldum cuþ*, plus the specifying *þæt*-clause in the following two lines in which there is further subordination in the divisive *þa Metod nolde* clause. We may also note that the presentation of the warriors as a grammatical object, *hie*, underlines their passivity. Against all this (*ac*) Beowulf's watchfulness and rage are set forth vigorously in normal subject-verb-object word order. Notable is the modifier *wæccende*, the only present participle in the whole passage, which in contrast to the *swæfon* describing the warriors' inaction, suggests (like Grendel's *scriðan*) duration, implies that Beowulf is wide awake and watching throughout all the following description even though he does not reappear until line 736b. The lexical collocation in line 708 is reinforced by the metrical and syntactical patterns: unlike line 703, where *sceadugenga* and *sceotend* were completely separated syntactically, *wæccende* and *wraþum* (*on andan*) here are grammatically related. The whole introductory part comes to a fitting climax in the phrase *beadwa geþinges*, which lexically, grammatically and metrically satisfies the expectations aroused by the *bad bolgenmod* of the a-verse of that line, and ideationally fulfills the whole drift of lines 702b–9, that is, the positioning of the three separate forces—striding, sleeping, watching—for conflict.

Activity and inactivity, purposeful movement and purposive watching, passive acceptance of God's will and enraged human alertness are compacted there into the brief opening section and made manifest by formal (grammatical) as well as by semantic means. The three 'agents'—Grendel, Geats, Beowulf—receive equal shares of the poet's lexical and syntactic attention. But in what follows, all attention is focused upon Grendel as he moves from the moor toward the hall. Interestingly enough, there is but one mention of the hall (*hornreced*) in lines 702b–9; now, the hall is referred to four times (ll. 713b, 714b, 715a, 717b) as Grendel's movements and intentions (*com, wod, gesohte, mynte*) culminate in his ironic findings (*fand*) in the rhetorical zeugma of the last line (719): 'heardran hæle, healðegnas fand ([never had he] found harder luck, [harder] hall-thanes)', which even includes a fifth reference to the hall in the compound *healðegnas*. Quirk has pointed out how in line 179, *hæþenra hyht; helle gemundon*, presenting the plight of the pagan Danes, their hope is metrically collocated with, and thus made equal to, hell, despite the syntactic division (represented by the semi-colon).[20] With even greater force here the 'harder luck' that Grendel encounters is grammatically connected in the rhetorical pattern with the hall guardians he finds, as well as being made equivalent to them metrically.

There is further syntactical significance in this section in lines 712–13, but it will best be discussed as part of a pattern set up in the whole passage later. First, the third *com* clause deserves some attention in its relation to what has preceded and as introductory to its own division of the overall structural pattern.

It is at this point, where Grendel is depicted as arriving at Heorot, that the poet brings the monster and the building into lexical, grammatical and metrical union at the centre of the poetic line, *Com þa to recede rinc siðian*, and applies to the *rinc* the epithetic formula *dreamum bedæled*. In the first presentation of the stalking monster, *com* and the stressed syllable of its complementary infinitive *scriðan* occupy the initial dip and lift of sequent b-verses and a-verses respectively; in the second presentation, *com* and the stressed syllable of *gongan* occupy the initial and second lifts of successive a-verses respectively; but in this third account *com* and the stressed syllable of *siðian* occupy the first and second lifts of sequent verses in the same line and, in fact, are part of a chiastic pattern of the whole line (verb-noun-noun-verb) that contrasts, in its syntactic suggestion of the swiftness with which Grendel reaches the hall, with the similar rhetorical pattern of line 703, which in its entirely different syntactic structure and lexical polarity opposes the striding *sceadugenga* and the sleeping *sceotend*.

If we look still further at the description of the subject on each of these occasions, we find, in another way, added poetic meaning. At first Grendel is presented simply as *sceadugenga*, a word that is a *hapax legomenon* (occurring only here) and, in its association with darkness, implies the murderous intention in the monster's heart.[21] At the same time, it also implies Grendel's outcast state, as one deprived of God's light. In the second representation, although Grendel's ruthlessness is made explicit in the following lines 712–13, the actual description of him in line 711 lies in the paratactic (co-ordinate) semi-formulaic clause *Godes yrre bær*,[22] which emphasizes the *reason* for his outcast state. Finally, in lines 720–1a, the common participial-phrase formula *dreamum bedæled*[23] describes the *rinc*, explicitly characterizing the effect of God's anger upon this descendent of Cain, his deprivation of joys. The progression from noun *hapax* to semi-formulaic clause to formulaic phrase thus presents a semantic pattern moving from implicit representation of Grendel's exiled condition to explicit reason therefore and explicit effect thereon. More than this, the poet has saved the most common associative formula for last, immediately after he has, through negative clauses in lines 716b following and in the zeugma of line 719, stated that Grendel has this time met his match. The impact of *dreamum bedæled* is thus twofold, suggesting not only, as a permanent epithet, the transgressor's habitual deprivation of joys, but the additional and final separation he is about to suffer at this time.

Grendel's entrance into Heorot itself is of some interest. It occurs in lines 721b–4a, three lines in a rough chiastic pattern, beginning and ending with a reference to the door of the hall. The first one and a half lines give us the scene objectively, as it were, *Duru* being the grammatical subject of the main clause and Grendel's action coming in the subordinate *syþðan*-clause.[24] In the remaining one and a half lines we are shifted to Grendel's point of view, as he becomes the grammatical subject of the main clause (his anger mentioned subordinately in the *þa*-clause); and the door, now presented in the highly appropriate metaphor *recedes muþan* (see the discussion of this in chapter 2), is the grammatical object of Grendel's action, *onbræd*, as the monster passes through it. In the remaining lines of this section, we are shown Grendel stepping onto the floor of the hall; and with attention focused on his eyes through the simile *ligge gelicost*, we are prepared for the description of what he sees in the following section.

The monster and his physical objective, victim(s) in the hall, syntactically as well as referentially separated at the very start of this whole passage, are here, finally, in all ways brought together in lines 728 following: *Geseah he in recede rinca manige....* Although *recede* and *rinca* provide a verbal and pattern echo of line 720, *Com þa to recede rinc siðian*, the syntax is quite different: the *rinca* in 728 are Beowulf's warriors and not Grendel, and they are the object, not the subject, of the action being described. There is a further verbal echo of line 712 in line 731, *mynte þæt he gedælde*, but again there is a difference. The full import of lines 728–34, however, necessitates our returning to examine lines 712–13, which I passed over earlier.

As Grendel comes from the moor bearing God's anger,

mynte se manscaða   manna cynnes
sumne besyrwan   in sele þam hean.   (ll. 712–13)

The intention, the evildoer and the race of men are metrically, grammatically and lexically linked; significant is the directness of the verbal expression of Grendel's intention, reflecting the directness and single-mindedness of the monster in his desire to trap someone in the high hall. There is no use of variation, no interrupting phrases or clauses: finite verb–subject–objective phrase–complementary infinitive–adverbial phrase is the word order. Grendel has presumably not found game plentiful in

Heorot since his initial ravages twelve years ago, as witness his modest hope of ensnaring *one* man (suggested by the masculine accusative *singular* form *sumne*). The verb *mynte* 'gives us our first sudden flash of insight into Grendel's mind. . . . He assumes that this evening will follow the usual pattern'.[25] To his surprise and delight, upon entering the hall he sees *many* warriors, and now has the expectation of a full-course dinner:

Geseah he in recede   rinca manige,
swefan sibbegedriht   samod ætgædere,
magorinca heap.   Þa his mod ahlog;
mynte þæt he gedælde,   ær þon dæg cwome,
atol aglæca   anra gehwylces
lif wið lice.   (ll. 728–33a)

Grendel's exultation at this unexpected human cornucopia is neatly captured by the triple variation of *rinca, swefan sibbegedriht* and *magorinca heap*. We can almost feel his glare lingering on the bounty of warriors fate has so generously bestowed upon him, as the variations pile up, slowing the pace of the verse. 'Then his heart laughed'—and in the following expression of his intention, the syntax and word order themselves imply the slow savouring by the monster of his windfall. For now the directness and simplicity of lines 712–13 are missing, and instead we find the verb *mynte* followed by a subordinate clause that is interrupted in its grammatical progress by *ær þon dæg cwome*, and includes a variation of *he* in *atol aglæca*. Additionally, the object of the verb *gedælde*, 'life from the body', is delayed for one and a half lines. Only when the implications of the syntactic structure have made themselves felt is an explicit statement made in a concluding subordinate clause, 'since to him had befallen the expectation of a feast'.

That this 'intentional' pattern is not fortuitous is suggested by the fact that the only other occurrence of the verb *mynte* in the whole poem is some thirty lines further on, again in application to Grendel's intentions. It provides an ironic echo against the first two *mynte*'s, for here the monster realizes the strength of the adversary who has him in his grip, and that infamous evildoer now has only the intention of fleeing:

Mynte se mæra   (þ)ær he meahte swa,
widre gewindan   ond on weg þanon

fleon on fenhopu;   wiste his fingra geweald
on grames grapum.   Þæt wæs geocor sið,
þæt se hearmscaþa   to Heorute ateah!

(That infamous one intended, wherever he might do so, to
move farther away and away thence flee to his fenny retreat;
he knew his fingers' power to be in a hostile one's grip. That
was a painful journey that that injurer had made to
Heorot!)

What Grendel originally intended when he began his journey from
the moors to Heorot, and what he intended when he saw the
many warriors lying asleep in the hall, is here contrasted with his
single-minded intention to escape with his life, and ironically
counterpoised by what this occasion made him know (*wiste*), the
end of his strength, power, and ultimately life.[26]

In this chapter I have tried to assess some of the implications
for meaning of the formal features of verse form and syntax in
Old English poems. I have suggested the roles that the norms of
the language as a whole and the norms established by a poem
itself can play in generating implications, especially through
interaction with 'deviations'. Other illustrations, of different
orders and magnitudes, might be adduced. For example, I think
there is even a suggestion of character difference between
Unferth and Beowulf via the different syntactic patterns in their
famous 'flyting'. Unferth's speech is direct, aggressive, in its use
of predominantly short clauses introduced by adverbs, like *ðær*
in lines 508, 513, 522, *ða* in line 518, *ðonon* in line 520, and *ðonne*
in line 525. Typical are lines 513ff.:

þær git eagorstream   earmum þehton,
mæton merestræta,   mundum brugdon,
glidon ofer garsecg;   geofon yþum weol,
wintrys wylm[um].   Git on wæteres æht
seofon niht swuncon;   he þe æt sunde oferflat,
hæfde mare mægen.   Þa hine on morgentid
on Heaþo-Ræmes   holm up ætbær;
ðonon he gesohte   swæsne eþel,
leof his leodum, . . .

(there you two enfolded the sea-stream with your arms,
measured the sea-paths, quickly moved your hands, glided

over the ocean; the sea welled with waves, the surges of winter. You two toiled seven nights in the power of the water; he bested you at swimming, had greater strength. Then in the morning the sea bore him up among the Heathoraemas; thence he sought his own native land, dear to his people. . . .)

By contrast Beowulf's speech is for the most part measured and thoughtful, making use of many *þæt*-clauses, particularly in such sentences as

> Hwæþere me gyfeþe wearð,
> þæt ic aglæcan   orde geræhte,
> hildebille.   (ll. 555b–7a)

(However it was granted to me that I reached the monster with my sword-point, my battle-blade.)

and

> Hwæþere me gesælde   þæt ic mid sweorde ofsloh
> niceras nigene.   (ll. 574–5a)

(However it was granted to me that I with my sword slew nine nicors.)

Other kinds of *þæt*-clauses in Beowulf's speech appear in lines 533, 537, 545, 563, 567, 571, 591, 595. And not one *þæt*-clause in all of Unferth's diatribe! Syntax may thus be taken as something of the measure of the man.

More, I think, could be done with character differentiation through syntax (Holofernes and Judith?), but the expectations and implications of syntactic patterns in scenes of activity versus scenes of inactivity, both within one poem and among different poems, might yield interesting information about the contribution of formal features to meaning. Of particular interest, it seems to me, are passages with verbal echoes within relatively short sequences where different syntactic arrangements, or surface structures, obtain, as in the *mynte* sections of the episode of Grendel's approach. Thus the critical investigator in this area has a wide choice of categories—from character to scenic activity to verbal situation—in which he can move. Even as with ambiguity, however, he must exercise restraint and show humility in handling linguistic patterns, weighing the various kinds of relevant evidence open to him. Nevertheless, I hope this chapter has shown that there *is* scope for considering syntactic and verse-form expectations and implications in the interpretation of Old English poems.

6

Generic Expectations
and the Quest for Allegory

Since the first chapter, in which I tried to assess the contribution
and limitation of the concept of *genre* to the interpretation of
poems, I have been concerned with the smaller components of
poetic composition, such as diction and formula, metaphor and
image, and such formal features as verse requirements, variation
and syntax. Three main points I hope have been established: (1)
that both present and historical meaning are compatible—
indeed are indispensable—in the understanding of Old English
poems; (2) that the process of analysis must weigh the many
different sets of expectations and implications that interact in the
totality of present-historical meaning at cruxes of interpretation;
and (3) that greater precision of meaning was available to the
Anglo-Saxon poet, despite his highly conventional poetic
counters, than is sometimes allowed. On this last matter
especially, I trust that by now it is possible to agree that, while
admitting the truth about inhibiting factors in a statement like
the following by Mrs Goldsmith, we must nevertheless make
some adjustment:[1]

> It is rather obvious that the rhythmic, alliterative, and
> syntactic frames within which the Anglo-Saxon poet has to
> work inhibit precise utterances; the compound word is more
> useful to him than the corresponding phrase, and
> inevitably less specific; a range of interchangeable words is
> required by the metre, so that fine distinctions are worn
> away; and the traditional vocabulary is relatively small.

For one thing, our modern use of phrases is no more precise: we
often need to get beneath their surface structures, via context,
to fathom their meanings, as in the standard linguistic illustration

of 'the shooting of the hunters'. More significantly, the good Anglo-Saxon poet could through context revivify worn-out language (as we have seen with the *Beowulf* poet's *recedes muþan*), and he was able to counterpoint his several expectational-implicational sets to arrive, in many cases, at a high degree of precision in meaning.

I should like to return now to generic expectations, to viewing Old English poems as wholes for the horizons of meaning their *Gestalten* provide for the interpretation of individual parts. For it is the configuration of the whole, or at least our conception of that configuration, that conditions our response to details of word, phrase, image and structure. Our predisposition to a particular generic classification can lead us to see realism where none is 'intended', as in many early interpretations of *The Wanderer* and *The Seafarer;* or it can equally cause us to concoct ingenious allegorical *significationes*. It is the latter of these generic predispositions on which I wish most to focus in this chapter. We shall find that the exploration will involve us once again in questions of precision, historicism, and intention; and we can hardly avoid problems of thematic and structural unity.

It is important to remember the constant interaction of part and whole in the critical interpreting mind. That is, to see that our view of a particular part may trigger an assumed *Gestalt* for the whole, just as our understanding of the whole may persuade us that the meaning of X is A rather than B. If we determine, for example, that the speaker of *The Husband's Message* is a piece of wood rather than a human agent—and this determination is a crucial one for the poem—then we may find with R. E. Kaske that the whole is a speech of the Cross *à la Dream of the Rood*.[2] (I say *may*, because there is still a leap of faith, as it were, from the horizon of prosopopoeia, wherein we willingly suspend our disbelief about inanimate objects' ability to converse—which necessarily follows—to that of the identification with the Cross.) On the other hand, if we conclude, by various deductions, that *The Wanderer* as a whole is about 'thought' in one way or another, then it is natural to select, as Bliss–Dunning have done in their recent edition of the poem, such meanings from the semantic ranges of the words *gehola, myne* and *waraõ* (ll. 31, 27, 32 respectively) as 'confidant', 'thought' and 'preoccupies'; but if we believe on other grounds that 'security' is the thematic horizon of meaning of the poem, it is equally natural to interpret these words in context as 'protector', 'love' and 'guards'.[3]

The concept of genre, as noted in chapter 1, reflects an author's intention to write a poem of a certain kind, one having affinities with others in such aspects as mood, scope, subject matter and techniques. Usually one thinks of genre as a formal category. In this respect, our analysis of Old English poetic genres is hampered by the limited number of poems thus capable of being accurately categorized, and by an absence of contemporary discussions of them. Most clearly of a kind, despite their heterogeneity of subject matter and technique, are the Exeter Book *Riddles*, whose natures reflect their bases in the contemporary Latin *aenigmata*.[4] Versified saints' lives also have common characteristics inherited from their Latin models; but it is dangerous to generalize too much even on this basis, since a poem like *Guthlac B*, as Rosier has observed, detaches itself from the tradition, and from its immediate source in Felix of Croyland's *Vita*, by reviewing the 'life' hurriedly and focusing on the death of the saint.[5] An even more serious difficulty arises, however, with poems like the elegies, as we saw in chapter 1; for here there are no ascertainable traditional sanctions, however much critics may plead similarity with the Latin *planctus* or complaint, the Germanic *Totenklagelied* (or 'Keening Song', as it were) or the Welsh lyric. If the elegies are a genre in Old English, they are so by force of our present, rather than determinate historical, perspective; that is, by our 'feel' for them as a group possessing certain features in common.[6] I shall have more to say about the concept of elegy later, however.

What is most problematical, as well as central, to our concern is the idea of allegory. The attempt to define allegory has occupied whole books,[7] and I do not wish to pursue that chimera here. Certainly for Old English literature *allegoria* cuts across formal categories, and we may best enlarge our concept of genre to include this designing spirit. We can refer to it either as a 'non-formal' genre or, with Mrs Goldsmith, as 'a *mode* of figurative writing which might inhere only intermittently in a given work'.[8] Whatever we call it, allegory, as relevant to the Old English Christian experience, is a message of special moral and/or mystical significance encoded in a seemingly 'otherwise' piece of narrative or description. That allegory as such was not alien to the Anglo-Saxon period and spirit, the preservation of the Old English *Phoenix* and the researches of numerous historical critics have placed beyond doubt. But whether the possibility of allegory calls, historically, for the necessary expectation that Old English poems were primarily vehicles for the kind of exegetical interpretation accorded the Bible and expounded by St Augustine in his *De doctrina christiana*—for this is the directional thrust that has been paramount in allegorical criticism—is another matter.

We might look at a recent line of argument that seems to be typical of the modern exegetical approach, that offered by Mrs Goldsmith in *The Mode and Meaning of Beowulf*—though her book has its own special contributions to make to the approach. The climate of Christian education in Anglo-Saxon England was such, the argument runs, that its aim was 'to teach men to look into the Scriptures and in the created world for the *invisibilia Dei* and to reject as delusive the temporal satisfactions of this life, in the hope of eternal reward' (p. 59). As part of the classical legacy bequeathed to the Middle Ages, pagan heroic poetry offered *exempla* of moral conduct, but there was a need to discover 'symbolic meaning in the more superstitious passages' of a poem like the *Aeneid* to make it consonant with Christian teaching (p. 64). For secular epic of itself was profitless reading, as Sulpicius Severus, the author of the influential Life of St Martin, averred; and therefore certain Christian writers like Sulpicius himself and the author of the Pseudo-Bede discourse on Psalm lii: 1–4 either wrote lives of holy men or collected 'biblical parables, similitudes and exempla taken from the common stock' to show patterns of holy faith and to encourage men toward true wisdom and divine virtue (pp. 65–6). The oral-formulaic background of a poem like *Beowulf* is no bar to the presence of allegorical-symbolic values, since a study such as Jan Vansina's *De la traditione orale*, dealing with the living poetry of Congo tribes, 'brings out very clearly that an initiated illiterate audience can accept and enjoy in poetry much that is obscure and allusive or symbolic in expression' (pp. 63–4); and the Christian poet of *Beowulf* in its transmitted form, with his probable knowledge of Sulpicius's *Vita S. Martini* and of material like that assembled in the Pseudo-Bede discourse, would necessarily have changed the meaning of the traditional secular symbols of heroic poetry into spiritual meaning by marrying them to Christian allegorical signification (pp. 64–6). Mrs Goldsmith concludes her argument in this part by saying,

> It will now, I think, be plain that *Beowulf*, if the religious element were removed, would fall into Sulpicius's category of secular works which offer the examples of great men for emulation and celebrate worldly glory. Beowulf himself earns and receives that *inanem ab hominibus memoriam* which Sulpicius contrasts with the *æternum præmium* which those who follow the example of the saints may hope to gain. Without the religious element, the poem would most surely teach its audience *pro obtinendi mundi gloria contendere* but with its 'Christian colouring' it seems to me to lead them *ad veram sapientiam et cælestem militiam divinamque virtutem*.
> (p. 67)

I hope I have done justice to Mrs Goldsmith's argument within this short space. If I have, certain questions present themselves. How great or pervasive *is* the religious element in *Beowulf*? Whallon, for example, has challenged the general acceptance of this intensive penetration.[9] Is a *poem* part of the 'created world'—since it is obviously not Scripture—into which men must look for the *invisibilia Dei*? What has the allegorical reading of the classical Virgil by the Christian Middle Ages got to do with the reading of *Beowulf*? There are other questions and problems, such as the degree of circularity involved in assessing the *Beowulf* poet's 'probable knowledge' on the basis of parallels supposedly 'found' in the text; but I shall not attempt to cope with these, for I wish to consider the allegorical case for Old English poetry in general, not just for *Beowulf*. But the Virgil reference is instructive, and may serve as a springboard for further discussion.

I think it is valid here to return to the concept of authorial intention. However much the medieval exegetes may have allegorized the *Aeneid* for Christian exemplary purposes, there can be no doubt that such was *not* Virgil's intention in writing his poem; and their reading of the epic was at least as 'modern' for their time—and certainly not historical—as, say, Renoir's psychological analysis of *Genesis B* is for ours (see chapter 1). But we may also question how extensive this 'non-historical' perspective on secular works was in Anglo-Saxon England; for surely the rationale set forth by Sulpicius and the Pseudo-Bede intimates that a large segment of the clerical population had a different interpretive approach, for Pseudo-Bede says, 'When I marked my clerics established in places of learning giving so much time to the acquisition of knowledge of secular compositions, which studiously teach their hearers to desire carnal things and to strive for worldly glory . . .'[10] How widespread, then, we may ask, was the poetical doctrine of the *De doctrina*?

An answer to this question has recently been advanced by Philip Rollinson in his challenging essay, 'Some Kinds of Meaning in Old English Poetry'[11]: not so wide as a church door, perhaps. Troubled by the Robertsonian emphasis on the 'sameness' of literary texts and its disregard of how the surface (*cortex*) 'may differ in various narrative and expository modes and consequently how the *nucleus* [*sensus, sententia*—the hidden message], depending on these different modes of presentation, is to be understood', Rollinson has questioned the validity of the Robertson-Huppé presentation of medieval poetics. He suggests that they have ignored, for example, Isidore of Seville's application to literature of terms and concepts of classical rhetoric and grammar. Rollinson finds a recognition in classical-medieval poetics of different kinds of narrative:

1 history—the narration of actual events;
2 fiction (*argumentum*)—narration of invented actions which did not but could have happened . . .
3 fables—narratives that are neither true (i.e. actual) nor probable or possible . . .

and he argues that 'Isidore follows these basic distinctions in his Grammar. He also makes further, significant subdistinctions concerning fables (I. xl) and expands the concept of *argumentum* to include narrative which treats of real persons and events in a fictitious manner (VIII. vii).'[12] He then yokes these genre categories with the medieval expectations of finding a literal (or literary) sense of words (*allegoria in verbis*) and/or a spiritual signification of things (*allegoria in res*), the former being dependent upon context, the latter consisting of mystical and Christological significations, and being an arbitrary imposition. The difference in these 'allegories' may be observed in Samson's riddle 'out of the eater came forth food and out of the bold one came forth sweetness': the verbal allegory, the answer to the riddle (which is a kind of fable), is 'honey out of the nest the bees made in the dead lion's mouth'; but apart from the riddle, the lion and the honey have 'given' Christological significance as *things in themselves*. The two kinds of significations, Rollinson further argues, were not necessarily part of *all* genre expectations:

> Considerable confusion and misunderstanding about the
> nature and goals of medieval fiction and allegory have
> resulted from the Robertsonian insistence that all 'serious'
> medieval literary texts are to be read in the same manner,
> this manner being like or identical to that of reading Holy
> Scripture. Such a position is deplorable. It attempts to
> controvert the demonstrable fact that medieval theorists
> were perfectly aware of the different kinds of literary
> narrative which were understood in their own unique ways.
> These literary techniques did not correspond in general
> to the methods of mystical exegesis of the Bible or involve
> double signification. (p. 21)

I shall refer to Rollinson's detailed arguments later in this chapter, but for now his evidence suggests reasonable grounds for a multi-dimensional *historical* perspective on the contribution of genre (or mode) to meaning. It is a perspective which seems to harmonize well with the modern theoretical views of R. S. Crane, who cautions us against critics who are 'reductive' in assuming narrowly-held positions on structure and genre. Crane sees this reductiveness in those[13]

> who equate poetic structure . . . exclusively with the
> conventions of verbal form or thematic arrangement which
> poets derive from earlier poetic tradition; in the critics,
> again, who look for fixed and unitary definitions of the
> poetic genres and discuss individual . . . [works] as more or
> less typical or perfect examples of these various quasi-
> Platonic forms; . . . in the many critics . . . who fix their
> attention on some part of the total structure—on one phase
> of the action or on the framework of its representation, on a
> principal character, a 'key' passage of thought, a

conspicuous train of imagery—and proceed to derive from this their formula for the whole.

Crane is talking here about the New Critics but, curiously enough, his strictures seem applicable to the Robertsonian exegetes as well, who perhaps have not escaped the 'solipsistic pit' as much as they have thought.

Let us turn, however, from these considerations of theory to the expectations of genre (mode) and structure in specific Old English poems. We may begin with one which clearly exhibits *allegoria in res*, where arbitrary moral or Christological meanings are assigned or superimposed upon 'things' or 'actions' within a poem. The Old English *Phoenix*, with its base in the Lactantian *De ave phoenice*, leaves no doubt about such expectations, since the *sensus spiritualis* 'concealed' within the cortex of the bird's life history is made explicit by the *sensus litteralis* of the poet's exegetical explanation in the second part of the poem. Rollinson assigns *The Phoenix*, along with the Old English *Physiologus*, to the genre *history*, since the birds and animals in these poems were considered to be 'real'.[14] J. E. Cross puts forward a further suggestion upon examining the various additions, deletions and changes the Old English poet made in his re-telling of the Lactantian descriptive narrative. The poet, he says, 'adapted the Latin poem to fit Christian reality and to place the Phoenix story within a Christian historical context'.[15] This 'Christian reality' begins with a description of the Earthly Paradise, which is not simply Lactantian but contains echoes of Genesis, Ezekiel and Revelation:[16]

Þæt is wynsum wong,   wealdas grene
rume under roderum.   Ne mæg þær ren ne snaw
ne forstes fnæst   ne fyres blæst
ne hægles hryre   ne hrimes dryre
ne sunnan hætu   ne sincaldu
ne wearm weder   ne winterscur
wihte gewyrdan,   ac se wong seomað
eadig ond onsund.   (ll. 13–20a)

(That is a pleasant plain, green forests spacious beneath the skies. There can neither rain nor snow nor breath of frost nor blast of fire nor fall of hail nor dropping of rime nor heat of sun nor unbroken cold nor warm weather nor winter shower injure aught, but the plain remains unscathed and flourishing.)

When the Phoenix is presented in the next section, it is associated with the sun: it bathes twelve times daily in the cold streams of Paradise before the sun rises, and then it mounts swiftly into the air, offering its adoration to God's bright token in song and carol. This routine continues for one thousand years when the bird, grown old, flies westward to a wood in Syria, attended for a while by a concourse of birds. Seeking seclusion, however, the Phoenix drives off its attendants and builds a nest atop a lofty tree named after itself. There, in section 3 of the poem, the bird's 'solarium' is enkindled by the sun; and nest, bird, and sweet herbs the lone dweller has gathered are consumed together on the pyre. In the cooled ashes, now, an apple's likeness appears, and from thence a wondrously fair worm emerges, which transforms itself into the fledgling Phoenix that eats naught but honeydew till, in section 4, it seeks again the terrestrial Eden whence it came, again attended by flocks of birds singing hosannahs unto this powerful leader. But the birds must once more retire when the Phoenix reaches its ideal land (section 5); and the self-containment of the bird, and its lack of fear of death, are praised by the poet as the 'paraphrase' of the Lactantian part of the poem runs its course.

The Phoenix, then, is a real bird to the Old English poet, a created being, one of the *visibilia* of this world in which, as the remainder of the poem shows, we may see *invisibilia Dei*. In that 'explication' of his story (or history), the poet's central significa-tion of the Phoenix is the good Christian who earns resurrection in his heavenly home after Doomsday. There is, additionally, a brief identification of the bird in its flight from the Earthly Paradise to the wood where it builds its nest with 'ða foregen-gan, / yldran usse [those forebears, our forefathers]' (i.e. Adam and Eve) in their expulsion from Paradise (ll. 428–42); and near the end of the poem a brief identification with Christ in his death and resurrection (ll. 642b–9). Cross, however, does not rest content with this 'loose' account of the poem's allegorical mean-ings(s), and insists that the poet is following the fourfold Scriptural exegetical method, that in addition to the historical level 'the representation of the Phoenix as the good Christian in his earthly nest is a *moral* or *tropological* interpretation, the bird as Christian in his heavenly dwelling is an *anagogical* interpretation, and the bird as Christ is a *typical* or *allegorical* interpretation'.[17] Surely if any Old English poem can be made to support such a tight and neat allegorical meaning or set of meanings, *The Phoenix* is the logical candidate. But I think this view of the poem's generic expectations suggests an intention of meaning which the poem itself will not clearly admit. It implies an order and structure too clean-cut for the actual poetic materials. We might link this view with Crane's warning about putting too-strait a jacket of genre onto a poem, about making a poem conform to expectations that, from the context of the poem, are illegitimate. Additionally, we might bear in mind Geoffrey Shepherd's timely warning that 'it seems very unlikely that the ingenuity and subtlety that a modern critic requires to demonstrate a unity was exercised by an Anglo-Saxon poet in composing ... The old poets often seem to do no more than make a verbal circumambulation of a well-known but rather ill-defined moral or spiritual situation.'[18]

Cross argues[19] that there is

a double interpretation of the Phoenix's nest (described only once in Lactantius and in the first section of the Old English poem) as a shelter for the good Christian on earth and as a place to live in heaven. On earth *Þær him nest wyrceð ... | dædum domlicum dryhtnes cempa* 'the warrior of the Lord makes a nest for himself by glorious deeds' (451–52) in the lofty tree of the favor of God in this world (446–47), *in þam halge nu | wic weardiað* 'in which the holy now have their dwelling' (447b–48a); but also *Beoð him of þam wyrtum wic gestaþelad | in wuldres byrig* 'a dwelling shall be built for them [*meotudes cempan* "the warriors of the Lord" (471b)] from the plants in the city of glory' (474–75a). The indication of a dividing line here in the good man's journey home is, of course, strengthened by a general observation that death for a Christian ends the continuous present but begins the everlasting future.

This interpretation seems attractive until we look more closely at text and context. Unfortunately, these do not support this clear line of demarcation between an earthly nest *in þam halge nu | wic weardiað* (ll. 447b-8a), and a heavenly nest, the dwelling in the city of glory, *wuldres byrig*. Let us look at the context of lines 447b–52. To do so, we must go back and start with line 437b, where we are told about our *foregengan* (Adam and Eve and the race of man ensuing) who had to leave the Earthly Paradise and journey into the power of wicked foes who often harmed them. Then, in lines 443ff., we find:

> Wæron hwæþre monge   þa þe Meotude wel
> gehyrdun under heofonum   halgum ðeawum,
> dædum domlicum,   þæt him Dryhten wearð,
> heofona Heahcyning   hold on mode.
> Ðæt is se hea beam   in þam halge nu
> wic weardiað   þær him wihte ne mæg
> ealdfeonda nan   atre sceþþan,
> facnes tacne   on þa frecnan tid,
> þær him nest wyrceð   wið niþa gehwam
> dædum domlicum   Dryhtnes ccmpa,
> þonne he ælmessan   earmum dæleð. . . .

(There were many under the heavens, however, who well obeyed the Creator in holy customs, with glorious deeds, so that the Lord, Highking of Heaven, became gracious in heart to them. That is the high tree in which now the holy ones have their dwelling, where none of the old foes can harm them at all with venom, with show of malice in that perilous time. There [=tree] by glorious deeds the warrior of God builds himself a nest against every hostility, when he gives aid to the poor. . . .)

Now, so far as I read this, the text is not suggesting a nest on earth: the phrase *there were many* refers to holy ones of the past who have departed from this earth, and their dwelling *now*, their nest, is clearly in Heaven, not on earth. Cross reads the *hea beam* (l. 447a) as 'the favor of the Lord on earth' (p. 140), but I think this is mistaken. For as Blake points out in his comparison of the poet's allegorical interpretation with his probable source in Ambrose's *Hexameron*, Book V, chs 79–80, although Ambrose likens Christ to the nest the Phoenix builds, the *Phoenix* poet likens Christ to the tree.[20] In other words, the favor of God to those who *did* his holy works, glorious deeds, was the 'high tree' (i.e., Christ) in which the holy ones *now* have their habitation, so that the enmity of Satan cannot touch them 'on þa frecnan tid [in that perilous time]' (not *this* perilous time, as some editors wrongly suggest by emending þa to þas), a phrase which corresponds to Ambrose's *in die male,* and refers, as Blake shows, to Doomsday.[21] The moral lesson is that those who follow the custom of those holy ones can also gain reward *þær him nest wycreð,* the *þær* being not on earth but in Christ.

As part of his argument Cross suggests that lines 455b–6: *forð onetteð, | lænan lifes leahtras dwæsceþ* have been misleadingly translated by Gordon and Gollancz as 'hasteneth forth from this frail life, blotteth out transgressions'; and he proposes instead that the 'phrase should clearly be read "strives always, quenches sins of this transitory life"'. But 'strives always' for *forð onetteð* seems strained, and it ignores the parallel statement about those who choose belief in the Lord over worldly wealth in lines 480b–1: 'ne biþ him wynne hyht / þæt hy þis læne lif long gewunien (nor do they have joy that they should long dwell in this transitory life)'. This latter passage, quite unambiguous in its meaning, suggests that *forð onetteð* might well mean in context 'hastens forth', or at least 'sets his goal in the next world'.

Thus, when the poet says in lines 474–5: *Beoð him of þam wyrtum wic gestaþelad | in wuldres byrig weorca to leane,* it seems more likely that the nest of the Phoenix is being equated with the dwelling in Heaven through Christ that the good works of the holy will command, and there is no distinction being made, thematically or structurally, between a nest on earth and one in Heaven. Rather than having a poem providing 'distinguishable tropological, anagogical, and typological explanations, so as to present a fourfold interpretation of a real and scriptural bird' (Cross, p. 145), we have in *The Phoenix* a circumambulation, to use Shepherd's felicitous term, on the theme of resurrection. The *Phoenix* poet has used allegorical equations of various sorts to make his point. He has quoted Scripture to his purpose in lines 548bff., where he cites the figure of Job, who, like the Phoenix, is certain in his faith, knowing he will rise again to enjoy happiness with the Lord (Job xxix.8). He incorporates an extended harvest and sowing image in the 'historical' part of the poem (ll. 243ff.) which 'appears as a figurative means for explaining and vivifying the rebirth of the bird which, in turn, functions as the major metaphoric framework for the doctrine of the resurrection, providing in each phase of its rebirth a typology for the good Christian and his Savior'.[22] The metaphor suggests that resurrection is a natural phenomenon, a familiar process of nature, as well as a mysterious and unique event like the mythical Phoenix or a biblical asseveration like Job's. The poet anthropomorphizes the Phoenix by applying to it terms from the heroic vocabulary, thus helping to identify the life of the bird and that of man, which it symbolizes in its life, its death and its resurrection.[23]

In summary, then, I suggest that although the mode or genre of *The Phoenix* is historical allegory, we do violence to its meaning when we attempt to see it as a perfect example of the highly structured fourfold exegetical genre. Such an approach, though professing to be historical, is, paradoxically, more modern than might appear in its catering to our desire to find a kind of aesthetic-thematic unity in a poem. And if this is the case with a relatively clear-cut allegorical poem like *The Phoenix*, what are we to make of such a secular-appearing poem as *The Husband's Message?*

It seems appropriate to turn to this poem now because Kaske has recently compared it with *The Phoenix* and with Cross's analysis of that poem: Kaske allegorizes *The Husband's Message* as a speech of the Cross (not J. E.!), and suggests three possible readings: 'as an address by the Cross to the Church following the Atonement, as a special and strongly hortatory vision of the Cross granted to an individual, and as an appearance of the Cross in the role of celestial convoy'; and he then proceeds to equate these 'with the famous "allegorical", "moral", and "anagogical" (eschatological) senses of medieval Biblical exegesis'. Thus, Kaske concludes, 'one is left wondering whether this brief and disarmingly "literal" poem may not in fact present an example of multiple allegory to set beside that of the Old English *Fenix*'.[24] This analysis is, I am afraid, not very convincing. Nevertheless, it is instructive about the interrelationship between the interpretation of parts of a poem and the concept of genre, as I have indicated earlier in this chapter, and provides us with a valuable caveat about critical procedures in arriving at the interpretation of Old English poems through genre predications.

The Husband's Message is a notoriously baffling poem for

several reasons. First, its starting point is not clear: is what is often called *Riddle 60*, the poem which precedes it in the Exeter Book, part of the 'message' or not? Related to this question are the paragraphing divisions at two other points in the lyric, which suggests that the scribe, at least, may have thought he was dealing with several other riddles as well, instead of with a single poem. Second, there is the problem of the speaker: is it a *beam* of some kind which prosopopoeically speaks the message from the exiled but now wealthy 'husband', or is it a human messenger? Third, what do the runes at the end of the poem signify, and how are they related to the speaker? There are additional problems connected with this text, including the loss of many words as a result of damage to the manuscript, but the burden of genre identification, and hence of horizon of meaning expectations, rests upon these three major questions. Since the poem is relatively short, it will be well to have it before us (without *Riddle 60*, to which I shall allude in the course of the discussion). I use Leslie's text for the most part[25] with one major change:

```
Nu ic onsundran      þe secgan wille
. . . . . . (n) treocyn.     Ic tudre aweox;
in mec æld[a] . . .     . . . . . . . sceal
ellor londes setta(n)     . . . . . . . . . lc,
sealte streamas     . . . . . . . . . . sse.                    5
Ful oft ic on bates [bosme]     . . . . . . gesohte,
þær mec mondryhten     min . . . . . . .
ofer heah h[a]fu;     eom nu her cumen
on ceolþele,     ond nu cunnan scealt
hu þu ymb modluf[a]n     mines frean                10
on hyge hycge.     Ic gehatan dear
þæt þu þær tirfæste     treowe findest.
   Hwæt, þec þonne biddan het,     se þisne beam agrof,
þæt þu sinchroden     sylf gemunde
on gewitlocan     wordbeotunga                         15
þe git on ærdagum     oft gespræcon,
þenden git moston     on meoduburgum
eard weardigan,     an lond bugan,
freondscype fremman.     Hine fæhþo adraf
of sigeþeode.     Heht nu sylfa þe                       20
```

lustum læra[n]   þæt þu lagu drefde,
siþþan þu gehyrde   on hliþes oran
galan geomorne   geac on bearwe.
Ne læt þu þec siþþan   siþes getwæfan,
lade gelettan,   lifgendne monn.   25
  Ongin mere secan,   mæwes eþel;
onsite sænacan,   þæt þu suð heonan
ofer merelade   monnan findest,
þær se þeoden is   þin on wenum.
Ne mæg him [on] worulde   willa [gelimpan]   30
mara on gemyndum,   þæsþe he me sægde,
þonne inc geunne   alwaldend God,
[þæt git] ætsomne   siþþan motan
secgum ond gesiþum   s[inc brytnian],
næglede beagas.   He genoh hafað   35
fædan gold[es], ...
[geon]d elþeode   eþel healde,
fægre folda[n]   . . . .
[hold]ra hæleþa,   þeahþe her min win(e)
. . . .   40
nyde gebæded,   nacan ut aþrong,
ond on yþa gel(a)g[u   ana] sceolde
faran on flotweg,   forðsiþes georn
mengan merestreamas.   Nu se mon hafað
wean oferwunnen;   nis him wilna gad,   45
ne meara, ne maðma,   ne meododreama
ænges ofer eorþan   eorlgestreona,
þeodnes dohtor,   gif he þin beneah.
Ofer eald gebeot   incer twega,
genyre ic ætsomne   .S.R. geador   50
.EA.W. ond .M.   aþe benemnan
þæt he þa wære   ond þa winetreowe,
be him lifgendum   læstan wolde,
þe git on ærdagum   oft gespræconn.

(Now I will tell you especially [or apart?] . . . species of
tree. From my childhood I grew up; in me of men . . . must
set elsewhere in the land . . . salt streams. . . . Full often
in the heart of a ship . . . I sought, where my liege-lord
me . . . over the high sea; I am now come here on board

ship, and now you shall know how you may think in your
mind about my lord's love. I dare promise you will find
there glorious faith. Lo, he bade me beseech you then, he
who inscribed this wood, that you should yourself recall in
your mind, treasure-adorned one, the promises which you
two in former days often spoke, while you two might dwell
in the mead-cities, occupy one and the same land, live out
your love. Feud drove him from the victorious people. He
himself bade [me] now joyfully to inform you that you
should cross the water after you have heard on the edge of
the hillside the sad cuckoo singing in the grove. Do not
allow any living man to keep you from the journey, hinder
your voyage. Seek the sea, the home of the seagull; board a
ship, so that south hence over the seapath you may find the
man where the prince is expecting you. No desire in the
world happens to be greater in his mind, as he said to me,
than that almighty God should grant you two that you
may afterwards distribute treasure, studded with bracelets,
to warriors and companions. He has sufficient of the
burnished gold . . . in a foreign land he holds his
dwelling, in a fair country . . . of dear warriors, though here
my lord . . . driven by need launched his ship and alone had
to travel on the expanse of waves, on the sea-way stir up the
sea-streams. Now the man has overcome woe; there is no
lack to him of desires: not of horses, nor of treasures, nor
of any of mead-joys [and] treasures over the earth, prince's
daughter, if only he may possess you. Concerning the old
promise between you two, I crowd together S.R.EA.W. and
M. to declare by oath that he the pact and pledge of fidelity
which you two in former days oft spoke will fulfill while he
lives.)

With the problems the poem presents, how should one proceed
critically? Kaske first mentions the dilemma of the nature of the
speaker thus:[26]

If, as has often been suggested, the poem itself is to be
thought of as a message spoken by a carved rune-staff or
other piece of wood, what is the relation between this total
message and the apparently distinct runic message of lines
[50–51]? If on the other hand the speaker is a human

messenger who carries a staff carved with these runes, what possible restoration of the damaged lines [2-3] can account for his use of the word *treocyn*, 'species of tree *or* tree,' in what is obviously a passage of self-description?

Kaske then alludes to the problem of the runic message and decides to begin his analysis with that. From his interpretation of the runes as meaning either '"I constrain *sigelrad* (heaven), *earwyn* (a delightful *or* joyous earth), and *mann* (man *or* mankind), all together, to declare by oath, etc."; or "I constrain into unity *sigelrad* (heaven), *earwyn* (a delightful *or* joyous earth), and *mann* (man *or* mankind)—[constrain] it to be declared by oath, etc."',[27] he jumps in his very next sentence to 'Now in the voluminous literature of the Cross produced during the first Christian millennium, one of the great seminal concepts is that of the Cross itself as a cosmic mystery embracing and binding into unity all creation, with particular emphasis on its joining heaven and earth'—and thus silently slides into the assumption that the speaker *is* indeed a piece of wood, and of a very special kind! Unfortunately, he never returns to considering the pros and cons of the speaker issue, except to say that the poem 'can be understood more easily than not as spoken by a tree or piece of wood' (p. 49), and insofar as he recognizes certain difficulties in connecting the Cross with some of the statements the speaker makes about itself (himself). He builds premise upon premise, including justifying *Riddle 60* as part of the poem, without sufficiently weighing the expectations in other directions. It seems to me this is methodologically unsound. (Cf. Crane, chapter 1, note 49, on the inadequacy of 'the doctrine of the sufficiency of positive corroboration'.) Kaske's interpretation is made further suspect by the dubiety of many of the so-called resemblances he adduces between words and phrases in the poem and those in other works: I have given one example of his employment of this 'fallacy of similarity' in chapter 1; but there are many more.

It would be well to remember at this point that, unlike *The Phoenix*, *The Husband's Message* presents no explicit interpretation of the narrative as allegory. Kaske himself admits that 'except for the runic passage, the particulars . . . are all parts of a relatively coherent literal message, which in itself might or might not be thought to demand allegorical significance' (p. 63). But since the runic passage *can* be explained as part of the 'relatively coherent literal message', the force of his argument for generic expectation of allegory (*allegoria in res*, really), is further diminished.

Let us examine the poem, beginning with the pros and cons of the textual evidence about the nature of the speaker. *Riddle 60* must be put aside for the moment. The only real support for the speaker-as-wood theory is the use of *treocyn* in line 2, 'in what is obviously a passage of self-description'—that is, if one does not punctuate as Leslie and I have done, but with Kaske and some other in this fashion:

Nu ic onsundran þe   secgan wille
[. . . .] treocyn   ic tudre aweox.

(Now I will tell you apart [or especially] how I grew up as a species of tree.)

As for the end of the poem, however one wishes to construe the *genyre ic* passage—to which I shall return—the *ic* may be *either* a human speaker who is referring to the runes on a piece of wood *or* the piece of wood speaking about its own incisions. On the other side of the argument, however, *se þisne beam agrof* (l. 13b), and *þæsþe he me sægde* (31b), seem more likely to be expressions uttered by a person: would a piece of wood, however personified, refer to itself as *þisne beam* 'this wood' when it had already used *mec*, or would it say that 'he *said* to me'? Possibly, and comparison with certain riddles might offer some support for this view, but this interpretation seems strained. But even more supportive of the human-agent theory are lines 6–9a: a piece of wood designed as a rune-stave (which is what the context of the poem demands in this case) would hadly have sought *ful oft* in a boat, saying further 'I *now* have come *here* on a ship'. (Kaske recognizes this particular difficulty in his interpretation in 'the apparent reference to earlier voyages of the Cross at its Lord's behest . . . I would suggest rather hesitantly that it may allude to some unrecorded legend concerning the earlier history of the Cross, broadly like those attached to the legend of Seth in the twelfth century and after' (p. 70). Well might he suggest this 'rather hesitantly'!) Further, there is the lord-retainer relationship suggested by *mondryhten min* (l. 7), *mines frean* (l. 10b) and *min wine* (l. 39b): although susceptible of a personification interpretation, these epithets seem much more indicative of a human speaker. (It might be noted that *Riddle 60* does *not* utilize such a relationship, but speaks rather of a general 'eorles ingeþonc [warrior's intention]' and 'for unc anum twam [before us two alone]', which implies a much more impersonal connection.)

What about *treocyn* then? This is the great stumbling block to the human-agent interpretation. Dobbie's note on line 2a seems to me relevant:

In the MS., *treo cyn* is at the end of a line, with a hole in the parchment after it. It is impossible to tell whether the final letter is *n*, or *m* with the final stroke lost, or whether or not any more letters followed the *n* or *m*. Between *wille* and *treco cyn* in the MS. there is space for about ten letters. The only suggested restoration which fits the indications in the MS. is Mackie's [*ymb þisum*] *treocyn* [*ne*].[28]

That is, lines 1–2a may thus read 'Now I will tell you especially [or apart?] about this species of tree [wood]'. Dobbie, like Kaske, does not put any punctuation at the end of line 2a but, with Leslie, I see no reason not to do so. Then the *human* speaker, having indicated his readiness to say something about the piece of wood he is carrying, goes into a presentation of his *own* pedigree and credentials. This is a sudden switch, to be sure, but it is less difficult to explain or accept than all the 'con' evidence. We notice that the second reference to the wood, in line 13b, is also brief, and the final explanation of its presence and meaning is not forthcoming till the end, with the presentation of the runic message. Might this be a device for climactic effect? Surely it is a possibility; and with the weight of evidence more heavily on the side of a human speaker, I submit that some such explanation is more to be sought than the many which are needed to account for the several contextual difficulties which arise when we postulate a prosopopoeic piece of wood.[29]

If we turn now to the climactic runic message, we may observe that Kaske does not see the runes as being engraved on the wood (which for him, of course, is the Cross): they are simply an adjuration by the speaker-Cross. Kaske thus makes no connection between the *agrof* 'incised' of line 13b and the runes, and instead of any literal meaning for *agrof*, he suggests that it 'may allude to the marks of the nails in the Cross' or to the INRI inscription at its top (p. 62). But a connection between *agrof* and the runes seems most probable, and if the runes are not inscriptions, one might legitimately ask why the poet used them at all. Now, accepting Kaske's reading of the MS. in line 50 as *genyre*, as I have done above (Leslie reads *gehyre*)[30] and his reading of the runes as *heaven*, *delightful earth* and *man*, we may still question his meaning for *genyre* of 'constrain', i.e., 'exhort'. According to *BTD* and *BTS*, there are three basic meanings of *genirwan*, the putative infinitive of this troublesome form: 'crowd together or contract' (with reference to space), 'diminish by contraction' and 'oppress by constraint'. Kaske's meaning simply does not occur elsewhere—he seems to have taken the last of these senses and deleted the idea of 'oppression'. But since the most common sense of the word, 'crowd together in space' does fit the context beautifully if the runic letters are incised on a piece of wood, by Occam's Razor we should accept this interpretation as valid. The probable human speaker is climactically showing his rune-stave and explaining its import to the princess he is addressing: 'I crowd together (the runes) S.R.EA.W. and M. (on this stave) to declare by oath, etc.'. We may in this context readily accept the significations of the runes themselves as both Kaske and Leslie read them, and see them, in their reference to heaven, earth, and the man himself, as the 'clincher' of the messenger's argument to persuade the *peodnes dohtor* (who evidently, from the whole context of the poem, *needs* persuasion) to join her husband in his newfoundland of prosperity. The poem thus presents a literal and intelligible story making no suggestion or hint of allegory.

If the speaker of *The Husband's Message* is indeed human, as I have argued, *Riddle 60*, the preceding piece in The Exeter Book, clearly cannot be a part of it. Leslie has argued strongly, in fact, that even if the speaker of *The Husband's Message* is a piece of wood, it still cannot relate to the riddle.[31] In the riddle the speaker-object, after giving an account of its early existence, says that it little thought it would ever speak 'mouthless'. It continues by telling

hu mec seaxe[s] ord   ond seo swiþre hond,
eorles ingeþonc   ond ord somod,

þingum geþydan   þæt ic wiþ þe sceolde
for unc anum twa[m]   ærendspræce
abeodan bealdlice,   swa hit beorna ma
uncre wordcwidas   widdor ne mænden.

(how the knife's point and the right hand, warrior's
intention and point together, performed these things so that
I might to you boldly announce a message before the two of
us alone, in such a way that others of men might not
communicate the words of us two more widely.)

Leslie's most crucial and telling point is that the *uncre wordcwidas*
of the last line indicates not the words of the speaker and the
addressee, but those of the speaker and the composer of the
message. Presumably if the speaker of the riddle were a rune-stave
bringing a message, the poet would have used *mine* instead of
uncre. For other reasons, too, Leslie concludes that the riddle-
object is a reed pen, and the riddle has an integrity of its own,
and thus in no way impinges upon the following lyric. I suspect
Leslie is correct, though I am somewhat bothered by the fact
that the riddle-object is fashioned with the point (*ord*) of a knife
and not the edge: the point suggests more the making of an
incision, like rune-marks on wood, than shaping a reed into a pen
point. Whatever the case here, there can be no connection
between *Riddle 60* and *The Husband's Message*, despite Kaske's
desire to unite them.

Where does all this leave us with regard to the horizon of
expectations we might posit for *The Husband's Message*? Certainly
the poem is not 'history', as *The Phoenix*, from a historical
perspective, can reasonably be viewed. The weight of various
sets of expectations argues against classifying it as 'fable' (riddle),
however much the Exeter Book scribe or his exemplar may have
confused it with a series of riddles. Since the speaker most
probably is human, the poem would seem to be a dramatic
monologue, a 'fiction' like other of the Old English elegies. Like
them it utilizes personal experience, whether real or assumed, as
a vehicle for imparting moral and/or religious wisdom about
man's condition in this world. Fortitude and courage in the face
of adversity are either explicitly or implicitly extolled in these
poems; the more 'Christian' of them, like *The Wanderer* and *The
Seafarer*, proceed further to suggest the superior values of the

heavenly life. What is basic to the elegies is their exemplary character: they are extensions, in an elegiac manner, of the *sapientia* of the figures of heroic fiction, whether saintly or secular.[32] They reveal a pattern of behaviour frequently reinforced by explicit gnomic wisdom, to which an Anglo-Saxon audience might reasonably have responded 'generically' without recourse to allegory. In the case of *The Seafarer*, some members of the audience might well have seen further, allegorical significance in the sea-journeys, but even here literal readings would no doubt have satisfied the exemplary generic expectations of other members.[33] *The Husband's Message*, although not as 'sorrowful' in tone as the others, nevertheless emphasizes, through the theme of exile and the sense of urgency of the messenger, the uncertainty of life and love and prosperity in this world, paying high tribute to the virtues of truthfulness and the keeping of vows (virtues both secular and Christian), even as the poem's 'companion piece', *The Wife's Lament*, extols the value of the same virtues by negative example.

Exemplary fiction is also to be found in the poeticized Old English saints' lives. Despite the historical background for these, Rollinson would classify them as fiction in the Isidorean sense, since they 'include the usual paraphernalia of Germanic heroic verse, such as epic boasts, beasts of battle, and vivid description of combat, and since in so doing they are accommodating the actual events of the legends to the terms of Old English culture and traditional narrative fiction. . . .'[34] These 'Lives' cannot by their very nature be 'allegorical'—they are, rather, exemplary of Christian behaviour:[35]

> the lesson of a saint's legend . . . whether it employs
> historical or fictional narrative, does not involve the *sensus
> spiritualis*. In the case of New Testament or other authentic
> historical account, although actual persons and events are
> the subject matter, *allegoria in res*, as usually understood,
> does not obtain, for the exemplary lesson is not
> allegorical at all in so far as it depends directly on the
> context of the *sensus litteralis*.

The case of Old Testament figures in poetry, however, might well admit of Christological interpretation, Rollinson continues; but he proposes[36] that even in such a poem as the Old English

Exodus, where the subject matter of the Red Sea crossing had a standard fourfold allegorical interpretation,[37]

> the first purpose of [the poem] seems to be to relate the exemplary (and exciting) story of a Jewish hero, of the heroic conflict between God's people and Satan's people, and of God's spectacular judgment, which decided that contest. The historical, literal level alone of the Old Testament account is re-presented in the heroic conventions and poetic expectations of a Germanic, if Christianized, tradition. In spite of the liturgical overtones, which could hardly be avoided, the essential meaning intended is surely not to emphasize the relationship of the poetic fiction to the rite of baptism.

Note Rollinson's insistence on 'first purpose' and 'meaning intended'. It is important because allegorical interpreters keep intimating or specifying authorial intentions in their approach. This insistence carries over into Rollinson's brief discussion of *Beowulf*, which he also sees as exemplary in its harmonizing of pagan and Christian values. Without the Christian values,[38]

> we should expect an exemplary meaning in the wisdom and courage of the hero and in the magnitude of his accomplishments. With such values present, we should expect an exemplary imitation of Christ. Beowulf, however, is not a saint but a secular hero. As has been frequently observed, he is exemplary in terms of Christian kingship.

Rollinson sees liturgical overtones in the poem, but these, he says,[39]

> should be judged in terms of this legitimate (medieval) generic expectation. . . . The Christological overtones serve to emphasize the magnitude and significance of the literal deeds themselves. Beowulf is not subsumed and his exploits forgotten in Christ; rather through the suggestion that his actions correspond to the Christ-like pattern he is magnified as himself.

So. Margaret Goldsmith, whose views I have summarized earlier, sees the Christian elements as *transforming* the basic poem into allegory; Rollinson sees them as *informing* a literal lesson. A third major genre approach views the Christian elements as interjections by the Christian poet in a poem whose meaning is basically heroic. G. V. Smithers has recently put forward such an interpretation: [40]

> ... Beowulf's life and death are explicitly represented as being governed by destiny, and ... his conduct throughout his life is represented as being in the highest degree honourable and as being crowned with the appropriate Germanic reward of heroic glory. The picture is an authentic and complete one of an exemplary hero according to the Germanic warrior code. Though the poet has interjected his own Christian values as well, as when from time to time he sets Beowulf's destiny under the omnipotence of God, the real dynamic impulse in Beowulf's life is the inherited pagan ethos. ... His death is a noble one, because he exercises the highest courage and thus fulfills his destiny. The fact of his death is painful, because of the human sympathies it arouses; but for Beowulf himself, as for the poet, all is well.
>
> The 'meaning' of *Beowulf* is thus already complete within the Germanic heroic ethos.

Smithers has arrived at his interpretation by examining the recurrence and context of words for 'destiny' and 'courage' throughout the poem. In a couple of earlier papers I had arrived at a somewhat similar account of the role of 'historic destiny' in the meaning of the poem: in one of these I viewed *Beowulf* comparatively with other epics and tragedies, to suggest a horizon of expectations of 'epic tragedy', in the other I focused more narrowly upon the feuds of the historic matter in the second part of the poem. [41] Mrs Goldsmith has arrived at her interpretation by seeing Hrothgar's homily as structurally central to the poem and needing intellectual and aesthetic fulfilment in the subsequent actions of the hero: she has focused upon the fight with the dragon/Dragon (as she sees it) as that literal and allegorical fulfilment, relegating the human feuds of the historical material to a secondary position. (It is of some interest that her index devotes one-third of a column to the item 'Devil' and less than two lines to 'feuds': one might reasonably ask whether, in terms of the text itself, this emphasis is not slightly disproportionate.) And, as I have remarked again and again, she uses 'similarities' with scriptural and patristic material to carry a large burden of her proof. Rollinson has taken the broad generic approach of medieval exemplary fiction, allowing symbolic, as distinct from allegorical, overtones to enhance the poem's meaning. Clearly we have here choices of different foci and of different relevant contexts, a matter we have raised earlier.

To deal adequately with *Beowulf*, one would need to take account of many other analyses, historically and/or aesthetically oriented, which have shed new, if sometimes murky, light on the poem in the past half-century—and this would require a monograph unto itself. I have merely used these three recent commentaries as illustrative of the wide range of views that would see *Beowulf* steadily and see it whole. My concern has been to indicate doubt about the validity of the current quest for allegory among critics, and their certitude of historical propriety which they invoke for this generic quest. I have at various points expressed my belief that there are methodological and logical fallacies in this critical approach, and have tried, by a few examples, to show that references to the text itself indicate the inadequacy or unreliability of supposed 'proof'. I might add that not the least of difficulties with an allegorical approach is that different critics in that vein arrive at diametrically opposed interpretations of the same image or act. Mrs Goldsmith, as we have seen earlier, sees the treasure hoard, for example, as an image of cupidity, a diabolical illusion that has tempted Beowulf's soul, and its re-burial as symbolic of its intrinsic worthlessness. But Charles Donahue sees the hoard as a means by which Beowulf advances towards Christian charity in his speech of thanksgiving for having achieved it, and he sees the re-burial as a 'sacrifice' on his people's part, an 'imitation' of Beowulf (-Christ)'s charity![42] It is no consolation in these circumstances to be told that one and the same image could have contradictory meanings in medieval exegesis.

There are difficulties with *Beowulf* as we have it; but so are there with *Hamlet* and with countless other literary masterpieces. Recognition of different strata in the extant poem may help us understand why some of the difficulties exist and suggest several generic expectations that should be weighed in the balance in determining meaning. There are, for example, folktale and myth which several observers have pieced out in the oral background of the poem.[43] We can recognize, with Smithers and others, the heroic point of view that is surely a central element in the meaning of *Beowulf*. We can also admit the explicit 'scripturizing', like having the scop in Heorot paraphrase Genesis, the placing of Grendel in the race of Cain, and Hrothgar's sermon; and the 'monotheizing' of Hrothgar and Beowulf—features which align the pagan perspective with Christian story and ethic. Perhaps we can call this level a *conscious processing*, whereby the received material has been adapted by the Christian poet—something akin to 'intention' but focusing not on the mind of the poet but upon the facts of the poem. At this level the poem is obviously exemplary, and its last words, even if reporting what Beowulf's men said about him and not being a direct comment of the poet's, are surely indicative of its meaning: Beowulf during his life demonstrated that he was the 'best of men of worldly kings'. There is no irony here. Beowulf's life is one worthy of imitation in this world. Anglo-Saxon poets were not shy when it came to expressing explicitly the superior values of the heavenly kingdom to the earthly at the conclusions of their poems. That the poem ends as it does is generically appropriate, and to try to see irony or a double perspective is to import dubious criteria into the criticism. For example, it is not convincing to argue that Wiglaf's statement that he and his men could not persuade Beowulf to leave the dragon alone is suggestive of the ironic view the poet wishes us to take of Beowulf's courage in his last fight; for the fact is that Hygelac, likewise, had tried to dissuade the hero from his earlier fight with Grendel! Both statements are *ex post facto*. Courage is courage, and to determine the essence of its value by the outcome of the conflict is perverse: the readiness is all, and Beowulf is exemplary in this respect as the best man among worldly kings.

At another level, beyond what I have called the conscious processing, there are overtones of meaning such as Rollinson and others would allow, symbolism as distinct from allegory. Such enrichment is possible, but, to revert to E. D. Hirsch's stricture (chapter 1), we must not conflate different texts as if they were one and the same. Margaret Goldsmith herself says, in refuting Father McNamee's allegorical interpretation of the poem as a Harrowing of Hell, that 'each reader must discover for himself how far the recollection of the great Pauline images seem to give perspective to the story of Beowulf'.[44] But effective criticism eschews the entirely personal 'discovery', as has been the burden of my song throughout this book.

This exploration of theory and of practice in the analysis of *The Phoenix*, *The Husband's Message* and *Beowulf* indicates that generic expectations have a limited applicability in the interpretation of Old English poems. For one thing, there is the inevitable circularity in the formulation of these expectations, since the interpenetration of 'meaning' of parts and whole, the impingement of one upon the other, is inescapable. When we go outside the poem itself, we are all too likely to try to fit our particular text upon the Procrustean bed of an 'ideal' type. And there has not been sufficient breadth of historical vision about the possibilities of medieval generic expectations from those who advocate and use allegorical exegesis as the supposedly valid way into the meaning of an Old English poem.

The interpretation of poems is at best a precarious business. A steady storm of correspondences flows from critical pens in attempts to bring the broad daylight of understanding to the dark poems of our Anglo-Saxon heritage. But to tell the cave from the winding path, we need to beware of false similitudes and to account for all important expectations and implications involved in the poetic instance. In this book I have by no means exhausted the possibilities for Old English poems. Themes, for example, which have been the object of much recent critical research, are absent from these pages. Inclusiveness has not been my goal, but rather methodology, with sample illustrations of my conception of valid critical procedure. While I do not expect that all readers will agree with all of my specific interpretations, I have at least tried to indicate and to weigh the various expectations and implications entering into each case, from generic considerations to those of word meaning and the implications of form. It is only in this way, I believe, that the critical eye may truly begin to see.

Notes

Chapter 1 Towards a Critical Framework

1 E.g. K. Crossley-Holland, *The Battle of Maldon and Other Old English Poems* (London, 1965), and M. Alexander, *The Earliest English Poems* (Penguin Classics, 1966).

2 E.g. C. L. Wrenn, 'On the Continuity of English Poetry', *Anglia* 76 (1958), 41–59.

3 H. C. Wyld, 'Diction and Imagery in Anglo-Saxon Poetry', *Essays and Studies* 11 (1925); quoted from reprint in *Essential Articles for the Study of Old English Poetry*, ed. J. B. Bessinger, Jun., and S. J. Kahrl, p. 186.

4 See Robertson's essay by this name in *English Institute Essays 1950* (New York, 1951). The term 'historical' is somewhat misleading: to Robertson and his followers it is equivalent only to 'exegetical' or 'allegorical'. For further strictures on the narrowness of the term as used by Robertson *et al.*, see throughout this chapter and particularly the R. S. Crane essay cited in note 49.

5 A. C. Spearing, *Criticism and Medieval Poetry* (London, 1964).

6 B. F. Huppé, *Doctrine and Poetry*.

7 Graham Hough, *An Essay on Criticism*.

8 See Eric Bentley's introduction to *The Importance of Scrutiny* (London, 1964).

9 George Watson, *The Study of Literature* (London, 1969), p. 16.

10 D. W. Robertson, Jun., 'Some Observations on Method in Literary Studies', *New Literary History* 1 (1969), 30–1.

11 M. A. K. Halliday, 'Descriptive Linguistics in Literary Studies', *English Studies Today* (Edinburgh, 1964); quoted from reprint in *Linguistics and Literary Style*, ed. D. C. Freeman (New York, 1970), p. 68. The roots of this new positivism in criticism may be traced back to the Russian Formalists, who 'studied the sound stratum, vowel harmonies, consonant clusters, rhyme, prose rhythm, and meter, leaning heavily on the results of modern linguisitics, its concept of the phoneme and its functional method. They were positivists with a scientific, almost technological ideal of literary scholarship': René Wellek, *Concepts of Criticism* (New Haven and London, 1963), p. 67.

12 On *gyng*, see Spearing, p. 7. On 'The Order of the World', see my review of N. D. Isaacs, *Structural Principles in Old English Poetry* (Knoxville, Tenn., 1968), in *JEGP* 68 (1969), 497.

13 W. K. Wimsatt, *The Verbal Icon*, p. 258.

14 Alain Renoir, 'The Self-Deception of Temptation: Boethian Psychology in *Genesis B*', in *Old English Poetry: Fifteen Essays*, ed. R. P. Creed (Providence, R.I., 1967), p. 65.

15 On the relationship between historic mimesis to modern moral meaning in a work of past literature, see Robert Weimann, 'Past Significance and Present Meaning in Literary History', *New Literary History* 1 (1969), 103.

16 Wimsatt, p. 257.

17 David Daiches, *A Study of Literature for Readers and Critics*, 2nd ed. (London, 1968), p. 79. We should recognize, however, that occasionally technique *is* the value of a poem, as in Donne's 'The Flea' or in the Old English riddle on the bookworm.

18 Wilbur Sanders, *The Dramatist and the Received Idea* (Cambridge, 1968), pp. 319–21.

19 For Gabriel Harvey, see *Pierce's Supererogation: or A New Prayse of the Old Asse* (London, 1593), p. 54; for Fulke Greville, *Life of Sir Philip Sidney* (Oxford, 1907), pp. 14–16. I owe this information to Thelma N. Greenfield.

20 Michael Cherniss, 'The Progress of the Hoard in *Beowulf*', *Phil Q.* 47 (1968), 473–86. He follows a suggestion first made by E. Leisi, 'Gold und Manneswert im *Beowulf*', *Anglia* 71 (1953), 259–73.

21 Margaret E. Goldsmith, *The Mode and Meaning of Beowulf*, pp. 94–6.

22 E. D. Hirsch, Jun., *Validity in Interpretation*, pp. 165–6.

23 Watson, p. 74.

24 Hirsch, pp. 222, 262.

25 Perhaps the earliest such designation is by J. J. Conybeare, in *Illustrations of Anglo-Saxon Poetry*, ed. W. D. Conybeare (London, 1826), p. lxxxi, where 'The Exile's Complaint' (='The Wife's Lament') is said to afford 'the only specimen [in Old English poetry] approaching to the character of the Elegiac ballad'. Cf. also pp. 244–5. Of some interest is the fact that the most famous of the elegies, *The Wanderer* and *The Seafarer*, were not recognized by Conybeare as such, but thought to be, following Wanley's account, part of 'a metrical Homily, treating on the doctrines of Theology': p. 204.

26 On *Deor* as a charm, see Morton Bloomfield, 'The Form of *Deor*', *PMLA* 79 (1964), 534–41; as a begging poem, see Norman E. Eliason, 'Two Old English Scop Poems', *PMLA* 81 (1966), 185–92,

and '*Deor*—a Begging Poem?' in *Medieval Literature and Civiliza-tion*, ed. D. A. Pearsall and R. A. Waldron (London, 1969), pp. 55–61. On *The Husband's Message* as allegory, see Robert E. Kaske, 'A Poem of the Cross in The Exeter Book: "Riddle 60" and "The Husband's Message"', *Traditio* 23 (1967), 41–71; for comments on this interpretation, see later in this chapter and in chapter 6. On *The Wanderer* and *The Seafarer* as allegories, see, e.g. G. V. Smithers, 'The Meaning of *The Seafarer* and *The Wanderer*', *Medium Ævum* 26 (1957), 137–53, and 28 (1959), 99–104; as penitential poems, see P. L. Henry, *The Early English and Celtic Lyric* (London, 1966); as wisdom literature, see Morton Bloomfield, 'Understanding Old English Poetry', *Annuale Mediaevale* 9 (1968), 5–25; as debate, see, e.g., John C. Pope, 'Dramatic Voices in *The Wanderer* and *The Seafarer*', in *Franciplegius: Medieval and Linguistic Studies in Honor of F. P. Magoun, Jr.*, ed. J. B. Bessinger, Jun., and R. P. Creed (New York and London, 1965), pp. 164–93. On the earlier interpretation of *Wulf and Eadwacer* as a riddle, see, e.g., H. M. Rieger, 'Über Cynewulf', *Zeitschrift für deutsche Philologie* 1 (1869), 215–19. On *The Wife's Lament* as a masculine rather than feminine monologue, see, e.g., Martin Stevens, 'The Narrator of *The Wife's Lament*', *NM* 69 (1968), 72–90. On all these poems as elegies, see my essay 'The Old English Elegies', in *Continuations and Beginnings: Studies in Old English Literature*, ed. E. G. Stanley, pp. 142–75.

27 Hirsch, pp. 44–102, 235–8.

28 On 'intentional fallacy', see the essay by that name in Wimsatt's *Verbal Icon*. For a brief but engaging discussion of these matters, see the chapter on 'Intention and Personality' in Hough's *Essay on Criticism*.

29 Hirsch, pp. 230, 238.

30 Ibid., pp. 239–40.

31 F. W. Bateson, *English Poetry: A Critical Introduction* (London, 1950), pp. 33–4.

32 Geoffrey H. Hartman, *Wordsworth's Poetry, 1787–1814* (New Haven, 1964), pp. 159–61.

33 Cf. D. G. Calder, 'Setting and Mode in *The Seafarer* and *The Wanderer*', *NM* 72 (1971), 264–75.

34 Hirsch, p. 126, note 37. This stricture applies to some degree even in the use of seminal terms by the same author in different poems, for as M. Riffaterre comments, one of the plagues of literary criticism is 'the proclivity to assume that a key word or verbal obses-sion must always have the same meaning for the author . . .': see his 'Describing Poetic Structures: Two Approaches to Baudelaire's *Les Chats*', *Yale French Studies* 36–37 (1966)–239.

35 Goldsmith, pp. 231–5.
36 Peter Clemoes, '*Mens absentia cogitans* in *The Seafarer* and *The Wanderer*', in *Medieval Literature and Civilization* (see note 26), pp. 62–73.
37 Ibid., pp. 63–4.
38 Ibid., p. 64.
39 Ibid., pp. 67–8.
40 Ibid., p. 72.
41 F. J. Sheed, *The Confessions of St. Augustine* (New York, 1943), p. 219.
42 Kaske (see note 26), p. 57.
43 E. B. Irving, Jun., 'Image and Meaning in the Elegies', in *Old English Poetry: Fifteen Essays* (see note 14), p. 154.
44 John Huntley, 'A Practical Look at E. D. Hirsch's *Validity in Interpretation*', *Genre* 1 (1968), 250.
45 Murray Krieger, *A Window to Criticism* (Princeton, 1964), pp. 15–16. Not all puns, I would hasten to add, establish such an 'elementing' semantic identity: many simply call attention to multiple meanings residing in a word where ordinarily one meaning is indicated by context, and others simply overlay one word's meaning with that of another phonetically similar word.
46 Ibid., pp. 29, 31.
47 Cf. Ibid., p. 64.
48 See Robert L. Allen, 'The Structure of Meaning', *Proceedings of the Ninth International Congress of Linguists* (Cambridge, Mass., 1962), pp. 421–6.
49 This chapter had been written and typed in final form when I belatedly discovered R. S. Crane's excellent essay 'On Hypotheses in "Historical Criticism": Apropos of Certain Contemporary Medievalists' in his *The Idea of the Humanities and Other Essays Critical and Historical*, II, pp. 236–59. Many of my points are made there in somewhat different terms, and I should like to cite a few of his statements about interpretational hypotheses in general. For one, he cautions that statistical probability 'applies only to classes of things and never to individuals within those classes. Although such probabilities are useful in inventing hypotheses, they cannot properly be given any deciding weight in our inquiries into particular matters of fact in history or literary criticism; these have to do wholly with individual happenings and productions . . .' (p. 240). For another, he inveighs against what he calls 'the doctrine of the sufficiency of positive corroboration' (p. 241), which he rightly says 'patently governs the practice of many literary scholars and of perhaps a majority of those who publish "interpretations" of texts'. This

doctrine leads to circularity in our criticism, and what is needed is
' a strong will to *dis*believe our own as well as other people's conjectures until, after a serious independent examination of the facts, that disbelief is no longer rationally possible' (pp. 243–4). 'The ideal', he continues, 'is to be able to say . . . about any interpretation of a given text, not merely that *if* its author's intention was such-and-such, he might very well have written as he did—that is still only hypothesis— but that *only if* his intention was such-and-such would he in all probability have written as he did' (p. 244).

50 A. E. Housman, 'The Application of Thought to Textual Criticism', quoted from F. R. Patterson, *Ben Jonson's Conversations with William Drummond of Hawthornden* (London, 1923), p. xlii.

51 I. A. Richards, 'Jakobson's Shakespeare: the Subliminal Structures of a Sonnet', *TLS* 28 May 1970, p. 590. A somewhat similar point is made by W. O. Hendricks in an interesting essay 'Three Models for the Description of Poetry', *Journal of Linguistics* 5 (1969), 1–2.

Chapter 2 Expectations and Implications in Diction and Formula

1 On the give and take between 'determinate meaning' and 'determinate metre' in the composition of a poem see section from J. C. Ransom's *The New Criticism* (1941) reprinted as 'Wanted: An Ontological Critic', in *Essays on the Language of Literature*, ed. S. Chapman and S. R. Levin (Boston, 1967), pp. 269–82.

2 The latest review of the formulaic situation may be found in A. C. Watts, *The Lyre and the Harp* (New Haven and London, 1969).

3 R. F. Lawrence, 'The Formulaic Theory and its Application to English Alliterative Poetry', in *Essays on Style and Language*, ed. Roger Fowler (London, 1966), pp. 177–8.

4 See, for example, Larry D. Benson, 'The Literary Character of Anglo-Saxon Formulaic Poetry', *PMLA* 81 (1966), 334–41.

5 *ELH* 26 (1959), 445–54. Creed's essay has been reprinted in at least three recent critical anthologies.

6 Ibid., p. 448.

7 Cf. R. L. Rogers, 'The Crypto-Psychological Character of the Oral Formula', *English Studies* 47 (1966), 89–102. Indeed, in this case it *does* evaporate, for if *þa* remains a constant, the only choice open to the poet was one of individual words; cf. Watts, pp. 74ff.

8 Creed, note 10.

9 See Klaeber's ed. of *Beowulf*, p. lxvi, on copulative alliterative phrases. The MS. reading, it should be noted, is *un hár*.

10 Cf. J. B. Hainsworth's conclusions about Homeric formulaic verse,

in *The Flexibility of the Homeric Formula* (Oxford, 1968), p. 128: '... even at the humbler level of the traditional diction there is ample room for virtuosity and skill or their opposites. The language may be flat or vigorous, dextrous or cumbersome'.

11 Fred C. Robinson makes an interesting case for translating *synsnædum* as 'with sinful morsels' in his 'Lexicography and Literary Criticism: A Caveat', in *Philological Essays in Honour of H. D. Merritt*, ed. J. L. Rosier (The Hague, 1970), pp. 102–5.

12 Donald K. Fry, 'Some Aesthetic Implications of a New Definition of the Formula', *NM* 69 (1968), 522.

13 E. G. Stanley, 'Old English Poetic Diction and the Interpretation of *The Wanderer, The Seafarer* and *The Penitent's Prayer*', *Anglia* 73 (1955); quoted from *Essential Articles for the Study of Old English Poetry*, ed. J. B. Bessinger, Jun., and S. J. Kahrl, pp. 476–7.

14 D. C. Collins, 'Kenning in Anglo-Saxon Poetry', *Essays and Studies*, n.s. 12 (1959), 17; William Whallon, 'The Diction of *Beowulf*', *PMLA* 76 (1961), 310.

15 S. B. Greenfield, 'The Formulaic Expression of the Theme of "Exile" in Anglo-Saxon Poetry', *Speculum* 30 (1955), 205.

16 Robinson, p. 99.

17 Ibid., pp. 101–2. A case parallel to that offered here on *lofgeornost* may be seen in the interpretation of the word *ofermod* in *The Battle of Maldon*, line 89: for an interesting argument against acceptance of the *BTD* meaning assigned *ofermod* here, and of the meaning assigned the unique *lytegian* (line 86) which is contextually related, see George Clark, '*The Battle of Maldon*: A Heroic Poem', *Speculum* 43 (1968), 52–71.

18 E. G. Stanley, 'Hæthenra Hyht in *Beowulf*', in *Studies in Old English Literature in Honor of A. G. Brodeur*, ed. S. B. Greenfield (Eugene, Ore., 1963), pp. 148–9.

19 In cases like this, one cannot really call upon the evidence in other Germanic languages. Although the OHG cognate *lob-gerni* glosses *iactantia* in a Notker gloss, there is a balancing appearance of the adjective used substantivally in the *Brot af Sigurðkviða* referring favourably to Sigurd as 'the seeker of glory'. The Old Icelandic adjective *lofgjarnligr*, and the simplices *lof* and *gjarn*, always seem to have favourable connotations, too. I should like to acknowledge a long and useful communication on the Old Icelandic uses from Mr Rory McTurk, of University College, Dublin.

20 Margaret E. Goldsmith, *The Mode and Meaning of Beowulf*, p. 224.

21 Robert E. Kaske, '*Sapientia et Fortitudo* as the Controlling Theme of *Beowulf*', *Studies in Philology* 55 (1958), 446–7.

22 See I. L. Gordon (ed.), *The Seafarer* (London, 1960), p. 41, note.

23 G. V. Smithers, 'The Meaning of *The Seafarer* and *The Wanderer:* Appendix', *Medium Ævum* 28 (1959), 103–4.

24 *Beowulf with the Finnsburg Fragment*, ed. A. J. Wyatt, revised by R. W. Chambers (Cambridge, 1914), p. 162.

25 Klaeber's edition of *Beowulf*, pp. 252–3.

26 See E. V. K. Dobbie, *The Anglo-Saxon Minor Poems* (*ASPR* VI) (New York, 1942), p. xvii; E. von Schaubert, *Heyne-Schückings Beowulf*, II, 15th ed. (Paderborn, 1961), p. 184. The commentator is William Whallon in his *Formula, Character, and Context* (Cambridge, Mass., 1969), p. 104.

27 E.g., H. Schilling, 'The Finnsburg-fragment and the Finn-episode', *MLN* 2 (1887), 146–50; M. Rieger, 'Zum Kampf in Finnsburg', *Zeitschrift für deutsches Altertum* 48 (1905–6), 12.

28 I suspect that the 'horizon of expectations' established by our notion of a poem's genre misleads us more often than we realize. Robinson furnishes another instance in the case of *scealcas* applied to the Vikings in *Maldon*, line 181. It is our desire to see the poet vilify the 'bad guys', he suggests, that has led us to acquiesce unthinkingly in the *BTD* ascription of 'a term of reproach' for the word *scealc* here, although in all other usages it means 'man, soldier, sailor, servant'; and all other epithets for the Vikings in *Maldon* 'seem curiously restrained and dispassionate'. If we were not thus misdirected, we would realize that the essential conflict in the poem is 'the tensions within the English ranks' and not one 'between virtuous Englishmen and evil Vikings'. Robinson, p. 100.

29 E.g., S. Bugge, 'Studien über das Beowulfepos', *Beiträge zur Geschichte der deutschen Sprache und Literatur* 12 (1887), 28; M. Trautmann, *Finn und Hildebrand*, Bonner Beiträge zur Anglistik 7 (1903), pp. 61–2.

30 S. B. Greenfield, 'The Canons of Old English Criticism', *ELH* 34 (1967), 146–8; Whallon, *Formula*, p. 107.

31 On collocation, congruity and complementarity, see Randolph Quirk, 'Poetic Language and Old English Metre', in *Early English and Norse Studies*, ed. A. Brown and P. Foote (London, 1963), pp. 150–71.

32 See note 21.

33 On *mægen* in this passage, Gordon comments that it 'probably refers to bodily strength, which grows weaker (*lytlað*) from wounds and exhaustion; but the word might refer to the English force which is steadily diminishing'. *The Battle of Maldon*, ed. E. V. Gordon (London, 1933, 1957), p. 61. Perhaps both meanings are 'intended'?

34 Henry L. Savage, *The Gawain-Poet* (University of North Carolina Press, 1956), pp. 37–8.

35 A. C. Spearing, *Criticism and Medieval Poetry* (London, 1964), p. 23.
36 E. B. Irving, Jun., 'The Heroic Style of *The Battle of Maldon*', *Studies in Philology* 58 (1961), 460.
37 E. V. Gordon, p. 45.

Chapter 3 The Uses of Variation

1 Cf. R. F. Leslie, 'Analysis of Stylistic Devices and Effects in Anglo-Saxon Literature', in *Stil- und Formprobleme in der Literatur*, ed. P. Böckmann (Heidelberg, 1959); quoted from reprint in *Old English Literature: Twenty-Two Analytical Essays*, ed. M. Stevens and J. Mandel (Lincoln, Nebr., 1968), p. 75.
2 W. K. Wimsatt, 'When is Variation "Elegant"?' from his *The Verbal Icon*, pp. 187–99.
3 Ibid., pp. 190–1. It is amusing to compare a similar but somewhat biased account of Old English variation that Conybeare gave one and a half centuries ago: '. . . the constant accumulation of equivalent, or nearly equivalent, words and phrases, which, as it generally constitutes the chief and earliest ornament of the poetry of rude and illiterate nations, appears in that of our Saxon ancestors to have supplied almost entirely the place of those higher graces and resources of composition, which are the natural results of a more advanced state of civil society, and a more extended range of information': J. J. Conybeare, *Illustrations of Anglo-Saxon Poetry*, ed. W. D. Conybeare (London, 1826), p. xxviii.
4 Ibid., p. 197.
5 Arthur G. Brodeur, *The Art of Beowulf* (Berkeley, 1959), p. 40.
6 E.g., Fred C. Robinson, 'Variation: A Study in the Diction of *Beowulf*' (Univ. of North Carolina diss., 1962), and W. Paetzel, *Die Variationen in der altgermanischen Alliterationspoesie*, Palaestra 48 (Berlin, 1913), would insist on the necessity for parallelism; Leslie and Brodeur, in the works cited above, would not.
7 Robinson, p. 18.
8 Brodeur, p. 279.
9 For an extensive and exhaustive categorization, see S. Colliander *Parallelismus im Heliand* (Lund, 1912).
10 Brodeur, p. 273; Whitney F. Bolton, ' "Variation" in *The Battle of Brunanburh*', *RES*, n.s. 19 (1968), 364.
11 Brodeur, p. 274.
12 Robinson, p. 82, note 98.
13 Caroline Brady, 'The Synonyms for "Sea" in *Beowulf*', in *Studies in*

Honor of A. M. Sturtevant (Lawence, Kans., 1952), p. 28; Robinson, p. 122, note 57.

14 Robert K. Gordon, *Anglo-Saxon Poetry* (London, 1926), p. 352; B. J. Timmer (ed.), *Judith*, 2nd ed. (London, 1961), glossary; R. N. Ringler, '*Him sēo wēn gelēah:* the Design for Irony in Grendel's Last Visit to Heorot', *Speculum* 41 (1966), 55, note 18.

15 Angus Fletcher, *Allegory: the Theory of a Symbolic Mode* (Ithaca, 1964), p. 117.

16 See my *A Critical History of Old English Literature*, pp. 139–40, and Rosemary Woolf, 'Doctrinal Influences on *The Dream of the Rood*', *Medium Ævum* 27 (1958), 151–2.

17 Paetzel, p. 123.

18 Bolton, p. 366.

19 On p. 371, Bolton does refer to this passage as indicating the sun's rise, transit and setting. I am indebted to a conversation with Dr G. C. Britton for convincing me of the viability of seeing variation in passages exhibiting movement.

20 Bolton, p. 371. The interpretation I have given above is my own, but cf. P. B. Taylor, 'Heroic Ritual in the Old English *Maxims*', *NM* 70 (1969), 406.

21 Robinson, p. 90.

22 Leslie, pp. 76–7.

23 On *ac* meaning 'for' as well as 'but', see P. J. Cosijn, *Aanteekeningen op den Béowulf* (Leiden, 1892), p. 22.

24 *The Complete Poetical Works of Spenser*, ed. R. E. Neil Dodge (Cambridge, 1908), p. 223.

25 Ruth Wallerstein, *Richard Crashaw: A Study in Style and Poetic Development* (Madison, 1935), p. 69.

Chapter 4 The Play of Sound and Sense

1 William Empson, *Seven Types of Ambiguity*, 3rd ed. (London, 1963), p. 1.

2 Fred C. Robinson, 'Lexicography and Literary Criticism: A Caveat', in *Philological Essays in Honour of H. D. Meritt*, ed. J. L. Rosier, p. 107. For an excellent discussion of puns in the Latin riddles of the Anglo-Saxons, see E. von Erhardt-Siebold, *Die lateinische Rätsel der Angelsachsen* (Heidelberg, 1925), index under *Worstpiel*.

3 Marijane Osborn, 'Some Uses of Ambiguity in *Beowulf*', *Thoth* 10 (1969), 18–19.

4 See Dorothy Bethurum, 'Wulfstan', in *Continuations and Beginnings*, ed. E. G. Stanley (London, 1966), p. 233.

5 *Anglo-Saxon Riddles of the Exeter Book* (Durham, N.C., 1963).
6 C. L. Wrenn, *A Study of Old English Literature*, p. 175.
7 M. J. Swanton, 'Ambiguity and Anticipation in "The Dream of the Rood"', *NM* 70 (1969), 407–25.
8 Ibid., pp. 421–2.
9 Empson, p. 58.
10 P. B. Taylor, 'Heroic Ritual in the Old English *Maxims*', *NM* 70 (1969), 398–9, note.
11 Osborn, p. 27.
12 'Ellipsis and Meaning in Poetry', *Texas Studies in Literature and Language* 13 (Spring 1971), 142.
13 Osborn, p. 34.
14 Neil D. Isaacs, 'The Convention of Personification in *Beowulf*', in *Old English Poetry: Fifteen Essays*, ed. R. P. Creed (Providence, R.I., 1967), pp. 215–48.
15 Robinson, 'Lexicography', p. 106.
16 Ibid., p. 107.
17 B. F. Huppé, *The Web of Words* (State University of New York Press, 1970), pp. 160–1.
18 Ibid., p. 161.
19 *Judith*, ed. B. J. Timmer, 2nd ed. (London, 1961), p. 19.
20 *ASPR* IV, p. 282.
21 Fred C. Robinson, 'The Significance of Names in Old English Literature', *Anglia* 86 (1968), 45.
22 Ibid., p. 52.
23 Ibid., p. 58.
24 Morton Bloomfield, '*Beowulf* and Christian Allegory: an Interpretation of Unferth', *Traditio* 7 (1949–51); quoted from reprint in *The Beowulf Poet*, ed. D. K. Fry (Englewood Cliffs, N.J., 1968), p. 69.
25 Ibid., p. 69.
26 Klaeber's ed., p. 148.
27 T. Forssner, *Continental-Germanic Personal Names in England, in Old and Middle English Times* (Uppsala, 1916), p. 236, note.
28 Osborn, p. 21. She also accepts the 'mar-peace' etymology.
29 See Kenneth Sisam, *The Structure of Beowulf*, pp. 40–3, for a denial of this treacherous implication.
30 H. B. Woolf, 'Unferth', *MLQ* 10 (1949), 146.
31 Sisam, p. 41.
32 E.g., J. L. Rosier, 'Design for Treachery: the Unferth Intrigue', *PMLA* 77 (1962), 1–7.
33 Sisam, p. 41.
34 See E. Förstemann, *Altdeutsches Namenbuch*, 2nd ed., vol. 1 (Bonn, 1900), p. 930.

35 Bloomfield, 'Unferth', p. 74.
36 Margaret Goldsmith makes the point, *contra* Bloomfield, that 'as Prudentius is thinking in terms of schism and heresy within the Church, the connection is not very likely': *Mode and Meaning*, p. 76, note 2.

Chapter 5 Verse Form, Syntax and Meaning

1 See my article 'Grammar and Meaning in Poetry', *PMLA* 82 (1967), 377–87, and my remarks at the end of chapter 1 of this book. For some attempts of grammatical-critical correlation see *Linguistics and Literary Style*, ed. D. C. Freeman (New York, 1970), and R. K. Fowler, *The Languages of Literature*.
2 See Noam Chomsky, 'Deep Structure, Surface Structure, and Semantic Interpretation', mimeo sheets reproduced by the Indiana University Linguistics Club (January 1969), p. 23 and passim. Not all such surface-structure differences reflect different semantic emphases, however: though Chomsky, e.g., says of the two sentences '(i) the sonata is easy to play on this violin' and '(ii) this violin is easy to play the sonata on' that 'These sentences share a single system of grammatical relations and, in some reasonable sense of paraphrase, may be regarded as paraphrases; they have the same truth conditions for example. However, they seem different in meaning in that one makes an assertion about the sonata, and the other about the violin' (p. 30), I think he is wrong. Both sentences are, despite differences in grammatical subjects, making assertions about the violin. The whole subject of semantic-syntactic relationships is unsettled, however, and the subject of recent interest, and dispute, among linguists; see, e.g., W. L. Chafe, *Meaning and the Structure of Language* (Chicago, 1970). I wish to thank Roger Fowler for the references to Chafe and Chomsky.
3 M. B. Emeneau, 'Style and Meaning in an Oral Literature', *Language* 42 (1966), 343.
4 J. B. Bessinger, '*Maldon* and the *Óláfsdrápa*: An Historical Caveat', *Compararative Literature* 14 (1962), 28–9; also in *Studies in Old English Literature in Honor of A. G. Brodeur*, ed. S. B. Greenfield (Eugene, Ore., 1963).
5 Winifred Nowottny, *The Language Poets Use*, p. 10.
6 See William O. Hendricks, 'Three Models for the Description of Poetry', *Journal of Linguistics* 5 (1969), 1–22.
7 Lydia Fakundiny, 'The Art of Old English Verse Composition', *RES*, n.s. 21 (1970), 261. On 'Kuhn's Law' about the placement of particles in Old English verse, see Desmond Slay, 'Some Aspects of

the Technique of Composition in Old English Verse', *Transactions of the Philological Society 1952*, pp. 1–4.

8 Fakundiny, p. 262.

9 Ibid., p. 264.

10 Ibid., p. 262.

11 Cf. M. Riffaterre, 'Criteria for Style Analysis', *Word* 15 (1959), 154–74, and 'Stylistic Context', ibid. 16 (1960), 207–18. J. P. Thorne goes so far as to suggest that we must postulate an independent grammar, an independent language, for each poem, a suggestion which seems to oppose Halliday's idea about the necessity for reading each poem against the background of the language as a whole (see *supra*). Thorne, 'Stylistics and generative grammar', *Journal of Linguistics* 1 (1965), p. 58.

12 Randolph Quirk, 'Poetic Language and Old English Metre', in *Early English and Norse Studies*, ed. A. Brown and P. Foote (London, 1963), pp. 150–71.

13 *The Wanderer*, ed. T. P. Dunning and A. J. Bliss.

14 *The Wanderer*, ed. R. F. Leslie (Manchester, 1966).

15 Cf. Bliss–Dunning, p. 110.

16 Bruce Mitchell, 'Some Syntactical Problems in *The Wanderer*', *NM* 69 (1968), 182–7.

17 On the position of the verb in a subordinate clause, see R. Quirk and C. L. Wrenn, *An Old English Grammar*, 2nd ed. (London, 1958), p. 94.

18 A. G. Brodeur, *The Art of Beowulf*, p. 90.

19 Alain Renoir, 'Point of View and Design for Terror in *Beowulf*', *NM* 63 (1962), 154–67.

20 Quirk, 'Poetic Language', p. 159.

21 Cf. Brodeur, p. 90.

22 The verse seems to combine two formulas: those with *bær* taking a direct object usually have an ale cup or a battle sark as the object (cf. *Beowulf*, ll. 1982, 2021, 2539). The two occasions on which *Godes yrre* is used apart from the present one refer to Adam and Eve and use the verb *habban* (*Genesis*, ll. 408b, 695b–96a).

23 On formulas of deprivation, see my 'The Formulaic Expression of the Theme of "Exile" in Anglo-Saxon Poetry', *Speculum* 30 (1955), 202, 205.

24 *Duru* is linked metrically (alliteratively) with *dreamum bedæled* in the line, suggesting the misery that is to befall the hall itself, as well as one of Beowulf's warriors.

25 R. N. Ringler, '*Him sēo wēn gelēah*: the Design for Irony in Grendel's Last Visit to Heorot', *Speculum* 41 (1966), 53.

26 Cf. ibid., p. 58.

Chapter 6   Generic Expectations and the Quest for Allegory

1 Margaret E. Goldsmith, *The Mode and Meaning of Beowulf*, p. 79.
2 Robert E. Kaske, 'A Poem of the Cross in The Exeter Book: "Riddle 60" and "The Husband's Message"', *Traditio* 23 (1967), 41–71.
3 See my review of *The Wanderer*, ed. T. P. Dunning and A. J. Bliss, in *Notes & Queries* (March, 1970), pp. 114–15.
4 See the discussion of riddles in my *A Critical History of Old English Literature*, pp. 204ff.
5 See James L. Rosier, 'Death and Transfiguration: *Guthlac B*', in *Philological Essays in Honour of H. D. Meritt*, ed. J. L. Rosier (The Hague, 1970), pp. 82–92.
6 Both Pilch's and my definitions and descriptions of the genre 'elegy' are of this sort: Herbert Pilch, 'The Elegiac Genre in Old English and Early Welsh Poetry', *Zeitschrift für celtische Philologie* 29 (1964), 209–24; S. B. Greenfield, 'The Old English Elegies', in *Continuations and Beginnings*, ed. E. G. Stanley, pp. 147–72.
7 E.g., Angus Fletcher, *Allegory: the Theory of a Symbolic Mode* (Ithaca, N.Y., 1964); Edwin Honig, *Dark Conceit: the Making of Allegory* (London, 1960).
8 Goldsmith, p. 76.
9 William Whallon, *Formula, Character, and Context* (Washington, D.C., 1969), pp. 117–38.
10 Cited from Goldsmith, p. 66.
11 Philip Rollinson, 'Some Kinds of Meaning in Old English Poetry', *Annuale Mediaevale* 11 (1970), 5–21. For an equally illuminating, but different kind of challenge to the *ex cathedra* pronouncements of Robertsonian 'historicism', see R. S. Crane's essay 'On Hypotheses in "Historical Criticism": Apropos of Certain Contemporary Medievalists', cited in note 49 of chapter 1.
12 Rollinson, p. 7.
13 R. S. Crane, *The Languages of Criticism and the Structure of Poetry* (Toronto, 1953), pp. 184–5.
14 Rollinson, pp. 12–13.
15 J. E. Cross, 'The Conception of the Old English *Phoenix*', in *Old English Poetry: Fifteen Essays*, ed. R. P. Creed (Providence, R.I., 1967), p. 139.
16 The text of *The Phoenix* used in this chapter is that of N. F. Blake (ed.), *The Phoenix* (Manchester, 1964).
17 Cross, pp. 135–6.
18 Geoffrey Shepherd, 'Scriptural Poetry', in *Continuations and Beginnings*, p. 15.

19 Cross, p. 135.
20 Blake, p. 20.
21 Ibid., p. 81.
22 J. S. Kantrowitz, 'The Anglo-Saxon *Phoenix* and Tradition', *Philological Quarterly* 43 (1964), 13.
23 Blake, p. 29.
24 Kaske, p. 70.
25 *Three Old English Elegies*, ed. R. F. Leslie (Manchester, 1961).
26 Kaske, p. 43. I have substituted for the line numbers Kaske uses (he makes *Riddle 60* part of the poem), those in the Leslie text above.
27 Kaske, p. 46.
28 *ASPR* III, p. 362.
29 On the whole matter of the difficulties in this problem, see Leslie, pp. 13–15.
30 Although Kaske is quite positive about the manuscript's reading *genyre* by virtue of ultra-violet photograph, I am not entirely convinced from my examination of the reproduction of that photograph with his article 'The Reading *genyre* in *The Husband's Message* Line 49', *Medium Ævum* 33 (1964), 204–6: the photograph faces p. 169.
31 R. F. Leslie, 'The Integrity of Riddle 60', *JEGP* 67 (1968), 451–7. See also F. H. Whitman, 'Riddle 60 and Its Sources', *Philological Quarterly* 50 (1971), 108–15.
32 While we cannot attach the Old English elegies in verse form or substance to those Latin poems called 'elegies', the classical grammarians recognized the suitability of couplets (instead of the heroic hexameter) for sad and sorrowful themes, which sometimes (as in Ovid's *Heroides*) related to heroic conflict and courage. Isidore of Seville recognizes this genre, too, in his *Etymologiae* I, xxxix. 14–15. Philip Rollinson, to whom I am greatly indebted for a long and thorough discussion of the possible lines of development of the genre *elegy*, comments, in a personal letter to me, that the Old English elegy 'was probably considered to be an excursus into various kinds of sad, thought-provoking sentiment-recalling, situations of the human condition. The situations involved, which occasion the sad remarks, may be taken as exemplary of the human condition, and the sad reflections themselves are typical responses to life's problems, transitory nature, tragedies or whatever, remarks with which the reader or listener will be expected to sympathize, wonder at, or feel a kindred response.' This seems to me to cover the situation of *The Husband's Message* very nicely.
33 For literal readings, see Dorothy Whitelock, 'The Interpretation of *The Seafarer*', in *Early Cultures of North-West Europe*, ed.' C. Fox and B. Dickins (Cambridge, 1950), pp. 261–72; P. L. Henry, *The*

Early English and Celtic Lyric (London, 1966). Daniel Calder makes a cogent argument against reading *The Wanderer* in any way other than literal, by comparing its structural setting and mode with those of *The Seafarer*. In his concluding paragraphs he states that 'Unlike *The Seafarer*, . . ., the structural pattern in the setting constitutes, in itself, the mode of *The Wanderer* and cannot be extrapolated to some other plane where one can construct an allegory . . . Nothing inherent in the structure of *The Wanderer* requires an allegorical reading, for the pattern that does exist makes itself immediately applicable to thematic interpretation. Christian didacticism stands by itself and is illustrated plainly by the several contrasts between the mutable and heavenly worlds . . . The recollective manner of the narrator's presentation of his past in *The Wanderer*, as opposed to the active involvement in present circumstances in *The Seafarer*, only heightens this conclusion . . .': D. G. Calder, 'Setting and Mode in *The Seafarer and The Wanderer*', NM 72 (1971), 274–5.

34 Rollinson, p. 14.
35 Ibid., pp. 15–16.
36 Ibid., p. 18.
37 Ælfric, for example, in his *Catholic Homilies*, II, p. 282, makes such an interpretation: see my *Critical History*, p. 50.
38 Rollinson, p. 19.
39 Ibid., pp. 19–20.
40 G. V. Smithers, 'Destiny and the Heroic Warrior in *Beowulf*', in *Philological Studies*, ed. J. L. Rosier, p. 80.
41 '*Beowulf* and Epic Tragedy', *Comparative Literature* 14 (1962), 91–105 (also part of *Studies in Old English Literature in Honor of A. G. Brodeur*, 1963); 'Geatish History: Poetic Art and Epic Quality in *Beowulf*', *Neophilologus* 47 (1963), 211–17.
42 Charles Donahue, '*Beowulf* and Christian Tradition: A Reconsideration from a Celtic Stance', *Traditio* 21 (1965), 107–8, 113.
43 E.g., Daniel R. Barnes, 'Folktale Morphology and the Structure of *Beowulf*', *Speculum* 45 (1970), 416–34; Ursula Dronke, 'Beowulf and Ragnarǫk', *Saga-Book of the Viking Society* 17 (1969), 302–25.
44 Margaret E. Goldsmith, 'The Choice in *Beowulf*', *Neophilologus* 48 (1964), 68.

Select Bibliography

The works mentioned below are but a sample from the many that might have been chosen as guides to the interpretation of Old English poems. I have tried to consider a variety of points of view as well as the variety of topics and approaches with which Old English criticism has concerned itself in modern times. Since this book has attempted to establish a critical framework, I have also listed those general works on criticism and interpretation which I have found most stimulating. The sections on *Beowulf* and *The Wanderer* and *The Seafarer* are designed to be representative not only of critical interpretations of those poems, but of other individual poems as well. For bibliographical leads to such other criticism, see Fred C. Robinson's excellent *Old English Literature: A Select Bibliography* (Toronto, 1970).

I.   General works on criticism:

Crane, R. S., 'On Hypotheses in "Historical Criticism": Apropos of Certain Contemporary Medievalists', in his *The Idea of the Humanities and Other Essays Critical and Historical*, II (Chicago and London, 1967), pp. 236–59. Has broad implications for *all* critical theories and analyses, suggesting limitations we should impose upon our critical flights.

Fowler, Roger, *The Languages of Literature* (London, 1971). In various essays, advocates sanely and soundly some of the ways in which linguistic studies may be useful in literary criticism.

Hirsch, E. D., Jun., *Validity in Interpretation* (New Haven and London, 1967). Theoretical, provocative, difficult in parts. Appendix I provides something of a microcosm of the book in very understandable form. For two insightful reviews, see John Huntley in *Genre* 1 (1968), 242–55, and Joseph Margolis in *Shakespeare Studies* 4 (1968), 407–14.

Hough, Graham, *An Essay on Criticism* (London, 1966). A short, eminently readable inquiry into the principles and problems of the various aspects of literary criticism.

New Literary History, I, No. 1 (October, 1969). Interesting essays relating literature to literary criticism; see especially those by J. M. Cameron ('Problems of Literary History'), D. W. Robertson, Jun.

('Some Observations on Method in Literary Studies'), Hallett Smith ('An Apologie for *Elizabethan Poetry*'), Sears Jayne ('Hallett Smith's Analysis of the Historical Assumptions behind his *Elizabethan Poetry*'), and Robert Weimann ('Past Significance and Present Meaning in Literary History').

Nowottny, Winifred, *The Language Poets Use* (London, 1962). A brilliant, sensitive analysis of the ways in which the elements of poetic language produce their effects.

Wimsatt, W. K., *The Verbal Icon* (Lexington, Ky., 1954; London, 1970). A collection of some of this outstanding modern critic's important studies in the meaning of poetry.

II.   Old English Criticism:

A.   Critical histories:

Greenfield, Stanley B., *A Critical History of Old English Literature* (New York, 1965; London, 1966). See particularly Chapter IV on 'The Nature and Quality of Old English Poetry'.

Wrenn, Charles L., *A Study of Old English Literature* (London, 1967). See especially Chapter 3 on 'Form and Style in Anglo-Saxon Literature'.

B.   Special topics:

Interpretational theory:

Huppé, Bernard F., *Doctrine and Poetry: Augustine's Influence on Old English Poetry* (New York, 1959). Argues for the pervasive influence of Augustinian theory, that the purpose of literature is the promotion of *caritas*, upon Old English poetry.

Rollinson, Philip, 'Some Kinds of Meaning in Old English Poetry', *Annuale Mediaevale* 11 (1970), 5–21. Argues that medieval exegetical theory allowed greater flexibility in the interpretation of poetic genres than the Huppé-Robertson allegorical (or 'historical') approach suggests.

Formula and Theme:

Benson, Larry, D., 'The Literary Character of Anglo-Saxon Formulaic Poetry', *PMLA* 81 (1966), 334–41. Through comparison of poetic translations with their Latin originals, argues, *contra* oral-formulaists, that written OE texts used formulas, and hence formulas are no necessary indication of oral composition.

Greenfield, Stanley B., 'The Canons of Old English Criticism', *ELH* 34 (1967), 141–55. Suggests that neither verbal nor syntactic formulas militate against precision of meaning. (Much of this essay subsumed in this book.)

—'The Formulaic Expression of the Theme of "Exile" in Anglo-Saxon Poetry', *Speculum* 30 (1955), 200–6. Considers the relationship between formulas and theme, between convention and originality in OE poetry.

Magoun, Francis P., Jun., 'Oral-Formulaic Character of Anglo-Saxon Poetry', *Speculum* 28 (1953), 446–67. The seminal essay for modern formulaic studies.

Diction and Variation:

Brodeur, Arthur G., *The Art of Beowulf* (Berkeley, 1959). Chapters I and II provide a very fine analysis of the range and scope of OE diction (including metaphoric expressions like the kenning) and of variation.

Robinson, Fred C., 'Lexicography and Literary Criticism: A Caveat', in *Philological Essays in Honour of H. D. Meritt*, ed. J. L. Rosier (The Hague, 1970), pp. 99–110. Asks critics to be sceptical about certain special dictionary definitions of OE words, and suggests the possibility of hitherto unconsidered aesthetic effects, such as synaesthesia, in OE poetry.

Stanley, Eric G., 'Old English Poetic Diction and the Interpretation of *The Wanderer*, *The Seafarer* and *The Penitent's Prayer*', *Anglia* 73 (1955–6), 413–66. A significant essay whose Part I investigates the nature of OE figurative diction and its relation to 'reality'.

Wyld, Henry C., 'Diction and Imagery in Anglo-Saxon Poetry', Essays and Studies, 11 (1925), 49–91. An overly exuberant and somewhat subjective, but nonetheless suggestive study of the sensibility and imagination of OE diction and imagery.

Style and Metre:

Bartlett, Adeline C., *The Larger Rhetorical Patterns in Anglo-Saxon Poetry* (New York, 1935). A valuable essay suggesting different rhetorical patterns which serve to unify meaningful segments of poems.

Campbell, Jackson J., 'Learned Rhetoric in Old English Poetry', *MP* 63 (1966), 189–201. Shows how OE poets used classical rhetorical figures. See also his article in *JEGP* 66 (1967), 1–20, for a more detailed background study.

Leslie, Roy F., 'Analysis of Stylistic Devices and Effects in Anglo-Saxon Literature', *Stil- und Formprobleme in der Literatur* (Heidelberg, 1959), pp. 129–36. A brief but stimulating discussion of the relation of style and structure in OE poetry.

Quirk, Randolph, 'Poetic Language and Old English Metre', in *Early*

English and Norse Studies. ed. A. Brown and P. Foote (London, 1963), pp. 150–71. Suggests the interrelationship between lexical, syntactic and metrical patterns in OE verse.

Slay, Desmond, 'Some Aspects of the Technique of Composition in Old English Verse', *Transactions of the Philological Society 1952*, pp. 1–14. Makes pertinent points about the syntactic-metrical placing of particles in OE verse.

Conceptual studies:

Cross, James E., 'Aspects of Microcosm and Macrocosm in Old English Literature', *Comparative Literature* 14 (1962), 1–22. Explores the manifestations of the concept in OE literature, relates them to Latin backgrounds, and makes suggestions for interpretations of several poetic cruxes in terms of this concept.

Robinson, Fred C., 'The Significance of Names in Old English Literature', *Anglia* 86 (1968), 14–58. Points up the concept of name meanings, especially etymologies in the exegetical tradition, in the interpretation of OE works. See also *NM* 69 (1968), 161–71.

Timmer, Benno J., 'Wyrd in Anglo-Saxon Prose and Poetry', *Neophilologus* 26 (1940), 24–33, and (1941), 213–28. A thorough exploration of the semantic range of the concept and word *wyrd* in OE literature.

C. Beowulf studies:

Bonjour, Adrien, *The Digressions in Beowulf* (Oxford, 1950). A landmark of critical study showing the artistic unity of the poem.

—*Twelve Beowulf Papers 1940–1960 with Additional Comments* (Neuchatel, 1962). Very perceptive analyses over a wide range of topics from sea images to stylistic and structural techniques to formulas to allegory.

Brodeur, Arthur G., *The Art of Beowulf* (Berkeley, 1959). A very careful and tolerant study of larger and smaller aspects of the poet's artistry.

Donahue, Charles, '*Beowulf* and Christian Tradition: A Reconsideration from a Celtic Stance', *Traditio* 21 (1965), 55–116. A typological interpretation based on an insular mode of Christianity, less rigorous than the Augustinian, in which the hero becomes, ultimately, a *figura* of Christ.

Goldsmith, Margaret E., *The Mode and Meaning of Beowulf* (London, 1970). An Augustinian-Gregorian based allegorical interpretation in which the hero is ultimately less than ideal.

Irving, Edward B., *A Reading of Beowulf* (New Haven, 1968). Uses modern critical approaches, suggesting a somewhat extensive permeation of irony and symbolism in the poem, for example, to heighten our awareness of the poem *qua* poem.

Select Bibliography

Kaske, Robert E., '*Beowulf*', in *Critical Approaches to Six Major English Works*, ed. R. M. Lumiansky and H. Baker (Philadelphia, 1968), pp. 3–40. Presents a convenient summary of previous full-scale interpretations, and then offers its own, which sees the theme *sapientia et fortitudo* as governing the poem's structure and meaning.

Sisam, Kenneth, *The Structure of Beowulf* (Oxford, 1965). A caveat against modern critical efforts to interpret the poem.

Stanley, Eric G., '*Beowulf*', in *Continuations and Beginnings: Studies in Old English Literature*, ed. E. G. Stanley (London, 1966), pp. 104–41. Particularly valuable for its suggestive stylistic analyses.

Tolkien, J. R. R., '*Beowulf*: The Monsters and the Critics', *Proceedings of the British Academy* 22 (1936), 245–95 [reprinted separately, Oxford, 1958, and in several anthologies]. The seminal essay for modern critical interpretations, which considers the poem's broad design as a balance of ends and beginnings and which sees the monsters, in their universal significance, as the proper aesthetic centre of the action.

D.   *The Wanderer* and *The Seafarer*:

The Wanderer, ed. T. P. Dunning and A. J. Bliss (London, 1969). The 104-page introduction is a model attempt to fuse textual, syntactic, semantic, thematic, and cultural approaches in interpretation. For a few reservations, see my review in *Notes and Queries* 215 (1970), 113–16.

Calder, Daniel G., 'Setting and Mode in *The Seafarer* and *The Wanderer*', *NM* 72 (1971), 264–75. Argues that the structure and method of presentation of the latter poem militate against an allegorical interpretation, whereas those of the former open it to such a view.

Cross, James E., 'On the Genre of *The Wanderer*', *Neophilologus* 45 (1961), 63–75. Sees the poem as a *consolatio*.

Greenfield, Stanley B., '*Min.*, *Sylf*. and Dramatic Voices in *The Wanderer* and *The Seafarer*', *JEGP* 68 (1969), 212–20. Argues that Pope's re-structuring of the poems in terms of two 'voices' is unsound.

Pope, John C., 'Dramatic Voices in *The Wanderer* and *The Seafarer*', in *Franciplegius: Medieval and Linguistic Studies in Honor of F. P. Magoun, Jr.*, ed. J. B. Bessinger, Jun., and R. P. Creed (New York, 1965), pp. 164–93. Provides some account of previous theories about structure and meaning in the course of suggesting that the poems are something of a dramatic debate.

Smithers, George V., 'The Meaning of *The Seafarer* and *The Wanderer*', *Medium Ævum* 26 (1957), 137–53, and 28 (1959), 99–104. The most persuasive allegorical interpretation of these poems, at least of the former, through comparisons with homiletic materials.

Stanley, Eric G., 'Old English Poetic Diction and the Interpretation of *The Wanderer, The Seafarer* and *The Penitent's Prayer*', *Anglia* 73 (1955-6), 413-66. Would place the two 'elegies' within the penitential tradition.

Whitelock, Dorothy, 'The Interpretation of *The Seafarer*', in *The Early Cultures of North-West Europe*, ed. Sir Cyril Fox and B. Dickins (Cambridge, 1950), pp. 261-72. The most persuasive literal interpretation of the poem, seeing the speaker as a pilgrim wishing to make a *peregrinatio* for the salvation of his soul.

Note: A good collection of essays is *Essential Articles for the Study of Old English Poetry*, ed. J. B. Bessinger, Jun., and S. J. Kahrl (Hamden, Conn., 1968). Several of the essays listed above (those by Cross, 'On Genre'; Greenfield, 'Formulaic Expression'; Leslie; Magoun; Pope; Stanley, 'Poetic Diction'; Timmer and Wyld), as well as many others, are reproduced therein.

Index

For individual lexicographical items, *see* Words and phrases. Items in Select Bibliography are not listed in this index.

Index

Index

Index

Index

Irony, 4, 30; in 'A slumber did my spirit seal', 17; in *Judith*, 72
Irving, E. B., Jun., 24, 56
Isaacs, N. D., 95, 161
Isidore of Seville, 138, 154, 173

Jakobson, R., 28
Job (Book of), 144
Judith (Book of), 97, 99
Judith: lines 28–32b and metaphoric word play, 96–100; variations in, 71–2; *see also* Words and phrases

Kantrowitz, J. S., 173
Kaske, R. E., 23–4, 43, 134, 145, 148–53
Keats, John, 112
Kenning, 36, 38, 39, 49–50, 62
Klaeber, F., 46, 48, 102, 164
Krapp, G. P., 117
Krieger, M., 26–7
Kuhn's Law, 170

Lactantius, *De ave phoenice*, 79, 140, 142
Language of individual text compared to language as whole, 5, 171; *see also* Deviation; Norms of language
Lawrence, R. F., 31
Layamon, *Brut*, 95
Leavis, F. R., 4
Leechdoms, 98
Leisi, E., 161
Leslie, R. F., 79, 117, 146, 150, 151, 152–3, 167
Lexicography, *see* Meaning
Linguistics and criticism, 2, 5–6, 17, 28–9, 109–10, 111–12
Literary history, 3, 4, 11

Mackie, W. S., 151
McNamee, M. B., 158
McTurk, R., 165
Maldon, 1, 10, 55–8, 110–11; formulaic repetition in, 55–7; Vikings' crossing of Pante, 110–

111; *see also* Intentional meaning; Words and phrases
Maxims II, 35–6
Meaning: determinate, 14, 25, 27; determinate metre and, 164; figurative *v.* literal in O.E. poetry, 37–8; formal, 31, 53, 110–11, 122; formal relationships in, 25–28, 29, 30, 45, 47–8, 54–8, 108; historical and present, 4–8, 27, 30, 37, 54, 57–9, 108, 119, 133; horizon of, 12–13, 16, 25, 101, 134, 146, 166; lexicography and, 39–40, 43, 44–5, 95–6; precision of in use of O.E. poetic diction, 30–5, 52, 133–4; referential, 45–51, 60, 110; surface structure and, 109; tone in, 7, 17, 19; typical attitudes in, 16, 18; versus significance, 13–14; *see also* Allegory; Context; Criticism; Diction; Expectations; Formula; Genre; Implications; Intentional meaning; Interpretation
Meters of Boethius, 42, 48, 49, 50
Metre and alliteration, 1, 2, 33–4, 38, 109–11; as formal requirements of O.E. poetry, 30, 60, 85; in *Maldon*, 57; *see also* Expectations; Implications
Milton, John: *Samson Agonistes*, 12; 'On his Blindness', 51
Mitchell, B., 118
Morte Arthur, alliterative, 54

Narrative, kinds of medieval, 138–139, 153–5
New Criticism, 2, 4, 8, 27, 30, 140
New Literary History, 4
New Testament, 154
Norms of language, 4, 14, 109; in O.E. verse, 112–14, 118–19; *see also* Deviation
Nowottny, W., 111

Old English poetry: continuity with English literature, 1–2; conventionality, conventions and

Index

Old English Poetry—*cont.*
traditions, 1–3, 9, 10–11, 30, 37–9, 112, 133, 154; formulas in Homeric, Yugoslavian and, 31; modern critical methods and, 2–3; originality in, 39; paratactic style in, 64; stylistic features of, 60

Old Testament: heroic figures in, 154–5; paronomasia in, 85; *sapientia* in Vulgate, 43

Oral composition, 30–1, 32

Oral delivery, 2, 30, 58

Order of the World, 6

Osborn, M., 93, 94, 103, 168

Paetzel, W., 76, 167

Paris Psalter, 98–9

Paronomasia, *see* Word play

Phoenix: as allegory, 12, 136, 140–5, 149, 153, 159; use of Scripture in, 140, 144–5; variation in, 79

Physiologus, 140

Piers Plowman, 1, 2

Pilch, H., 172

Pope, J. C., 34, 162

Prosopopoeia, 12, 146

Prudentius, 107, 170

Psalms, 19, 20, 97–9; O.E. translation of, 97–9

Pseudo-Bede, discourse on Psalm 52: 1–4, 136–7, 138

Psychology: of dreams in medieval literature, 13; in interpretation of *Genesis B*, 7–8

Punctuation and O.E. texts, 44, 77

Puns, *see* Word play

Quirk, R., 115–16, 126

Ransom, J. C., 164

Received idea, 8

Renoir, A., 7–8, 122, 137

Richards, I. A., 4, 28

Riddles, O.E.: as genre, 12, 135; on bookworm, 161; rich in word play, 86–8; *Riddle 60*: relation to

Husband's Message, 146, 150, 151, 152–3; *Riddle 84*, 44

Rieger, M., 101, 162

Riffaterre, M., 162, 171

Ringler, R. N., 72, 171

Robertson, D. W., Jun., 2, 4–5, 16, 138, 139, 140

Robinson, F. C., 39–41, 42, 43, 65, 66, 68–9, 73, 78, 83, 85, 95, 100–101, 106

Rogers, R. L., 164

Rollinson, P., 138–9, 140, 154–5, 157, 158, 173

Rosier, J. L., 135, 169

Ruin, genre identification of, 12

Saints' Lives, O.E., 135, 154

Sanders, W., 8

Savage, H. L., 53

Schaubert, E. von, 166

Schilling, H., 166

Schücking, L. L., 41

Scripture: as aid in interpreting O.E. poetry, 3, 11, 18, 23, 139; etymolgies of, 101; *see also* Job; Judith; New Testament; Old Testament; *Phoenix*; Psalms

Seafarer, 12, 18, 20–3, 42, 43–5, 63, 88–90, 107, 121, 153–4; as exemplary fiction, 154; bird sounds in lines 19b–22, 63; genre identification of, 12; interpretation of lines 58–64a, 20–3, 43–5; word play in, 88–90; *see also* Allegory; *Wanderer*; Words and phrases

Semantic-syntactic relationships, *see* Expectations; Implications

Sensus literalis, *see* Allegory, *allegoria in verbis*

Sensus spiritualis, *see* Allegory, *allegoria in res*

Shakespeare, William: *Hamlet*, 157; *Macbeth*, 9; *Midsummer Night's Dream*, 7; *Much Ado About Nothing*, 25

Sheed, F. J., 163

Shepherd, G., 142, 144

Index

Index